# My Samsung
# Galaxy Note® 5

Craig James Johnston
Guy Hart-Davis

800 East 96th Street,
Indianapolis, Indiana 46240 USA

# My Samsung Galaxy Note® 5

## Copyright © 2016 by Pearson Education, Inc.

ISBN-13: 978-0-7897-5820-0
ISBN-10: 0-7897-5820-2

Library of Congress Control Number: 2015956433

Printed in the United States of America

First Printing: December 2015

## Trademarks

All terms mentioned in this book that are known to be trademarks or service marks have been appropriately capitalized. Que Publishing cannot attest to the accuracy of this information. Use of a term in this book should not be regarded as affecting the validity of any trademark or service mark.

All Galaxy Note 5 images are provided by Samsung Electronics America.

## Warning and Disclaimer

Every effort has been made to make this book as complete and as accurate as possible, but no warranty or fitness is implied. The information provided is on an "as is" basis. The authors and the publisher shall have neither liability nor responsibility to any person or entity with respect to any loss or damages arising from the information contained in this book.

## Special Sales

For information about buying this title in bulk quantities, or for special sales opportunities (which may include electronic versions; custom cover designs; and content particular to your business, training goals, marketing focus, or branding interests), please contact our corporate sales department at corpsales@pearsoned.com or (800) 382-3419.

For government sales inquiries, please contact governmentsales@pearsoned.com.

For questions about sales outside the U.S., please contact international@pearsoned.com.

**Editor-in-Chief**
Greg Wiegand

**Acquisitions Editor**
Michelle Newcomb

**Development and Copy Editor**
Charlotte Kughen, The Wordsmithery LLC

**Managing Editor**
Sandra Schroeder

**Project Editor**
Mandie Frank

**Indexer**
Erika Millen

**Proofreader**
Katie Matejka

**Technical Editor**
Christian Kenyeres

**Editorial Assistant**
Cindy Teeters

**Designer**
Mark Shirar

**Compositor**
Tricia Bronkella

# Contents at a Glance

# Table of Contents

## 14   Using S Health     457

## Index     493

# About the Authors

**Craig James Johnston** has been involved with technology since his high school days at Glenwood High in Durban, South Africa, when his school was given some Apple ][ Europluses. From that moment, technology captivated him, and he has owned, supported, evangelized, and written about it.

Craig has been involved in designing and supporting large-scale enterprise networks with integrated email and directory services since 1989. He has held many different IT-related positions in his career, ranging from sales support engineer to mobile architect for a 40,000-smartphone infrastructure at a large bank.

In addition to designing and supporting mobile computing environments, Craig cohosts the CrackBerry.com podcast as well as guest hosting on other podcasts, including iPhone and iPad Live podcasts. You can see Craig's previously published work in his books *Professional BlackBerry*, *My iMovie*, and many books in the *My* series covering devices by Apple, BlackBerry, Palm, HTC, Motorola, Samsung, and Google.

Craig also enjoys high-horsepower, high-speed vehicles and tries very hard to keep to the speed limit while driving them.

Originally from Durban, South Africa, Craig has lived in the United Kingdom, the San Francisco Bay Area, and New Jersey, where he now lives with his wife, Karen, and a couple of cats.

Craig would love to hear from you. Feel free to contact Craig about your experiences with *My Samsung Galaxy Note 5* at http://www.CraigsBooks.info.

All comments, suggestions, and feedback are welcome, including positive and negative.

**Guy Hart-Davis** is the author of more than 100 computer books, including *Android Tips and Tricks* and *Windows 10 Tips and Tricks*.

# Dedication

*"I love deadlines. I like the whooshing sound they make as they fly by."*
—Douglas Adams

# Acknowledgments

We would like to express our deepest gratitude to the following people on the *My Samsung Galaxy Note 5* team, who all worked extremely hard on this book:

- Michelle Newcomb, our acquisitions editor, who worked with us to give this project an edge

- Christian Kenyeres, our technical editor, who double-checked our writing to ensure the technical accuracy of this book

- Charlotte Kughen, who developed and edited the manuscript skillfully

- Mandie Frank, who kept the book project on schedule

- Tricia Bronkella, who combined the text and art into colorful pages

# We Want to Hear from You!

As the reader of this book, *you* are our most important critic and commentator. We value your opinion and want to know what we're doing right, what we could do better, what areas you'd like to see us publish in, and any other words of wisdom you're willing to pass our way.

We welcome your comments. You can email or write to let us know what you did or didn't like about this book—as well as what we can do to make our books better.

*Please note that we cannot help you with technical problems related to the topic of this book.*

When you write, please be sure to include this book's title and author as well as your name and email address. We will carefully review your comments and share them with the author and editors who worked on the book.

Email: feedback@quepublishing.com

Mail: Que Publishing
ATTN: Reader Feedback
800 East 96th Street
Indianapolis, IN 46240 USA

# Reader Services

Register your copy of **My Samsung Galaxy Note 5** at quepublishing.com for convenient access to downloads, updates, and corrections as they become available. To start the registration process, go to quepublishing.com/register and log in or create an account*. Enter the product ISBN, 9780789758200, and click Submit. Once the process is complete, you will find any available bonus content under Registered Products.

*Be sure to check the box that you would like to hear from us in order to receive exclusive discounts on future editions of this product.

In this chapter, you become familiar with the external features of the Galaxy Note 5 and the basics of getting started with the Android operating system. Topics include the following:

→ Getting to know your Galaxy Note 5's external features
→ Getting to know your Galaxy Note 5's S Pen (stylus)
→ Learning the fundamentals of Android 5.1.1 (Lollipop) and TouchWiz
→ Setting up your Galaxy Note 5 for the first time
→ Installing desktop synchronization software

# Getting to Know Your Galaxy Note 5

Let's start by getting to know more about your Galaxy Note 5 by examining the external features, device features, and how the Android 5.1.1 operating system works.

In addition to Android 5.1.1 (Lollipop), this chapter covers the Samsung TouchWiz interface, which is overlaid on top of Android to adjust the way things look and function.

## Your Galaxy Note 5's External Features

Becoming familiar with the external features of your Galaxy Note 5 is a good place to start because you will be using them often. This section covers some of the technical specifications of your Galaxy Note 5, including the touchscreen, camera, and S Pen. There are many versions of the Samsung Galaxy Note 5, but no matter which one you own or which wireless carrier you use to connect it, the exterior, functionality, and look and feel of the interface are exactly the same.

# Front

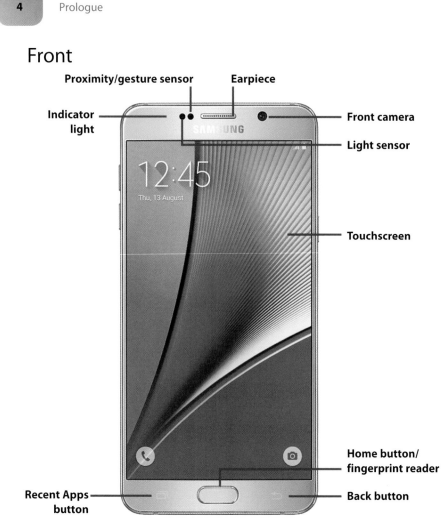

- **Proximity/gesture sensor**—Detects when you place your Galaxy Note 5 against your head to talk, which causes it to turn off the screen so that your ear doesn't inadvertently activate any onscreen items. This sensor also allows you to use gestures (in conjunction with the accelerometer). Gestures are covered later in the chapter.

- **Light sensor**—Adjusts the brightness of your Galaxy Note 5's screen based on the brightness of the ambient light.

- **Earpiece**—The part you hold against your ear while on a call.

- **Indicator light**—Indicates new events (such as missed calls, new Facebook messages, and new emails).

- **Front camera**—A 5-megapixel front-facing camera that you use for video chat, taking self-portraits, and even unlocking your Galaxy Note 5 using your face.

- **Touchscreen**—The Galaxy Note 5 has a 5.7" 1440×2560 pixel Quad HD Super AMOLED (Super Active-Matrix Organic Light-Emitting Diode) screen that incorporates capacitive touch.

- **Back button**—Tap to go back one screen when using an application or menu. This is a touch-sensitive button.

- **Recent Apps button**—Tap to see a list of apps you recently used. You can then touch to jump to them or swipe them off the screen to close them. Touch and hold to see additional options for the current screen.

- **Home button/fingerprint reader**—Press to go to the Home screen. The application that you are using continues to run in the background. Press twice to launch S Voice. Press and hold to launch Google Now. A fingerprint reader is built in to the Home button; you can read more about it in Chapter 2, "Customizing Your Galaxy Note 5." This is a physical button.

## Back

Rear camera

LED camera flash

Volume up/down buttons

Power button

Heart rate sensor

- **Volume up/down buttons**—Control the audio volume on calls and while playing audio and video.

- **Power button**—Press once to wake up your Galaxy Note 5. Press and hold for one second to reveal a menu of choices. The choices enable you to put your Galaxy Note 5 into Silent mode or Airplane mode, or to power it off completely.

- **Rear camera**—Take clear pictures up close or far away with the 16-megapixel camera with autofocus and Optical Image Stabilization (OIS).

- **LED (light-emitting diode) camera flash**—Use the flash to illuminate your surroundings when you're taking pictures in low light.

- **Heart rate sensor**—While using the S Health app, place your finger over the heart rate sensor to allow S Health to detect your heart rate.

## Top

Noise-canceling microphone        SIM card tray

- **SIM card tray**—Use the SIM card tray ejection tool provided in the box to eject the SIM card tray and insert a new or replacement SIM card.

- **Noise-canceling microphone**—Use in conjunction with the regular microphone to reduce background noise during phone calls. This micro-phone is also used when you record videos.

## Bottom

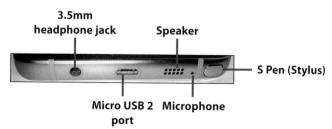

3.5mm headphone jack    Speaker      S Pen (Stylus)

Micro USB 2 port    Microphone

- **Micro USB 2 port**—You can use the Micro USB 2 port to synchronize your Galaxy Note 5 to your desktop computer and charge it.

- **Microphone**—You use the microphones when you are on a call and hold-ing your Galaxy Note 5 to your ear.

- **Speaker**—The speaker is used to play all audio and when you use the speakerphone function for phone calls.

- **S Pen (Stylus)**—Press the S Pen to reveal a pull-out grip, and then pull the S Pen out of its holder to draw on the screen and interact with apps. Read more about the S Pen in the next section.

# S Pen

Your Samsung Galaxy Note 5 comes with a stylus, which Samsung calls the S Pen. The S Pen is stored in the Galaxy Note 5 on the right side, and you pull it out from the lower right. This section covers some of the S Pen's features and functions.

## Getting to Know the S Pen

Let's take a look at the S Pen itself and learn about its features.

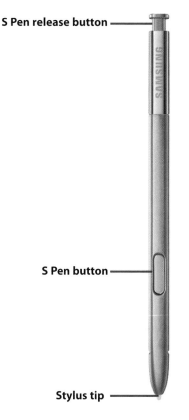

S Pen release button

S Pen button

Stylus tip

- **Stylus tip**—The S Pen stylus tip is what makes contact with the screen as you write and draw. The stylus tip is pressure sensitive, so it knows how hard or soft you are pressing. This is particularly useful for drawing because pressure translates into line thickness.

- **S Pen release button**—The release button enables you to easily remove and replace the S Pen. When the S Pen is in your Note 5, press the release button and then pull out the S Pen. When you re-insert the S Pen into your Note 5, press the release button again.

- **S Pen button**—The S Pen button adds extra functionality to the S Pen. When you press the button as you drag the pen on the screen, you can perform functions, such as moving between screens, taking screenshots, and even cutting out parts of any screen.

# Air Command

When you remove your S Pen, Air Command is the first thing that pops up. Air Command gives you quick access to useful S Pen functionality. You can also access Air Command any time by hovering your S Pen over the screen and pressing the S Pen button or by tapping the pencil icon.

- **Action Memo**—Write a note and tell your Note 5 to take action on what you write. For example, write a phone number and tell Action Memo to dial that number.

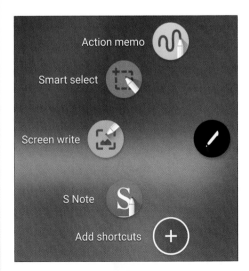

- **Smart Select**— Capture a part of the screen by drawing around the area you want to capture. You can then write on the captured image, save the captured area of the screen to the Scrapbook or Gallery apps, or share the captured image.

- **Screen Write**—Capture the entire screen and then write on the image of the captured screen. You can then save the image to the Scrapbook or Gallery apps, or share it.

**Write something first...**

**...and then tap More...**

Link to action ———— **...and then tap Link to Action...**

**...and finish by choosing an action.**

**Draw around an area on the screen.**

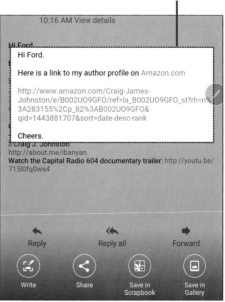

- **S Note**—S Note is a full-featured note-taking app. You can create notes that contain your handwriting or text (or both). You can insert voice notes, videos, and photos into your notes.

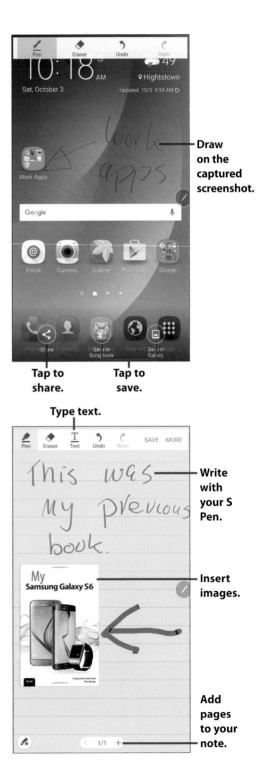

Draw on the captured screenshot.

Tap to share.    Tap to save.

Type text.

Write with your S Pen.

Insert images.

Add pages to your note.

## Take a Note on the Lock Screen

S Note has a feature that enables you to write a note directly on your Note 5's Lock screen, so you can take a note without first having to unlock your Note 5 and launch the S Note app. To take a note while your Note 5 is locked, simply remove the S Pen and start writing.

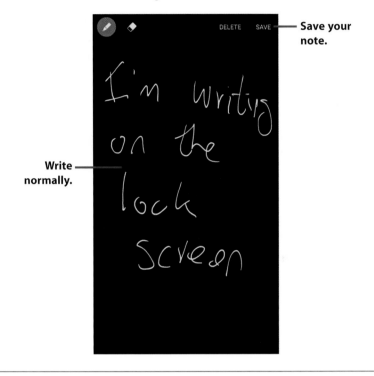

**Save your note.**

**Write normally.**

# Air View

Air View is a feature that shows you a preview of information about an object and enables you to interact with it when you hover the S Pen or your finger near the screen over an object that is Air View enabled. Make sure that Air View is turned on in Settings before you try to use it. Refer to Chapter 2 to see how to turn on Air View and customize how it works. This section shows you some examples of using Air View.

**Hover over an album**
**in the Gallery app.**

**Album preview**
**is shown.**

**Information about**
**the icon is shown.**

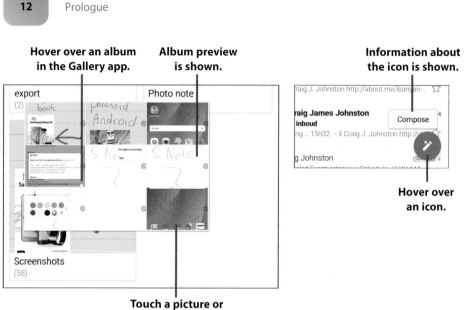

**Hover over**
**an icon.**

**Touch a picture or**
**video to open it.**

## Air View Is Not Always Available

Apps must be specifically written to support Air View. For example, Samsung has rewritten the Gallery app to support Air View; however, the Photos app, which Google has moved to, does not support Air View.

## Scrolling Using the S Pen

You can scroll up and down by hovering your S Pen at the top or bottom of an area of the screen that scrolls, such as a message list. For this gesture, you must not press the S Pen button on the screen—just hover at the top or bottom of the scroll area. You see an arrow indicating that the scrolling gesture has been recognized.

**Hover to**
**scroll up.**

# Gestures and Motions

Gestures and motions allow you to quickly use certain functions or features by making hand gestures or moving the Note 5 in a specific way.

- **Direct Call**—While you are looking at a missed call, reading an SMS (text message) from someone, or viewing someone's contact information, if you lift your Note 5 to your ear and hold it there, the phone number being viewed will be dialed.

- **Smart Alert**—If you have missed calls or messages, when you pick up your Note 5 from a flat surface, it vibrates.

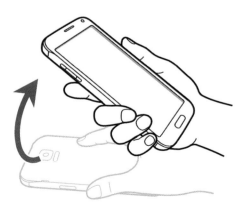

- **Mute**—To mute incoming calls and alarms, either place your hand over the screen or turn your Note 5 over.

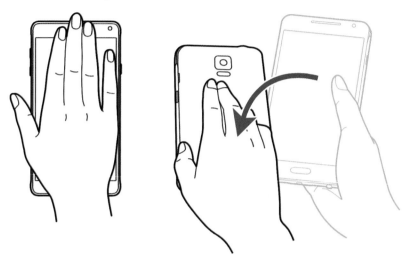

- **Palm Swipe to Capture**—You can capture a screenshot by holding your palm perpendicular to the screen, touching it on the screen and swiping it from left to right or right to left. The captured screenshot goes to the Screenshots album, which you can view using the Gallery or Photos app.

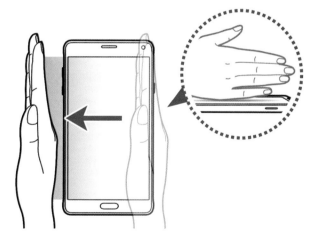

# First-Time Setup

Before setting up your new Samsung Galaxy Note 5, you should have a Google account because your Galaxy Note 5 running Android is tightly integrated with Google. When you have a Google account, you can store your content in the Google cloud, including any books and music you buy or movies you rent. If you do not already have a Google account, go to https://accounts.google.com on your desktop computer and sign up for one.

1. Press and hold the Power button until you see the animation start playing.

2. Scroll up and down to change your language if needed.

3. Tap the right arrow to continue.

4. Tap a Wi-Fi network you want to connect to during setup. If you'd rather not connect to a Wi-Fi network, tap Next and continue at step 8.

## Why Use Wi-Fi During Setup?

As you go through the first-time setup of your Note 5, you might want to restore a backup of a previous device to your Note 5, and at the end of the device setup, a number of apps might need to be updated. Both of these activities can use a lot of data. Using Wi-Fi speeds up these activities as well as saves you the cost of the cellular data charges. Therefore, although you do not have to connect to a Wi-Fi network for device setup, it is advisable.

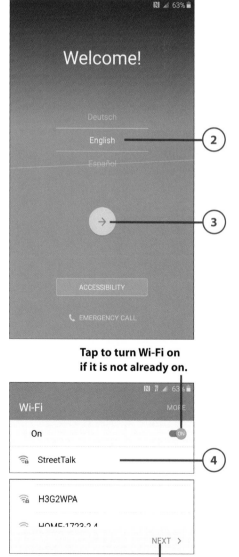

**Tap to turn Wi-Fi on if it is not already on.**

**Tap to skip and use cellular data.**

5. Enter the password for the Wi-Fi network using the onscreen keyboard.

6. Tap Connect. Your Galaxy Note 5 connects to the Wi-Fi network.

7. Tap Next.

**StreetTalk**

Password
••••••••

☐ Show password

☐ Show advanced options

CANCEL    CONNECT

**Wi-Fi**   MORE

On   ON

StreetTalk
Connected

**Indicates that you
are connected to
the network.**

ARGF4

H3G2WPA_2GEXT

HOME-1010

NEXT →

# >>>Go Further
## SMART NETWORK SWITCH

Smart network switch is a feature that, once enabled, allows your Note 5 to seamlessly switch between the two Wi-Fi bands (2.4GHz and 5GHz) and cellular data to maintain a stable Internet connection. Your Note 5 constantly analyzes its connection to the Internet and switches between Wi-Fi networks operating on 2.4GHz and 5GHz to provide the best connection, and if the Wi-Fi connectivity becomes poor, it switches to the cellular data network. Bear in mind that with this option enabled you might start seeing higher cellular data usage, especially in areas where Wi-Fi is unstable, slow, or overcrowded. To enable Smart Network Switch, before you continue with step 7, tap More, and tap Smart Network Switch to enable it.

**8.** Tap to check the box to give Samsung consent to collect diagnostic and usage data from your Note 5.

**9.** Tap Next after you have read and understood the End User License Agreement (EULA).

**10.** If you have another Android device (phone or smartphone) running Android 5.0 (Lollipop) or later and you want to transfer the data from it to your Note 5, follow the instructions on this screen, or tap Skip to continue.

Terms and conditions

**End User License Agreement**

Read the End User License Agreement carefully. It contains important information.

Learn more

**Diagnostic data**

☑ CONSENT TO PROVIDE DIAGNOSTIC AND USAGE DATA
Samsung Electronics Co., Ltd. and its affiliates ("Samsung") would like your help in improving the quality and performance of its products and services. Your device includes diagnostic software that may, with your consent, automatically collect diagnostic and usage data from your device. Diagnostic software may send this data to

NEXT >

**8**        **9**

Tap & Go

Quickly copy any Google Accounts, backed up apps and data from your existing Android device. To copy:

1. Make sure your other device is on and unlocked.

2. Briefly place the two devices back-to-back until you hear a tone, then set aside.

Learn more

<        SKIP →        **10**

11. Enter your Google account email address (your Gmail address).

12. Tap Next.

13. Enter your Google account password.

14. Tap Next.

15. Tap Accept if you understand and accept the Google Terms of Service and Privacy Policy.

N 🛜 ⊿ 62% 🔋

Add your account                    ⋮

Go gle

Sign in to get the most out of your device. ⓘ

Enter your email

editor.ford.prefect@gmail.com ————————— 11

Or create a new account

‹                              NEXT → 12

**Tap to create a new Google account.**

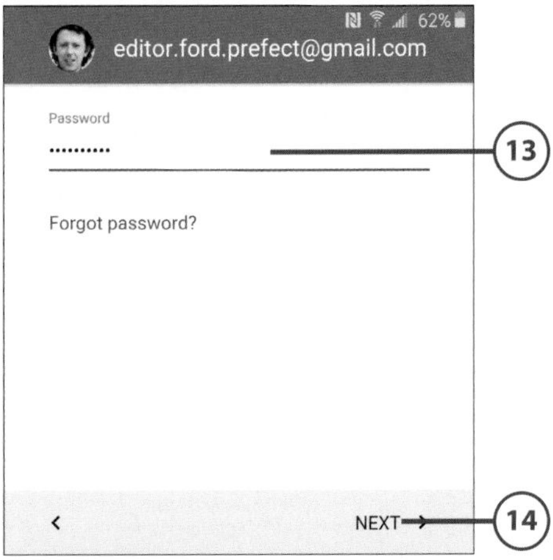

N 🛜 ⊿ 62% 🔋

editor.ford.prefect@gmail.com

Password

●●●●●●●●● —————————————— 13

Forgot password?

‹                              NEXT → 14

N 🛜 ⊿ 62% 🔋

editor.ford.prefect@gmail.com

By signing in, you agree to the
Terms of Service and Privacy Policy.

Don't sign in

**Tap to read the terms of service and privacy policy.**

‹                            ACCEPT → 15

**16.** Tap Set Up as New Device if you are not restoring from a back of another device.

**17.** Tap Next to continue setting up your Note 5 as a new device.

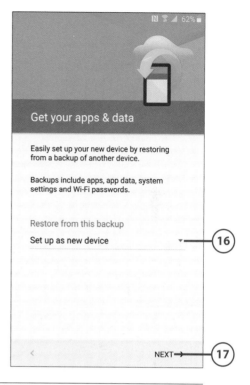

## Beware of the Restore

If you are switching from a non-Samsung Android device to your new Galaxy Note 5, be careful when restoring apps and data from your previous device. If you decide to restore your apps and data in step 16, make sure that you first unselect some of the core Android apps such as Calendar and Contacts because Samsung has rewritten many of the core Android apps to support special Samsung features like the S Pen and to have a different look and feel. If you don't unselect these apps, you might end up with duplicate apps.

Restore from this backup

SM-N920T  Last used 6 days ago  ——— **Select your old device.**

Also include

All apps  44  ——— **Choose apps to restore.**

18. Tap Set Screen Lock Now to choose a method for securing your Note 5. If you decide not to secure your Note 5, skip to step 23.

19. Tap Fingerprints. The fingerprint method of securing your Note 5 is used in this example because it is by far the easiest and most secure method for securing your device.

20. Follow the on-screen instructions for capturing your fingerprint. This involves lightly placing your thumb or finger on the Home button and then lifting it when you see the percentage on the screen increase. You repeat this process until the percentage reaches 100%.

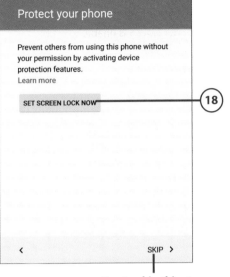

**Protect your phone**

Prevent others from using this phone without your permission by activating device protection features.

Learn more

SET SCREEN LOCK NOW — 18

‹                              SKIP ›

Tap to skip this step.
**Use other screen lock methods.**

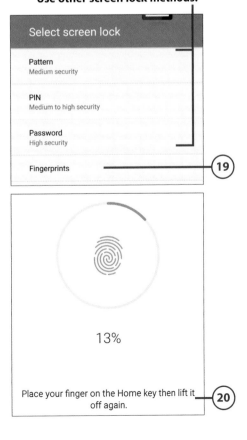

**Select screen lock**

Pattern
Medium security

PIN
Medium to high security

Password
High security

Fingerprints — 19

13%

Place your finger on the Home key then lift it off again. — 20

**21.** Enter a password that you can use if your Note 5 is unable to read your fingerprint.

**22.** Tap Continue.

**23.** Choose whether you want notifications and their content to appear on the Lock screen. You can select Show Content to show notifications and their content, Hide Content to show the notifications but not their content, or Do Not Show Notifications keep the Lock screen free of notifications.

**24.** Tap Next.

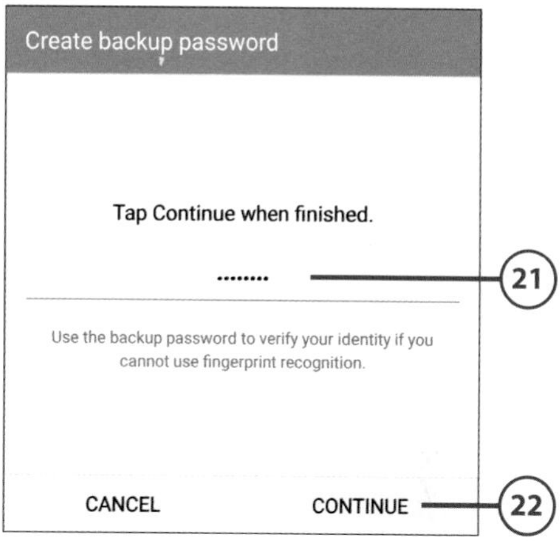

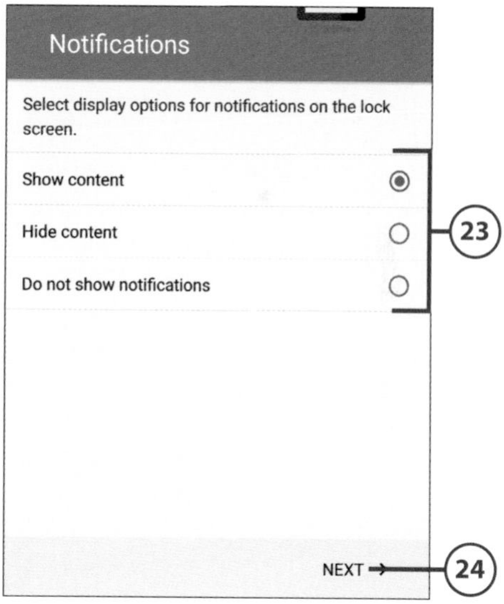

Create backup password

Tap Continue when finished.

........

Use the backup password to verify your identity if you cannot use fingerprint recognition.

CANCEL          CONTINUE

Notifications

Select display options for notifications on the lock screen.

Show content

Hide content

Do not show notifications

NEXT →

**25.** Check the box if you want the data on your Note 5 to be backed up to your Google account.

**26.** Check the box if you want to use Google's location services.

**27.** Tap More.

**28.** Tap to sign in to your Samsung account if you have one, or tap Skip and jump to step 36.

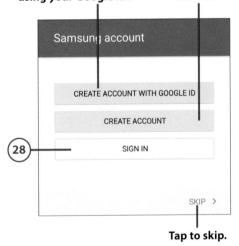

This phone may also receive and install updates and apps from Google, your carrier, and your phone's manufacturer. Some apps may be downloaded and installed if you continue, and you can remove them at any time.

25 ☑ **Back up your phone's apps, app data, settings, personal dictionaries, and Wi-Fi passwords** using your Google Account so you can easily restore later. Learn more

26 ☑ **Use Google's location service** to help apps determine location. This means sending anonymous location data to Google, even when no apps are running. Learn more

< MORE ∨

27

**Create a Samsung account using your Google ID.** **Create a Samsung account.**

Samsung account

CREATE ACCOUNT WITH GOOGLE ID

CREATE ACCOUNT

28 SIGN IN

SKIP >

**Tap to skip.**

# >>>Go Further

## DO I NEED A SAMSUNG ACCOUNT?

Android was designed to be used with a Google account. Your Google account enables you to access the Google ecosystem of Android apps, music, movies, and books; plus, your phone's settings are backed up to the Google cloud. If you change devices, your new device reverts to the way you had your old device set up. A Samsung account does a similar thing, but it uses the Samsung ecosystem. If you would like to take advantage of the extra Samsung services on your Note 5—such as the Galaxy app store, the ability to locate your lost device, or to keep track of your S Health diet and health information—you should sign up for a Samsung account.

**29.** Enter the email address you used for your Samsung account.

**30.** Enter your Samsung account password.

**31.** Tap Sign In.

**32.** Check the box to enable enhanced Samsung account features. If you enable this, Samsung collects your phone number, contact list, and text messages. Samsung's enhanced features include Profile Sharing where you can see your friends' contact pictures, as long as they also have Samsung phones, and Simple Sharing that allows you to use the Contacts app to share files with friends who have Samsung phones.

**33.** Tap Agree if you understand and accept the Samsung terms and conditions.

**Samsung account**

editor.ford.prefect@gmail.com — 29

•••••••••• — 30

☐ Show password

Forgot your ID or password?

CANCEL                    SIGN IN → 31

32

Terms and Conditions, Terms of Service, and Samsung Privacy policy.

☑ Enhanced features. If you activate the service, your phone number, contact list and messages will be automatically collected. It may result in data and text message charges.

DECLINE                    AGREE → 33

**34.** Tap the on/off button to enable or disable automatically backing up your data to your Samsung account.

**35.** Tap Next.

**36.** Tap Set to set your wake-up command for Samsung's S Voice. When this is set, you can say your wake-up phrase (such as "Hi Galaxy") plus a command like "Call Charlie mobile" and your Note 5 performs that task for you. You can also tap Later and skip to step 40.

⟨R⟩ 📶 61% 🔋

## Back up and sync

By storing your data on a Samsung server, Back up and sync allows you to manage your data. You can choose what data will be "backed up and synced" via the Settings option.

Learn more

Back up and sync ⬤ **(34)**

If you want to restore your backed up data on your previous device, please click the next button below.

LATER                    NEXT → **(35)**

## Set wake-up command

S Voice helps you control your device with your voice. Use your voice to easily wake up your device, open apps, make calls, and more.

LATER                    SET → **(36)**

**Tap to set
this up later.**

**37.** Hold your Note 5 about 8–12 inches (20–30 cm) from your mouth and tap Start.

**38.** Follow the on-screen prompts that guide you to say your wake-up command four times. The screen automatically advances when you're done.

**39.** Tap Done after you have read some of the examples of using your voice to command your Note 5.

**40.** Tap the on/off switch if you want your Note 5 to use Easy mode. Easy mode uses a simplified Home screen layout, plus enlarges the text and size of the app icons. You can always disable Easy mode later if you decide it's not for you.

**41.** Tap Finish.

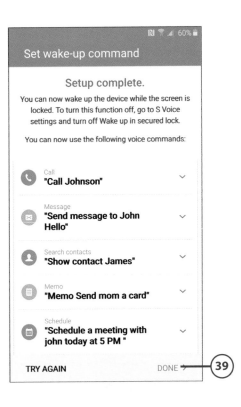

# Fundamentals of Android 5.1.1 and TouchWiz

Your Galaxy Note 5 is run by an operating system called Android. Android was created by Google to run on any smartphone, and your Galaxy Note 5 uses a version called Android 5.1.1 (or Lollipop). Samsung has made many changes to this version of Android by adding extra components and modifying many standard Android features. They call this customization TouchWiz.

## The Lock Screen

If you haven't used your Galaxy Note 5 for a while, the screen goes blank to conserve battery power. This task explains the different ways to interact with the Lock screen.

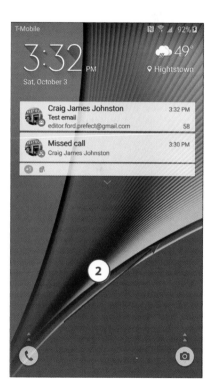

1. Press the Power button or Home button to wake up your Galaxy Note 5.

2. Swipe your finger across the screen in any direction to unlock your Galaxy Note 5. If you have set a PIN, password, or pattern lock, you need to enter or draw it to unlock your Note 5.

### If You Use Your Fingerprint Always Use the Home Button

If you have chosen to unlock your Note 5 using your fingerprint, then it does not make sense to wake up your Note 5 using the Power button. Because the fingerprint reader is in the Home button, you can wake up and unlock your Note 5 in one step by pressing the Home button. If you do not want to unlock your Note 5 but just want to see what is on the Lock screen, press the Power button.

3. Tap a notification, such as the missed call and new email notifications in the figure, and then unlock your Note 5 (swipe the screen, type passcode, use fingerprint) to go directly to the app.

4. Swipe down from the down arrow to see more notifications, if there are more than two.

5. Swipe up from the Camera icon to launch the Camera app. You can launch the Camera app from the Lock screen without unlocking your Note 5.

6. Swipe up from the Phone icon to launch the Phone app. You still need to unlock your Note 5 to use the Phone app.

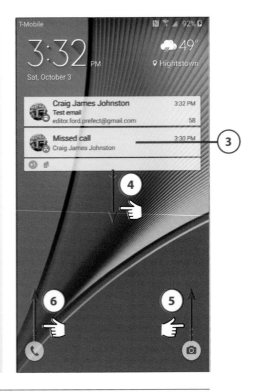

## Working with Quick Settings on the Lock Screen

You can work with Quick Settings right on the Lock screen. Swipe down from the top of the screen to reveal the Quick Settings. Make the changes you want to make. Read more about Quick Settings later in the "Work with Notifications" section.

**Swipe down to see Quick Settings.**

## Answering a Call from the Lock Screen

If your Galaxy Note 5 is locked when a call comes in, you have three choices: Drag the green icon to answer the incoming call; drag the red icon to reject the incoming call and send it straight to voicemail; or drag up from the bottom of the screen to reject the call and send a preset text message (SMS) to the caller.

Drag to answer.

Drag to reject.

Slide up to reject and send a text message.

# The Home Screen(s)

After you unlock your Galaxy Note 5, you are presented with the Home screen. Your Galaxy Note 5 has three Home screen panes (although you can create more). The Home screen panes contain application shortcuts, a Launcher icon, Notification bar, Shortcuts, Favorites Tray, and widgets.

Notification icons

Notification bar

Widgets

App shortcut

App folder

Swipe left and right to see all Home screen panes.

Favorites Tray

Launcher icon

- **Notification bar**—The Notification bar shows information about Bluetooth, Wi-Fi, and cellular coverage, as well as the battery level and time. The Notification bar also serves as a place where apps can alert or notify you using notification icons.

- **Notification icons**—Notification icons appear in the Notification bar when an app needs to alert or notify you of something. For example, the Phone app can show the Missed Calls icon, indicating that you missed a call.

- **Widgets**—Widgets are mini-apps that run directly on the Home screen panes. They are specially designed to provide functionality and real-time information. An example of a widget is one that shows the current weather or provides a search capability. You can move and sometimes resize widgets.

- **App shortcut**—When you tap an app shortcut, the associated app launches.

- **App folders**—You can group apps in a folder as a way to organize your apps and declutter your screen.

- **Favorites Tray**—The Favorites Tray is visible on all Home screen panes. You can drag apps to the Favorites Tray so that they are available no matter which Home screen pane you are viewing. You can rearrange and remove apps in the Favorites Tray.

- **Launcher icon**—Tap to show application icons for all applications that you have installed on your Galaxy Note 5.

# Work with Notifications

To interact with notifications that appear in the Notification bar, place your finger above the top of the screen and drag to pull down the Notification bar and reveal the notifications. Swipe individual notifications off the screen to the left or right to clear them one by one, or tap Clear to clear all of them at once. The Notification bar also includes Quick Settings such as the ability to turn on or off Wi-Fi or Bluetooth.

**Tap to edit which Quick Settings are visible.**

**Swipe left and right to see more Quick Settings.**

**Tap to see all Settings.**

**Quick Settings**

**Use two fingers to pull down a notification to see more of it and actions you can take on it.**

**Tap to launch the associated app.**

**Swipe a notification left or right off the screen to clear it.**

**Tap to clear all notifications.**

## What Are Quick Settings?

Quick Settings are icons that allow quick on/off actions. Examples are turning Wi-Fi on or off and turning Bluetooth on or off. You can also change the settings for the services represented by their icons (for example Wi-Fi), by touching and holding an icon.

# Create App Shortcuts

Tap the Launcher icon to see all of your apps. Touch and hold on the app you want to make a shortcut for. After the Home screen appears, drag the app shortcut to the location you want the shortcut to be on the Home screen, drag it to an app folder, or drag it left or right off the screen to move between Home screen panes. Release the icon to place it.

Touch and hold an app icon.

Drag to where you want it and release it.

Drag between Home screen panes.

# Create App Folders

To create a new app folder, drag one icon on top of another. After you give your app folder a name, the folder displays on your Home screen. Now you can drag other app shortcuts into that folder. To open the folder, tap it to reveal the shortcuts in that folder.

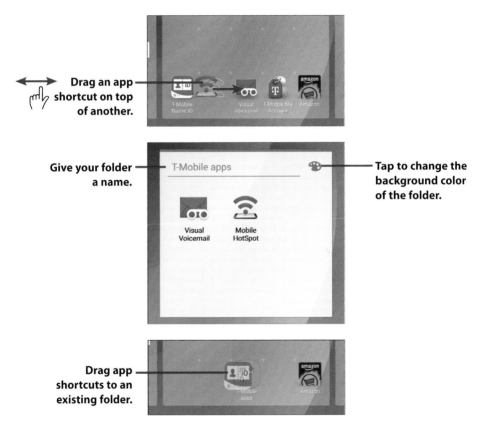

**Drag an app shortcut on top of another.**

**Give your folder a name.**

**Tap to change the background color of the folder.**

**Drag app shortcuts to an existing folder.**

## Remove an App Shortcut and Add a New Home Screen Pane

To remove an app shortcut, touch and hold the app shortcut icon, and then drag it to the trash can icon (labeled Remove). To create a new Home screen pane, touch and hold an app shortcut icon, drag it all the way to the right-most pane, and then release it. A new Home screen pane is created and your app shortcut icon is placed on it.

# Use the Touchscreen

You interact with your Galaxy Note 5 mostly by touching the screen, which is known as making gestures on the screen. You can tap, swipe, pinch, touch and hold, double-tap, and type.

- **Tap**—To start an application, tap its icon. Tap a menu item to select it. Tap the letters of the onscreen keyboard to type.

- **Touch and hold**—Touch and hold to interact with an object. For example, if you touch and hold a blank area of the Home screen, a menu pops up. If you touch and hold an icon, you can reposition it with your finger.

- **Drag**—Dragging always starts with a touch and hold. For example, if you touch the Notification bar, you can drag it down to read all of the notification messages.

- **Swipe or slide**—Move your finger across the screen quickly to scroll the contents of the screen. Be careful not to touch and hold before you swipe or you will reposition something. You can also swipe to clear notifications or close apps when viewing the recent apps.

- **Double-tap**—Double-tapping is like double-clicking a mouse on a desktop computer. Tap the screen twice in quick succession. For example, you can double-tap a web page to zoom in to part of that page.

- **Pinch**—Zoom in and out of images and pages by placing your thumb and forefinger on the screen. Pinch them together to zoom out or spread them apart (unpinch) to zoom in. Applications such as Browser, Gallery, and Maps support pinching.

- **Rotate the screen**—If you rotate your Galaxy Note 5 from an upright position to being on its left or right side, the screen switches from Portrait view to Landscape view. Most applications honor the screen orientation. The Home screens and Launcher do not.

# Use the Keyboard

Your Galaxy Note 5 has a virtual or onscreen keyboard for those times when you need to enter text. You might be a little wary of a keyboard that has no physical keys, but you will be pleasantly surprised at how well it works.

Most applications automatically show the keyboard when you need to enter text. If the keyboard does not appear, tap the area where you want to type and the keyboard slides up, ready for use.

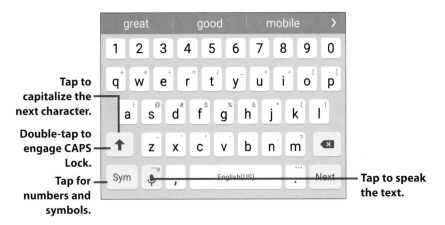

**Tap to capitalize the next character.**

**Double-tap to engage CAPS Lock.**

**Tap for numbers and symbols.**

**Tap to speak the text.**

Using the virtual keyboard as you type, your Galaxy Note 5 makes word suggestions. Think of this as similar to the spell checker you would see in a word processor. Your Galaxy Note 5 uses a dictionary of words to guess what you are typing. If the word you were going to type is highlighted, tap space or period to select it. If you can see the word in the list but it is not highlighted, tap the word to select it.

**Tap to select an alternative suggested word.**

**List of suggested words**

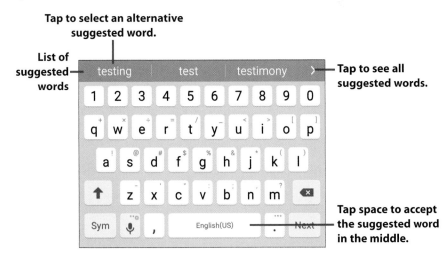

**Tap to see all suggested words.**

**Tap space to accept the suggested word in the middle.**

# >>>Go Further

## NEXT WORD SUGGESTION

When you are between typing words, the keyboard tries to predict the next word you want to type. (In this example I typed "This is a test"; the keyboard is suggesting that the most obvious word I want to type next is "drive," but it is also showing that I might want to type "of" or end the sentence with a period.) All you need to do is tap the correct word, and the keyboard types it for you. If the keyboard is not showing a word that you want to use, simply continue typing. The more you type, the more the keyboard learns how you write and the better it will become at suggesting the next words you are likely to type.

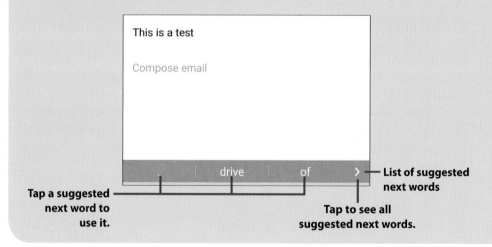

**List of suggested next words**

**Tap a suggested next word to use it.**

**Tap to see all suggested next words.**

To make the next letter you type a capital letter, tap the Shift key. To make all letters capitals (or CAPS), double-tap the Shift key to engage CAPS Lock. Tap Shift again to disengage CAPS Lock.

To type symbols, tap the Symbols key. When on the Symbols screen, tap the 1/2 key to see extra symbols. There are two screens of symbols. Tap the ABC key to return to the regular keyboard.

**Tap to see more symbols.**
**Tap to return to letters.**

## Quick Access to Symbols

If you want to type commonly used symbols, touch and hold the period key. A small window opens with those common symbols. Tap a symbol to type it or tap the Sym icon to see all symbols.

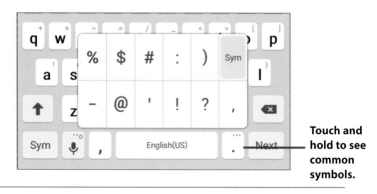

**Touch and hold to see common symbols.**

To enter an accented character, touch and hold any vowel or the C, N, or S key. A small window opens, enabling you to select an accented or alternative character. Slide your finger over the accented character and lift your finger to type it.

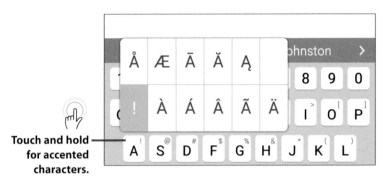

**Touch and hold for accented characters.**

To reveal other alternative characters, touch and hold any other letter, number, or symbol.

## Want a Larger Keyboard?

Turn your Galaxy Note 5 sideways to switch to a landscape keyboard. The landscape keyboard has larger keys and is easier to type on.

## Swipe to Type

Instead of typing on the keyboard in the traditional way by tapping each letter individually, you can swipe over the letters in one continuous movement. This is called Swiftkey Flow. It is enabled by default; to use it, just start swiping your finger over the letters of the word you want to type. As you swipe, your finger is followed by a blue trail to help you see what keys your finger has passed over. Lift your finger after each word. No need to worry about spaces because your Galaxy Note 5 adds them for you. To type a double letter (as in the word *pool*), loop around that letter on the keyboard.

## Dictation—Speak Instead of Type

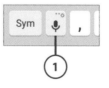

**Tap to select a different dictation language.**

Your Galaxy Note 5 can turn your voice into text. It uses Google's speech recognition service, which means you must have a connection to the cellular network or a Wi-Fi network to use it.

1. Tap the microphone key.

2. Wait until you see Speak Now and start speaking what you want to be typed. You can speak the punctuation by saying "comma," "question mark," "exclamation mark," or "exclamation point."

# Edit Text

After you enter text, you can edit it by cutting, copying, or pasting the text. This task describes how to select and cut text so you can paste over a word with the cut text.

1. While you are typing, touch and hold a word you want to copy.

2. Slide the blue end markers until you have selected all of the text you want to copy.

3. Tap to cut the text. Cutting text places it in the Clipboard, just like a Copy action would do, but it also removes the text from its current position.

4. Touch and hold the word you want to paste over.

5. Tap to paste what you cut earlier.

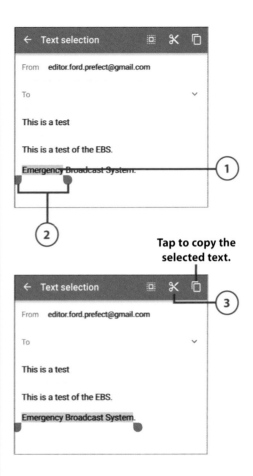

**Tap to copy the selected text.**

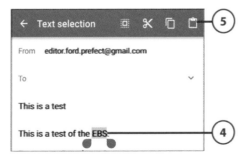

## Placing a Cursor

You can also simply place a cursor on the screen and move it around to do manual text editing, such as backspace to delete letters or manually insert a new word. To do this, tap the screen in the text area. A single blue marker displays; drag that marker to the point in the text you want to make changes to. Now start typing or tap backspace, and the action occurs at the cursor position.

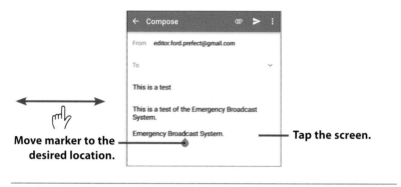

Move marker to the desired location.

Tap the screen.

## Writing Instead of Typing

As discussed earlier in this chapter, your Galaxy Note 5 comes with the S Pen stylus. Instead of typing on the keyboard, you can use handwriting recognition to write. To enable Handwriting mode, pull out the S Pen from its holder and tap the Back key to dismiss the Air Command window. Then hover the S Pen over the screen in the text area until you see the handwriting icon. Tap the icon with your S Pen. Any text you have typed appears to be in handwriting. Now write in your own handwriting on the screen and it is turned into text. Tap Done to return to typing.

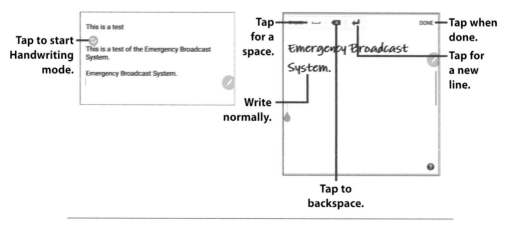

Tap to start Handwriting mode.

Tap for a space.

Write normally.

Tap to backspace.

Tap when done.

Tap for a new line.

# Keyboard Tricks

You can write instead of typing, use emoticons (smiley faces), and enable a one-handed keyboard.

1. Touch and hold the microphone key (to the right of the Sym key).

2. Tap to use dictation.

3. Tap to use Handwriting mode.

4. Tap to see everything you have previously copied to the clipboard. If there is text, you can tap it to paste it at the cursor position.

5. Tap to type emoticons (smiley faces).

6. Tap to change keyboard settings, including choosing a new keyboard.

# Menus

Your Galaxy Note 5 has two types of menus: app menus and context menus. All applications use an app menu. To see the app menu, tap the Menu icon, which is normally on the top-right of the screen.

**Tap to see the app menu.**

Add from Contacts

Save draft

Discard

Settings

Help & feedback

**Tap a menu item.**

A context menu applies to an item on the screen. If you touch and hold something on the screen (in this example, a link on a web page), a context menu appears. The items on the context menu differ based on the type of object you touched.

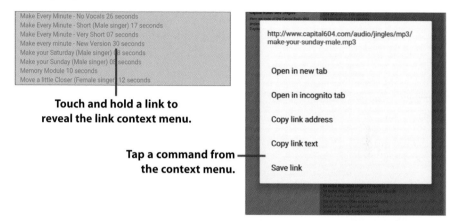

**Touch and hold a link to reveal the link context menu.**

**Tap a command from the context menu.**

# Switch Between Apps

You can use the multitasking feature to switch between running apps and close apps.

1. Tap the Recent Apps button (to the left of the Home button).

2. Swipe up and down the list of running apps.

3. Tap an app to switch to it.

4. Touch and hold an app icon to see memory and processor usage for each active app.

5. Tap to open the app in split-screen mode. This opens the app so that it only takes up the top half of the screen. See more about running multiple apps at the same time in the next section.

6. Close an app by swiping the app left or right off the screen or tapping the X on the top right of the app.

**Tap to end all running apps.**

# Run Multiple Apps on the Screen at the Same Time

Your Galaxy Note 5 has a feature called Multi Window that allows certain apps to run on the same screen at the same time. They can either run in a split-screen configuration, in multiple separate small windows, or a combination of both.

## Run Two Apps on a Split-Screen

This section explains how to run two apps at the same time in a split-screen configuration.

1. Touch and hold the Recent Apps button while on the Home screen, to see apps that support Multi Window.

2. Tap an app you want to run. The app launches in the top half of the screen.

The current screen does not support split screen view. Select two apps to open in split screen view.

**Scroll left and right
to see all apps.**

## Choose Apps That Are Already Running

When choosing which apps to start in Multi Window mode, if you keep scroll-ing right so that you see the left-most screen, it looks very much like the Recent Apps screen. Tap an app that is already running to switch it to Multi Window mode.

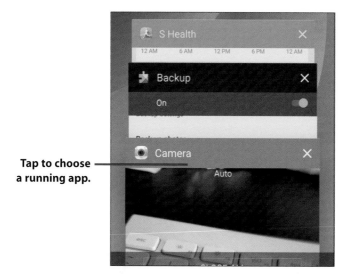

**Tap to choose a running app.**

## *It's Not All Good*

**Not All Apps Support Multi Window**

Apps must be specially written to take advantage of Samsung's Multi Window mode because Multi Window mode is not part of the Android operating sys-tem. This means that you might not see the apps you are looking for until the developer updates the app to support Samsung's Multi Window mode.

3.   Tap a second app icon to launch it in the bottom half of the screen.

4.   Drag the circle up or down to give more or less room to each app.

5.   Tap the circle to reveal extra Multi Window features.

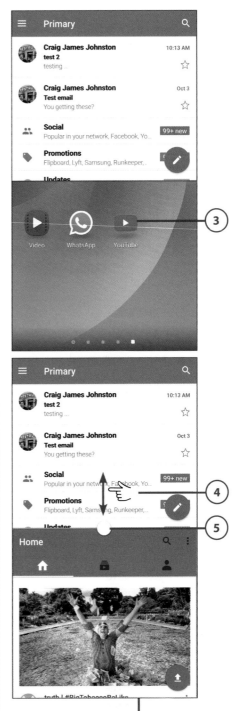

The blue outline indicates which app is active.

6. Tap to swap the position of the apps on the screen.

7. Tap to enable dragging content (such as text or an image) between windows.

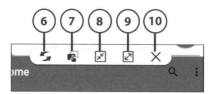

8. Tap to minimize the selected app to a small draggable circle on the screen. A blue box indicates which app is selected.

9. Tap to maximize the selected app to full screen. A blue box indicates which app is selected.

10. Tap to close the app in the selected window. The selected app has a blue box around its perimeter.

## How To Tell Which App Is Selected

When you have two apps open on the screen at the same time, you can tell which one is active by looking for a blue border around the active app. It is important to know which app is active when you are using the controls in steps 8, 9, and 10.

## >>>Go Further

### MINIMIZED APPS

When you choose to minimize an app as shown in step 8, the app shrinks to a small circle on the screen. You can drag the minimized app anywhere on the screen. If you touch and hold the app, a trash can icon appears; drag the app to the trash can to close the app. If you tap the minimized app, it enlarges to a pop-up window instead of maximizing back to its original window in the split screen. You can then continue working on the app in its small window. When an app is in a pop-up window, you can resize it by dragging the blue border around the app. Minimized and pop-up apps continue to be shown no matter what screen you are on and what app you are running.

Minimized apps

App in a pop-up window

## Quicker Way of Running Multi-Window

If you only want to use apps that are already running in Multi Window, you can do this more quickly. Tap the Recents Apps button. Tap the Multi Window icon on any running app. That app switches to Multi Window mode and displays in the top-half of the screen. Next, tap a second app to run in the bottom half of the screen. Remember that not all apps support Multi Window, so some apps might not have the Multi Window icon.

Tap to select app for Multi Window.

Choose a second app.

Tap to turn Wi-Fi
on or off.

Tap to turn NFC
on or off.

Tap to turn
Bluetooth
on or off.

Tap to turn all
radios on or off.

In this chapter, you discover the connectivity capabilities of your Galaxy Note 5, including Bluetooth, Wi-Fi, VPN, and NFC. Topics include the following:

→ Pairing with Bluetooth devices
→ Connecting to Wi-Fi networks
→ Using Near Field Communications (NFC) and beaming
→ Working with cellular networks
→ Working with virtual private networks (VPNs)
→ Using your Galaxy Note 5 as a Wi-Fi hotspot
→ Setting up and using Android Pay or Samsung Pay

# Working with Different Networks, NFC, and Contactless Payments

Your Galaxy Note 5 can connect to Bluetooth devices, such as headsets, computers, and car in-dash systems, as well as to Wi-Fi networks and 2G, 3G, and 4G cellular networks. It has all the connectivity you should expect on a great smartphone. Your Galaxy Note 5 can also connect to virtual private networks (VPNs) for access to secure networks. You can share files or pay at the check-out counter using your Note 5's NFC radio. Your Galaxy Note 5 can even share its cellular data connection with other devices over Wi-Fi.

## Connecting to Bluetooth Devices

Bluetooth is a great personal area network (PAN) technology that allows for short-distance wireless access to all sorts of devices, such as headsets, other phones, computers, smartwatches, Google Glass, and even car in-dash systems for hands-free calling and playing music. The following tasks walk you through pairing your Galaxy Note 5 to your device and configuring options.

## Pair with a New Bluetooth Device

Before you can take advantage of Bluetooth, you need to connect your Galaxy Note 5 with that device, which is called pairing. After you pair your Galaxy Note 5 with a Bluetooth device, the two devices can connect to each other automatically in the future.

---

### Putting the Bluetooth Device into Pairing Mode

Before you pair a Bluetooth device to your Galaxy Note 5, you must first put it into Pairing mode. If you are pairing with a Bluetooth headset, you normally have to hold the button on the headset for a certain period of time. Consult your Bluetooth device's manual to find out how to put that device into Pairing mode.

---

**1.** Pull down the Notification bar.

**2.** Touch and hold the Bluetooth icon to configure Bluetooth.

**3.** Tap to turn the Bluetooth radio on, if it is not already on.

**4.** Tap the Bluetooth device you want to connect to. This example uses a JBL Flip 2 Bluetooth Speaker.

**5.** If all went well, your Galaxy Note 5 should now be paired with the new Bluetooth device.

**Devices your Note 5 is already paired with.**

**Your Galaxy Note 5's Bluetooth name.**

🖾          ✳ 🔃 ⁑ ⏶ 100%🔋 11:17 AM

← Bluetooth                              STOP

On                              ○ ⬤ON   ③

Your device (Galaxy Note5) is currently visible to nearby devices.

Paired devices

Gear Live 10C9                        ⚙

Available devices

🖳  Craig's iMac

🎧  JBL Flip 2

▤  iPhone

▤  iPhone

▤  A0:18:28:EF:2E:02

▤  B8:78:2E:25:01:F9

④          **Discovered Bluetooth devices**

**Successfully paired**

Paired devices

🎧  **JBL Flip 2**                       ⚙
    Connected for call and media audio

○  Gear Live 10C9                     ⚙

Available devices

## Bluetooth Passkey

If you are pairing with a device that requires a passkey, such as a car in-dash system, smartwatch, other smartphone, or a computer, the screen shows a passkey. Make sure the passkey is the same on your Galaxy Note 5 and on the device you are pairing with. Tap OK on your Galaxy Note 5 and confirm the passkey on the device you are pairing with.

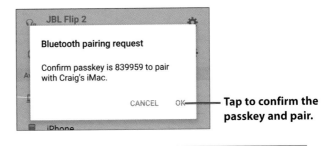

Tap to confirm the passkey and pair.

## All Zeros

If you are pairing with an older Bluetooth headset, you might be prompted to enter the passkey. Try using four zeros; it normally works. If the zeros don't work, refer to the headset's manual.

# >>>Go Further
## REVERSE PAIRING

The steps in this section describe how to pair your Galaxy Note 5 with a Bluetooth device that is in Pairing mode, listening for an incoming pairing command. You can also pair Bluetooth by having someone else with a Bluetooth device search for your Note 5 and initiate the pairing.

# Change Bluetooth Device Options

After a Bluetooth device is paired to your Note 5, you might be able to change a few options for it. The number of options depends on the Bluetooth device you are connecting to. Some have more features than others.

1. Tap the Settings icon to the right of the Bluetooth device.

2. Tap to rename the Bluetooth device to something more descriptive.

3. Tap to disconnect and unpair the Galaxy Note 5 from the Bluetooth device. If you do this, you won't be able to use the Bluetooth device again until you redo the pairing as described in the "Pair with a New Bluetooth Device" task.

4. Tap to use or not use the device's features. Sometimes Bluetooth devices have more than one profile. You can use this screen to select which ones you want to use.

Paired devices

🎧 **JBL Flip 2**
Connected for call and media audio    ⚙ —①

⌚ Gear Live 10C9    ⚙

🔒 📶    ❄ 📶 📶 100% 🔋 11:21 AM

← Paired device

Rename    ——②
JBL Flip 2

Unpair    ——③

Use for

📞 Call audio    ON

🎧 Media audio    ON    ④

## Bluetooth Profiles

Each Bluetooth device can have one or more Bluetooth profiles. Each Bluetooth profile describes certain features of the device. This tells your Galaxy Note 5 what it can do when connected to the device. A Bluetooth headset normally only has one profile, such as Phone Audio (or Call Audio). This tells your Galaxy Note 5 that it can only use the device for phone call audio. Some devices might have this profile but also provide other features such as a Phone Book Access profile, which would allow it to synchronize with your Galaxy Note 5's address book. The latter is typical for a car's in-dash Bluetooth device. The example shown in step 4 of the "Change Bluetooth Device Options" task is a Plantronics Bluetooth headset that has two Bluetooth profiles: Call Audio and Media Audio. Media Audio allows your Galaxy Note 5 to play media such as sounds your Note 5 makes and other media such as music, audio from a video, and so on. You might decide that you want to use the headset only for phone calls (Call Audio) and would prefer the media audio to continue to be directed to your Note 5's built-in speaker. In that case, you would uncheck Media Audio.

## Quick Disconnect

To quickly disconnect from a Bluetooth device, tap the device on the Bluetooth Settings screen and then tap OK.

# Wi-Fi

Wi-Fi (Wireless Fidelity) networks are wireless networks that run within free radio bands around the world. Your local coffee shop probably has free Wi-Fi, and so do many other places, such as airports, train stations, malls, and other public areas. Your Galaxy Note 5 can connect to any Wi-Fi network and provide you faster Internet access speeds than the cellular network.

# Connect to Wi-Fi

The following steps explain how to find and connect to Wi-Fi networks. After you have connected your Galaxy Note 5 to a Wi-Fi network, you automatically are connected to it the next time you are in range of that network.

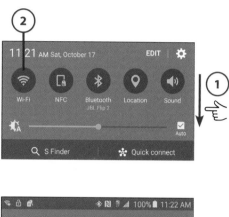

1. Pull down the Notification bar.

2. Touch and hold the Wi-Fi icon.

3. Tap to turn Wi-Fi on if the slider is in the off position.

4. Tap the name of the Wi-Fi net-work you want to connect to. If the network does not use any security, you can skip to step 10.

## You Are Prompted to Log In

If you are in a hotel, on a plane, or in some other place that provides Wi-Fi, many times even though the Wi-Fi net-work does not use any security, right after step 4, you are redirected to a login page. The login page is typically there for you to charge the cost of the Wi-Fi usage to your hotel room or some other account. Sometimes it is just to display a terms of use message for you to accept. If the login page is not displayed and you find that your Internet access is not working, open a web browser (Chrome or the default Internet browser) and type any website (such as abc.com). This should prompt the Wi-Fi network to dis-play the login page.

5. Enter the Wi-Fi network password.

6. Tap to configure advanced options such as to use a specific web browsing proxy server or to use static IP settings. If you don't need to configure advanced options, skip to step 9.

7. Tap to use a special web browsing proxy server while connected to this Wi-Fi network.

8. Tap to decide whether to let the Wi-Fi network router provide you with an IP address and IP settings or to use a static IP address and enter your own IP settings.

9. Tap to connect to the Wi-Fi network.

10. If all goes well, you see the Wi-Fi network in the list with the word "Connected" under it.

**Tap to show the password if you think you might be typing it incorrectly.**

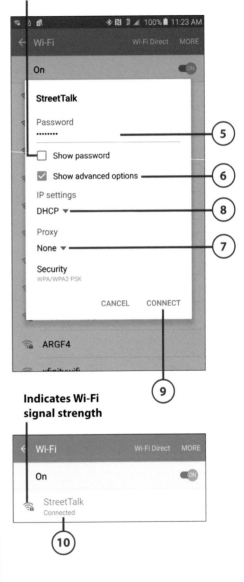

**Indicates Wi-Fi signal strength**

## Adding a Hidden Network

If the network you want to connect to is not listed on the screen, it might be purposely hidden. Hidden networks do not broadcast their name—which is known as their Service Set Identifier (SSID). Tap More, and tap Add Network, type in the SSID, and choose the type of security that the network uses. You need to get this information from the network administrator before you try to connect.

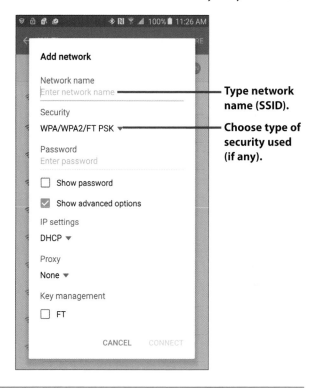

Type network name (SSID).

Choose type of security used (if any).

# Configure Wi-Fi Network Options

1. Tap a Wi-Fi network to reveal a pop-up that shows information about your connection to that network.

2. Tap Forget to tell your Galaxy Note 5 to not connect to this network in the future.

3. Touch and hold on a Wi-Fi network to reveal two actions.

4. Tap to forget the Wi-Fi network and no longer connect to it.

5. Tap to change the Wi-Fi network password or encryption key that your Galaxy Note 5 uses to connect to the network.

6. Tap to write the Wi-Fi network's information to an NFC tag.

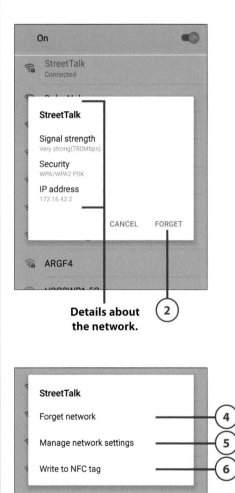

**Details about the network.**

---

## Writing Wi-Fi Information to an NFC Tag

In step 6, there is an option called Write to NFC Tag. This option enables you to write the information about the selected Wi-Fi network to a Near Field Communications (NFC) tag. This is useful if you want to pass out the tags to people so they can more easily connect to your Wi-Fi network, or stick a tag on the wall so people passing by can tap on the tag and quickly connect to your Wi-Fi network without knowing the network name or password.

# Configure Advanced Wi-Fi Options

Your Galaxy Note 5 enables you to configure a few advanced Wi-Fi settings that can actually help preserve your battery life.

1.  Tap More.

2.  Tap Advanced.

3.  Tap to enable or disable the ability for your Galaxy Note 5 to automatically notify you when it detects a new Wi-Fi network.

4.  Tap to let your Note 5 automatically connect to Wi-Fi networks that support Passpoint.

5.  Tap to change the Wi-Fi sleep policy. This enables you to choose whether your Galaxy Note 5 should keep its connection to Wi-Fi when it goes to sleep.

6.  Tap to choose whether to allow Google and apps running on your Note 5 to scan for Wi-Fi networks, even if you have turned Wi-Fi off.

7.  Tap to install certificates for authentication onto Wi-Fi networks that are provided by your administrator, and that you earlier stored on the SD card (external memory).

8.  Use this Wi-Fi MAC address if you need to provide a network administrator with your MAC address in order to be able to use a Wi-Fi network.

9.  This shows the IP address that has been assigned to your Galaxy Note 5 when it connected to the Wi-Fi network.

10. Tap to save your changes and return to the previous screen.

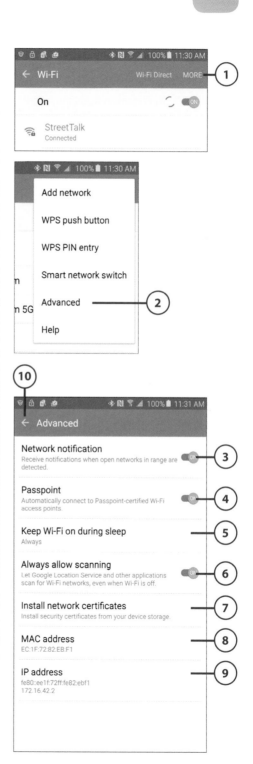

## Should You Keep Wi-Fi on During Sleep?

In step 5 of the "Configure Advanced Wi-Fi Options" task, you can choose how your Galaxy Note 5 handles its connection to Wi-Fi when it goes to sleep. Because Wi-Fi is much faster and more efficient than 3G or 4G, and is free, you should keep this set to Always. However, battery usage can be affected by always being connected to Wi-Fi, so you might want to set this to Only When Plugged In, which means that if your Galaxy Note 5 is not charging, and it goes to sleep, it switches to the cellular network for data; when the Galaxy Note 5 is charging and it goes to sleep, it stays connected to Wi-Fi. If you choose Never for this setting, when your Galaxy Note 5 goes to sleep, it switches to using the cellular network for all data. This can lead to more data being used out of your cellular data bundle, which might cost extra, so be careful.

# >>>Go Further

## WHAT ARE IP AND MAC ADDRESSES?

A Media Access Control (MAC) address is a number burned into your Galaxy Note 5 that identifies its Wi-Fi adapter. This is called the *Physical Layer address* because it is a physical adapter. An Internet Protocol (IP) address is a secondary way to identify your Galaxy Note 5. Unlike a Physical Layer address or MAC address, the IP address can be changed at any time. Modern networks use the IP address when they need to deliver some data to you. Typically when you connect to a network, a device on the network assigns a new IP address. On home networks, this is typically your Wi-Fi router.

Some network administrators use a security feature to limit who can connect to their Wi-Fi network. They set up their network to only allow connections from Wi-Fi devices with specific MAC addresses. If you are trying to connect to such a network, you will have to give the network administrator your MAC address, and he will add it to the allowed list.

## What Is Passpoint?

Passpoint is a technology that is being used increasingly by operators of Wi-Fi hotspots, and its purpose is to let your Note 5 (and other Passpoint-enabled smartphones and tablets) to automatically roam onto the hotspots with no need for you to search for them or log in to them using the typical hotspot login web page. Simply based on the SIM card in your Note 5, you are automatically authenticated onto these hotspots and provided a secure encrypted connection.

# Wi-Fi Direct

Wi-Fi Direct is a feature that allows two Android devices running version 4.1 (Jelly Bean) or later to connect to each other using Wi-Fi so they can exchange files. Because Wi-Fi is much faster than Bluetooth, if you are sending large files, using Wi-Fi Direct makes sense. You do not need to be attached to an existing Wi-Fi network to use Wi-Fi Direct.

## It's Not All Good

**Wi-Fi Direct Is Not Working**

At the time of writing, Wi-Fi Direct was not working on the Galaxy Note 5. I made several attempts to send files to a number of different Android devices that were running different versions of Android, and the sending always failed. If you search for Wi-Fi Direct in the Google Play app store, you can find a number of third-party solutions that use Wi-Fi Direct but make the connections between devices themselves instead of relying on Android to do it.

# Send a File Using Wi-Fi Direct

Follow these steps to connect to an Android device running version 4.1 (Jelly Bean) or later via Wi-Fi Direct and send it files from your Note 5.

1. Ask the other person to enable Wi-Fi Direct on his Android device. The Wi-Fi Direct screen is normally under the Wi-Fi Settings or Wi-Fi Advanced Settings.

2. Tap the Share icon for the item you want to send. This can be a picture in the Gallery app, for example.

3. Tap the Wi-Fi Direct icon.

4. Tap the other user's device name to invite it to connect with your Galaxy Note 5 via Wi-Fi Direct and send the file to that device.

5. Ask the other person to tap Accept or Connect on the device you are inviting.

6. If the Wi-Fi Direct connection is made successfully, the file is sent to the other device.

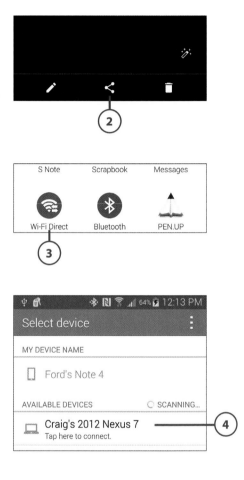

# Receive a File Using Wi-Fi Direct

Follow these steps to receive files from an Android device running 4.1 (Jelly Bean) or later.

1. Pull down the Notification bar.

2. Touch and hold the Wi-Fi icon.

3. Tap the Menu icon.

4. Tap Wi-Fi Direct and wait for the other person to invite you.

5. Tap Connect when the other person invites you to connect using Wi-Fi Direct. One or more files should now start copying to your Note 5.

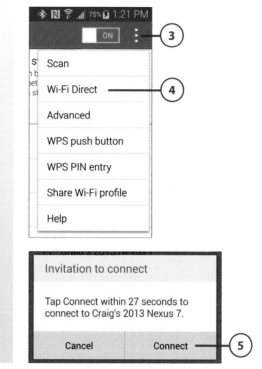

### Does Wi-Fi Direct Work for All Android Devices?

Theoretically, all Android devices running version 4.1 should be able to send or receive files via Wi-Fi Direct; however, some devices do have reported issues.

# Near Field Communications (NFC)

Your Galaxy Note 5 has the ability to swap data via its NFC radio with other phones that use NFC or read data that is stored on NFC tags. You can also use NFC to pay for items you have purchased. Android Beam also uses NFC to send files between Android devices by setting up the sending process automatically via NFC and then continuing it via Bluetooth or Wi-Fi Direct.

## Enable NFC and Android Beam

To get the full benefit from NFC, you need to enable the NFC radio. You should also enable Android Beam.

1. Pull down the Notification bar.

2. Touch and hold the NFC icon.

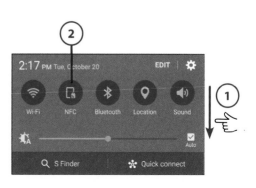

3. Tap to enable NFC if the switch isn't already in the On position.

4. Tap to enable Android Beam. (See the next section for more about Android Beam.)

5. Tap to choose which contactless payment service you want to use. If you have set up both Android Pay and Samsung Pay, you can use the option to choose which one is used at the checkout counter. Learn more about contactless payments later in this chapter.

6. Tap to save your changes and go back to the main Settings screen.

# >>>Go Further

## WHAT IS ANDROID BEAM?

All Android devices running version 4.0 (Ice Cream Sandwich) or later have a feature called Android Beam. This feature sends small bits of data via NFC (such as links to YouTube videos or links to apps in Google Play) to enable you to effectively share content, but it also automates sending actual files (such as pictures and videos) between devices via Bluetooth.

## Use Android Beam to Send Links to Content

You can use Android Beam to send links to content—such as apps, music, and video in the Google Play Store or website links—to another device. Android Beam only works between devices that are both running Android 4.0 (Ice Cream Sandwich) or later. The following example shows you how to send a website link.

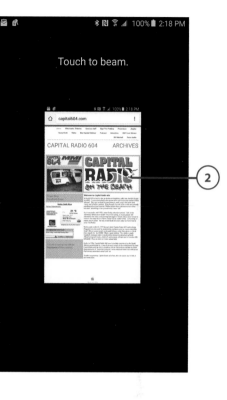

1. Open a website that you'd like to share the link to. Put the back of your Galaxy Note 5 about 1" from the back of another NFC-enabled device. You know that the two devices have successfully connected when the web page zooms out.

2. Tap the web page after it zooms out.

3. The browser on the other device opens and immediately loads the link you shared.

## Beam Google Play Content and YouTube Videos

If you like a song, movie, book, or app that is in the Google Play Store, you can beam it to someone. Simply open the song, movie, book, or app in Google Play, tap your devices together, and tap to beam. To beam a YouTube video, open the video in the YouTube app, tap the devices together, and tap to beam. The other device opens YouTube and jumps directly to the video.

# Use Android Beam to Send Real Files

You can also use Android Beam to send real content such as pictures, music, and video that's stored on your Galaxy Note 5. Sending real files using Android Beam only works between devices that are running Android 4.1 (Jelly Bean) or later. This task describes how to beam a picture.

1. Open the picture you want to beam. Then put the back of your Galaxy Note 5 about 1" from the back of another NFC-enabled phone. You know that the two devices have successfully connected when the picture zooms out.

2. Tap the picture after it zooms out.

3. Pull down the Notification bar to see the progress of the file transfer.

# >>>*Go Further*

## QUICK CONNECT

Quick Connect is a Samsung app that enables you to quickly share content with your friends' phones or tablets; you can also share content to a Chromecast. To use Quick Connect, pull down the Notification bar and tap Quick Connect. After the screen refreshes you should see phones, tablets, and devices in your area. Tap a friend's phone or tablet to send them variety of content including pictures, video, an S Note, a calendar event, a contact card, a document, and any other file. You can also share a Wi-Fi profile that you have saved on your Note 5 with your friend. Tap your Chromecast to view a picture or play audio or video on the television connected to the Chromecast.

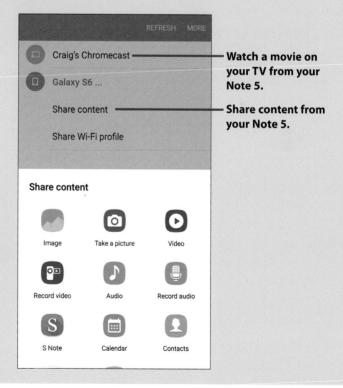

**Watch a movie on your TV from your Note 5.**

**Share content from your Note 5.**

# Cellular Networks

Your Galaxy Note 5 can connect to many different cellular networks around the world. The exact networks that it can connect to are determined by the variant of Galaxy Note 5 you have because not all carriers use the same technology. To complicate things even more, many network carriers use different frequencies from one another.

## Change Mobile Settings

Your Galaxy Note 5 has a few options when it comes to connecting to cellular (or mobile) networks.

1. Pull down the Notification bar.

2. Tap the Settings icon.

3. Tap Mobile Networks.

4. Tap to enable or disable cellular data roaming. If this is unchecked, your Galaxy Note 5 does not attempt to use data while you roam away from your home cellular network.

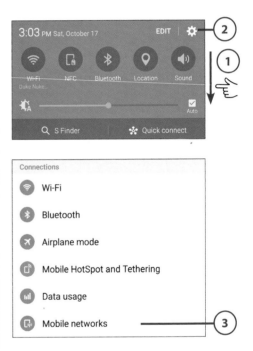

5. Tap to view, edit, and add APNs. It is unlikely that you need to make any APN changes.

6. Tap to change the network mode. This setting enables you to choose to force your Note 5 to connect to a slower 2G network (GSM Only) to save battery, but it also allows you to manually select whether you want your Note 5 to only connect to 3G networks (WCDMA Only), automatically select between 3G and 2G (WCDMA/GSM Auto Connect), or let your Note 5 automatically select between 4G, 3G, and 2G networks (LTE/WCDMA/GSM Auto Connect).

7. Tap to view and choose mobile operators to use manually.

8. Tap to save your changes and return to the previous screen.

## What Is an APN?

APN stands for Access Point Name. You normally don't have to make changes to APNs, but sometimes you need to enter them manually to access certain features. For example, if you need to use tethering, which is where you connect your laptop to your Galaxy Note 5, and your Galaxy Note 5 provides Internet connectivity for your laptop, you might be asked by your carrier to use a specific APN. Think of an APN as a gateway to a service.

## Can I Disable Mobile Data?

If you disable mobile data, you can save on battery life; however, you effectively kill the functionality of any app that needs to be connected all the time, such as instant messaging apps (Yahoo! or Google Talk) or apps such as Skype. You also stop receiving email in real time. When this feature is disabled, about 5 minutes after your Galaxy Note 5 goes to sleep, it disconnects from the mobile data network; however, it remains connected to the mobile voice network.

## >>>Go Further
### WHY SELECT OPERATORS MANUALLY?

When you are roaming in your home country, your Galaxy Note 5 automatically selects your home cellular provider. When you are roaming outside your home country, your Galaxy Note 5 registers on a cellular provider based on its name and how it scores alphabetically. The lowest score always wins. For example, a carrier whose name starts with a number is always chosen over carriers whose names start with letters. A carrier whose name starts with the letter *A* is chosen over a carrier whose name starts with the letter *B*, and so on. As you roam, your home carrier might not have a good roaming relationship with a carrier that your Galaxy Note 5 has chosen based on its name, so it's better for you to choose the carrier manually to ensure the best roaming rates and, many times, basic connectivity. You will notice that sometimes carriers are represented not by their names but by their operator codes (or Public Land Mobile Network [PLNM] number). For example, 53024 is actually 2Degrees in New Zealand, and 53005 is Telecom New Zealand.

## >>>Go Further
### BOOST YOUR DOWNLOAD SPEEDS

Your Galaxy Note 5 has a feature called Download Booster. When you enable it, it allows your Galaxy Note 5 to download content over both the cellular data and Wi-Fi networks at the same time. Because the downloads are transferring over both networks, the time it takes to download content is faster, sometimes double the speed of just Wi-Fi, depending on circumstances. Of course, if you have a limited cellular data plan, you might want to be cautious using this feature, or keep it disabled. To enable Download Booster, pull down the Notification bar and tap the Settings icon. Then tap More connection settings, and tap Download booster. Choose whether you want to turn it on or off.

# Virtual Private Networks (VPNs)

Your Galaxy Note 5 can connect to virtual private networks (VPNs), which are normally used by companies to provide a secure connection to their inside networks or intranets.

# Add a VPN

Before you add a VPN, you must first have all the information needed to set it up on your Galaxy Note 5. Speak to your network administrator to get this information ahead of time (and save yourself some frustration). The information you need includes the type of VPN protocol used, the type of encryption used, and the name of the host to which you are connecting.

1. Pull down the Notification bar.

2. Tap the Settings icon.

3. Tap More Connection Settings under the Connections section.

4. Tap VPN. If you have not secured your Note 5 with a PIN, password, pattern, or fingerprint, you are prompted to take care of that when you tap VPN. After you take care of securing your Note 5, you can continue with the next step.

---

## Why Do You Need to Set a PIN or Password?

If you don't already have a screen lock PIN, password, or pattern set up before you create your first VPN network connection, you are prompted to create one. This is a security measure that ensures your Galaxy Note 5 must first be unlocked before anyone can access a stored VPN connection. Because VPN connections are usually used to access company data, this is a good idea.

---

5. Tap More.

6. Tap Add VPN.

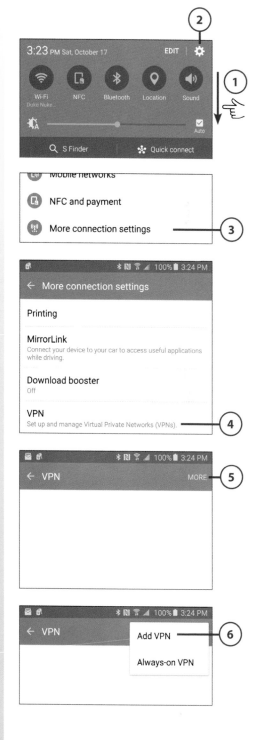

7. Enter a name for your VPN network. You can call it anything, such as Work VPN, or the name of the provider, such as PublicVPN.

8. Tap to choose the type of encryption technology used to create the VPN.

9. Enter the remaining parameters that your network administrator has provided.

10. Tap Save.

## Connect to a VPN

After you have created one or more VPN connections, you can connect to them when the need arises.

1. Pull down the Notification bar.

2. Tap the Settings icon.

3. Tap More Connection Settings under the Connections section.

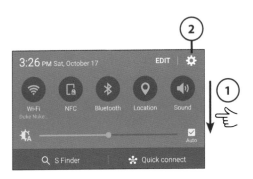

4. Tap VPN.

5. Tap a preconfigured VPN connection.

6. Enter the VPN username.

7. Enter the VPN password.

8. Tap Connect. After you're connected to the VPN, you can use your web browser and other applications normally, but you now have access to resources at the other end of the VPN tunnel, such as company web servers or even your company email.

Printing

MirrorLink
Connect your device to your car to access useful applications while driving.

Download booster
Off

VPN ————— ④
Set up and manage Virtual Private Networks (VPNs).

Default messaging app
Messages

---

✱ 🄽 📶 100% 3:27 PM

← VPN                                    MORE

Public VPN ————— ⑤
PPTP VPN

---

← VPN                                    MORE

P
PF

**Connect to Public VPN**

Username
fprefect ————— ⑥

Password
•••••••••• ————— ⑦

☑ Save account information

CANCEL    CONNECT ————— ⑧

**Check to save username and password.**

## >>>Go Further

## HOW CAN YOU TELL IF YOU ARE CONNECTED?

After your Galaxy Note 5 successfully connects to a VPN network, you see a key icon in the Notification bar. This indicates that you are connected. If you pull down the Notification bar, you can tap the icon to see information about the connection and to disconnect from the VPN.

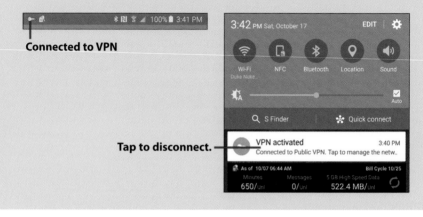

**Connected to VPN**

**Tap to disconnect.**

## Editing or Deleting a VPN

You can edit an existing VPN or delete it by touching and holding the name of the VPN. A window pops up with a list of options.

**Touch and hold a VPN.**

**Make a selection.**

## It's Not All Good

**No Quick Way to Start a VPN Connection**

The Galaxy Note 5 does not have a way to add a shortcut to your Home screen to jump straight to the VPN screen. There may be third-party solutions in the form of apps you can install that add this functionality. Check the Google Play Store.

# Mobile Wi-Fi Hotspot

Your Galaxy Note 5 has the ability to share its cellular data connection with up to eight devices over Wi-Fi. Before you use this feature, you need to normally sign up for a tethering or hotspot plan with your cellular provider, which is normally an extra monthly cost.

## Start Your Mobile Wi-Fi Hotspot

After your Wi-Fi hotspot is set up the way you want it, you can start it and begin sharing your Internet connection.

1. Pull down the Notification bar.

2. Tap the Settings icon.

3. Tap Mobile HotSpot and Tethering under the Connections section.

4. Tap Mobile HotSpot to configure and start your hotspot.

## What Is USB Tethering?

USB tethering is a feature that enables you to share your Note 5's Internet connection with a computer via the USB port. To use this, connect your Note 5 to the computer using the supplied USB cable and enable USB tethering. On the computer there will be some extra setup to do, which includes choosing your Note 5 as an Internet access point. (And on older Windows computers you might need to install a device driver. Be sure to consult the computer's manual for instructions.)

5. Tap More to preconfigure your hotspot before starting it (recommended). If you would rather just start the hotspot now, skip to step 17.

6. Tap Configure Mobile HotSpot.

**Mobile HotSpot and Tethering**

Mobile HotSpot
Off — 4

USB tethering
USB connected, check to tether    OFF

**Tap to enable USB tethering**

**Mobile HotSpot**    MORE — 5

Off    OFF

I come in pieces
Allow all devices to connect.

Password

bubblegum

**Mobile HotSp**    Allowed devices

Off    Configure Mobile HotSpot — 6

I come in pieces
Allow all devices to connect.

Password

bubblegum

Help

**7.** Choose a network name (also known as the SSID) for your mobile hotspot. You can leave it set to the auto-generated name or change it to something more friendly.

**8.** Tap to enable or disable broadcasting your hotspot's network name (its SSID). If you choose not to broadcast it, your network will be hidden, but you have to take more steps to connect to it.

**9.** Tap to choose the type of security to use for your mobile hotspot or choose Open to use no security.

**10.** Enter a password for your portable hotspot if you chose to use a security method in step 9.

**11.** Tap to show advanced options for your hotspot.

**12.** Choose either the 2.4GHz or 5GHz radio bands for your hotspot. Because the 2.4GHz bands can be overcrowded, choosing the 5GHz bands can help with performance.

**13.** Swipe up for more options.

**14.** Tap to change the maximum number of people who can connect to your hotspot. Because Wi-Fi is a shared network, fewer people normally means faster performance for everyone.

**15.** Tap to change the number of minutes of inactivity that must pass before the hotspot turns itself off.

**16.** Tap to save your hotspot settings.

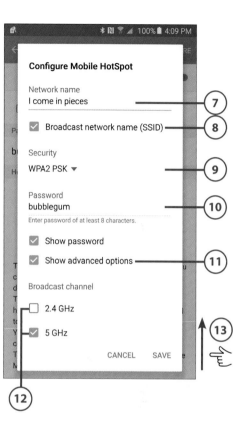

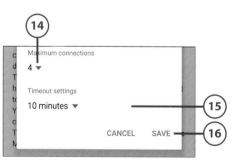

**17.** Tap to turn your hotspot on. Provide the hotspot connection information at the bottom of the screen to people you want to connect to your hotspot.

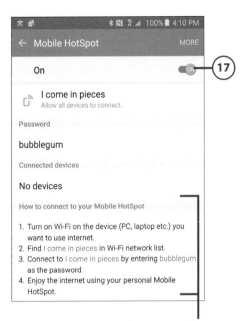

**Give these instructions to people who want to use your HotSpot.**

## Limit Who Can Connect

People can only connect to your hotspot after you give them the connection information; however, you can further limit who can connect to your hotspot by allowing devices that have specific MAC addresses.

**1.** From the Mobile HotSpot screen, tap the plus symbol to add an already connected device to the allowed devices list. Because the devices are already connected, your Note 5 already knows its MAC address.

**2.** Tap More and then tap Allowed Devices to add devices to the allowed list manually. You need to ask the device owner for her MAC address.

3. Tap the name of the hotspot to choose what devices are allowed to connect to your hotspot.

4. Tap Allowed Devices Only to limit the devices to the ones on the allowed list.

> ⚡ 🔵      ⚹ 📶 📶 100% 🔋 4:18 PM
>
> ←   Mobile HotSpot        MORE
>
> On      ⬤ON
>
> ⌗   I come in pieces ———— ③
>
>     Allow all devices
>
> Pass
>
> bub   Allowed devices only —— ④

# Contactless Payments

You can pay for items at the checkout counter just by holding your Note 5 close to the contactless terminal. For this functionality you can choose to use Android Pay or Samsung Pay. This section describes how to set up Android Pay and Samsung Pay.

## Set Up Android Pay

Android Pay is available for any Android device, regardless of manufacturer. If you think that you might change to a non-Samsung device in the future, consider using Android Pay.

1. Tap the Android Pay icon. If you don't see the icon, install Android Pay from the Google Play Store.

2. Tap the plus symbol to add a new credit or debit card for use with Android Pay.

> Add a credit or debit card
> Then you'll be ready to quickly and securely pay with your phone   + ② 

3. On the next screen, hold your Note 5 so that the card you want to add is lined up in the view finder. Your Note 5 should be able to read the information off the card. (not shown).

> rates, or other fees, when you use your Card through a Mobile Device.
>
>     CANCEL        ACCEPT ④

4. Tap Accept to accept your bank's terms and conditions for using your card with Android Pay.

5. Tap Got It to indicate that you understand that you must secure your Note 5 using a PIN, password, pattern, or fingerprint to use Android Pay.

Android Pay requires screen lock to be turned on.

For your security, Android Pay monitors your screen lock settings. You may be asked to unlock your phone to pay.

Since your phone can be used to pay when it's unlocked, you may want to change how quickly it locks in your settings.

GOT IT — 5

6. Choose a verification method; a code will be sent to you to verify the card you are adding. You can choose an email or text message.

7. After you receive the verification code, enter it and tap Submit.

Verify your card
Choose a verification method

Email

Text message

Text message — 6

8. Repeat steps 2 through 7 to add additional credit and debit cards to Android Pay.

← VISA-

Enter verification code
An email was sent to

SUBMIT — 7

# Set Up Samsung Pay

Samsung Pay is only available on Samsung devices like your Note 5. If you think that you might change to a non-Samsung device in the future, you may consider using Android Pay, or try out Samsung Pay now.

Samsung Pay — 1

1. Tap the Samsung Pay icon.

2. The first time you run Samsung Pay you have to decide whether you want to use your fingerprint for verification or you want to type in a PIN. It is highly recommended to use your fingerprint. To use your fingerprint, place your finger on the Home button so your fingerprint can be verified.

Skip and use Samsung Pay PIN.

USE FINGERPRINT

**Tap to use a PIN**

3. Tap Add Card to add a new credit or debit card for use with Samsung Pay.

4. On the next screen, hold your Note 5 so that the card you want to add is lined up in the view finder. Your Note 5 should be able to read the information off the card.

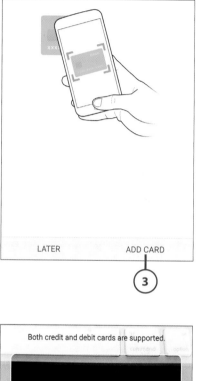

LATER                ADD CARD

③

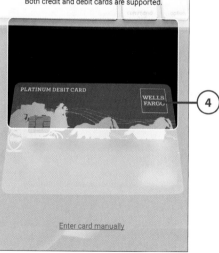

Both credit and debit cards are supported.

PLATINUM DEBIT CARD

WELLS FARGO

④

Enter card manually

5. Verify the information captured from your card, and enter any missing information.
6. Tap Next.
7. Tap Agree to All to accept your bank's terms and conditions for using your card with Samsung Pay.
8. Choose a verification method; a code will be sent to you to verify the card you are adding. You can choose an email or text message.

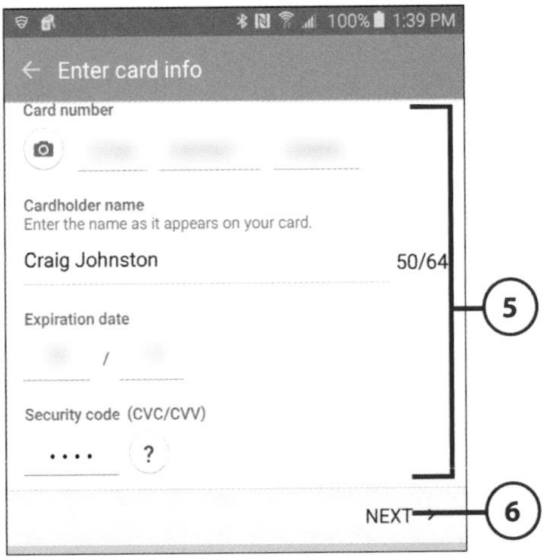
100% 1:39 PM
Enter card info
Card number
Cardholder name
Enter the name as it appears on your card.
Craig Johnston
50/64
Expiration date
Security code (CVC/CVV)
NEXT
5
6

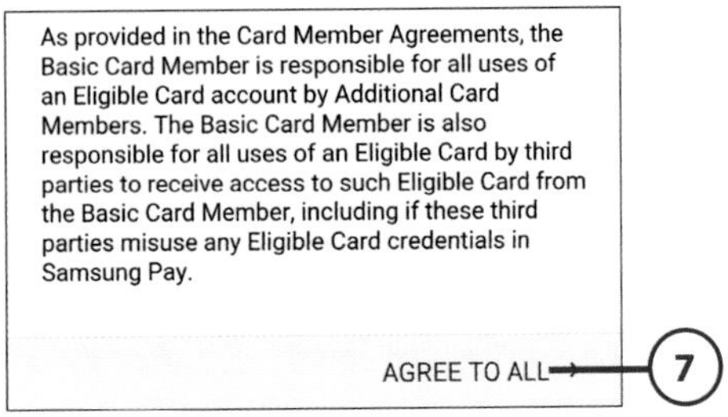
As provided in the Card Member Agreements, the Basic Card Member is responsible for all uses of an Eligible Card account by Additional Card Members. The Basic Card Member is also responsible for all uses of an Eligible Card by third parties to receive access to such Eligible Card from the Basic Card Member, including if these third parties misuse any Eligible Card credentials in Samsung Pay.
AGREE TO ALL
7

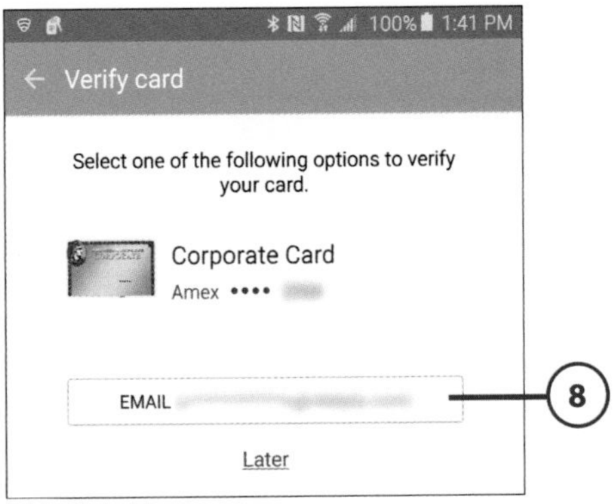
100% 1:41 PM
Verify card
Select one of the following options to verify your card.
Corporate Card
Amex ••••
EMAIL
Later
8

9. After you receive the verification code, enter it and tap Done.

10. Tap Done.

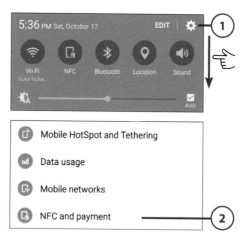

Tap to add another card.

# Choose Android Pay or Samsung Pay

If you have set up both Android Pay and Samsung Pay on your Note 5, you need to decide which one to use before you go shopping. If you set up only one payment service, you can skip these steps.

1. Pull down the Notification bar and tap the Setting icon.

2. Tap NFC and Payment under the Connections section.

3. Tap Tap and Pay.

4. Choose Android Pay or Samsung Pay.

5. Tap the back icon to save your change.

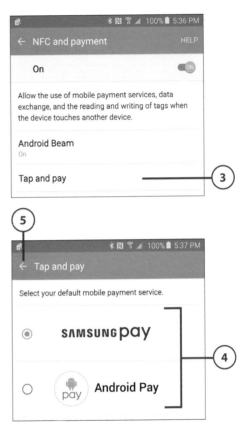

## Using Android Pay

1. Unlock your Note 5. Depending on how your set it up, you might use a PIN, password, pattern, or your fingerprint.

2. Tap your Note 5 against the terminal that has the contactless pay logo.

## Using Samsung Pay

1. Swipe up from the bottom of the screen to reveal your credit or debit card. You can do this from any Home screen or the Lock screen.

2. If you have more than one card and you want to use a different card to pay, swipe left and right to choose a different card.

3. Put your finger on the Home button to verify your identify, or if you chose to use a PIN, type in the PIN to get ready to pay (not shown).

4. Put your Note 5 close to a terminal that has the contactless payment logo on it, or hold it close to the magnetic strip reader of an older credit/debit card reader.

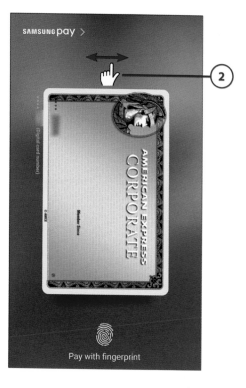

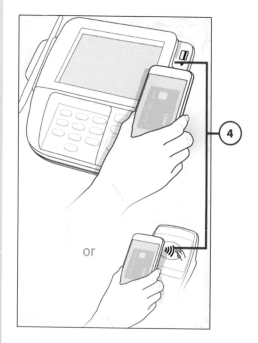

Tap to choose where
to use the wallpaper.

Tap to choose a new
wallpaper.

In this chapter, you find out how to customize your Galaxy Note 5 to suit your needs and lifestyle. Topics include the following:

→ Using wallpapers and live wallpapers
→ Replacing the keyboard
→ Adjusting sound and display settings
→ Setting the region and language
→ Using the fingerprint scanner

# Customizing Your Galaxy Note 5

Your Galaxy Note 5 arrives preconfigured to appeal to most buyers; however, you might want to change the way some of the features work, or even personalize it to fit your mood or lifestyle. Luckily, your Galaxy Note 5 is customizable.

## Changing Your Wallpaper

Your Galaxy Note 5 comes preloaded with a cool wallpaper. You can install other wallpapers, use live wallpapers that animate, and even use pictures in the Gallery application as your wallpaper.

1. Touch and hold in an open area on the Home screen.

2. Tap Wallpapers.

3. Tap to select where you want to change the wallpaper. You can choose a new wallpaper for the Home screen only or the Lock screen only, or you can use the same new wallpaper for both the Home and Lock screens.

4. Use the steps in one of the following three sections to choose the type of wallpaper to use as well as to select your new wallpaper.

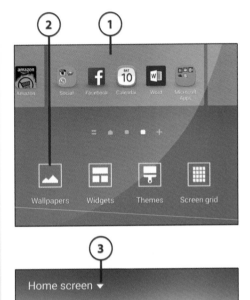

## What Is Wallpaper Motion Effect?

Wallpaper Motion Effect is an effect that creates the illusion that your icons and widgets are floating above the wallpaper. When the effect is turned on, as you move your Note 5 in your hand, the wallpaper appears to move, creating the perspective illusion. Some people are sensitive to this effect and might feel dizzy or disoriented. If you don't care for this effect, you can turn it off. This effect also uses processing power, which translates into a draw on battery charge, so turning off the effect might extend your battery life a little bit.

# Set Up Wallpaper from Gallery Pictures

You can use any picture in your Gallery as a wallpaper.

1. Swipe from left to right over the wallpaper thumbnails until you see one labeled From Gallery.

2. Tap From Gallery.

3. Navigate your photo albums and tap a photo you want to use for your wallpaper.

4. Drag the picture around with your finger to adjust what part of the picture you want to use as your wallpaper.

5. Zoom in and out of the picture using the pinch gesture. Sometimes if the photo you choose is very large, you are not able to zoom in or out.

6. Tap Set as Wallpaper when you have finished adjusting the picture.

**Turn on or off the Wallpaper motion effect.**

**Turn the Wallpaper motion effect on or off.**

# Set Up Live Wallpaper

Live wallpaper is wallpaper with some intelligence behind it. It can be a cool animation or even an animation that keys off things such as the music you are playing on your Galaxy Note 5, or it can be something simple such as the time. There are some very cool live wallpapers in Google Play that you can install and use.

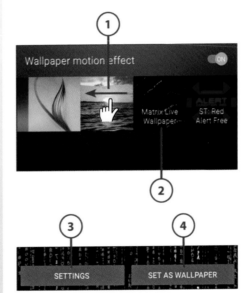

1. Swipe from left to right over the wallpaper thumbnails until you see the thumbnails with titles. Live wallpapers are kept on the right side of the wallpaper thumbnails.

2. Tap the live wallpaper you want to use.

3. Tap Settings to change the way the live wallpaper works. (Not all live wallpapers have settings that you can adjust.)

4. Tap Set as Wallpaper to use the live wallpaper.

## Finding More Wallpaper

You can find wallpaper or live wallpaper in the Google Play Store. Open the Google Play Store app and search for "wallpaper" or "live wallpaper." Read more on how to use the Google Play Store in Chapter 11, "Working with Android Apps."

## Set Up Wallpaper

Choose a static wallpaper that is pre-loaded and sized correctly for your screen.

1. Swipe left and right over the wallpaper thumbnails to see static wallpaper options. Static wallpapers are in between the From Gallery option and the live wallpapers.

2. Tap a wallpaper to preview it.

3. Tap Set as Wallpaper to use the wallpaper.

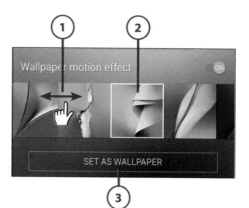

# Changing Your Keyboard

If you find it hard to type on the standard Galaxy Note 5 keyboard, or you just want to make it look better, you can install replacement keyboards. You can download free or purchase replacement keyboards from the Google Play Store. Most, if not all, keyboards come with their own installation wizard that walks you through adding and activating a keyboard, but if the one you installed does not have a wizard, or when you want to manually switch keyboards in the future, you need to use these steps.

1. Pull down the notification bar and tap the Settings icon.

2. Tap Language and Input.

3. Tap Default keyboard.

4. Tap Set Up Input Methods.

5. Tap the on/off switch next to a keyboard you have previously installed from the Google Play Store (this example uses SwiftKey Keyboard) to make that keyboard available for use.

6. Tap the back arrow to return to the previous screen.

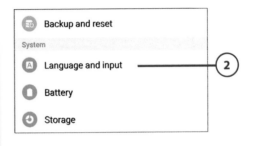

## Doing Your Research

When you enable a new keyboard in step 5, the Galaxy Note 5 gives you a warning telling you that nonstandard keyboards have the potential for capturing everything you type. Do your research on any keyboards before you download and install them.

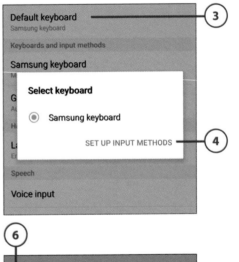

7. Tap Default Keyboard to change the default keyboard to the one you have just enabled.

8. Tap the name of your new keyboard to select it to be the default.

## What Can You Do with Your New Keyboard?

Keyboards you buy in the Google Play Store can do many things. They can change the key layout, change the color and style of the keys, offer different methods of text input, and even enable you to use an old T9 predictive input keyboard that you might have become used to when using an old "dumb phone" that had only a numeric keypad.

9. Tap the new keyboard name to make changes, including customizing it. Sometimes the keyboard's customization wizard launches when you tap the keyboard name.

10. Tap the back arrow to save your changes.

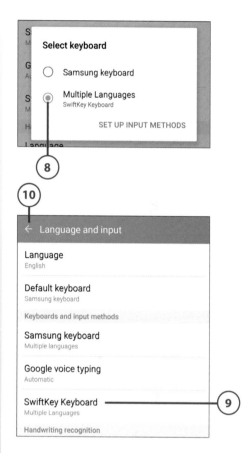

# Adding Widgets to Your Home Screens

Some applications that you install come with widgets that you can place on your Home screen panes. These widgets normally display real-time information, such as stocks, weather, time, and Facebook feeds. Your Galaxy Note 5 also comes preinstalled with some widgets. The following tasks explain how to add and manage widgets.

## Add a Widget

Your Galaxy Note 5 should come preinstalled with some widgets, but you might also have some extra ones that have been added when you installed applications. Here is how to add those widgets to your Home screen panes.

1. Touch and hold an open area on the Home screen.

2. Tap Widgets.

3. Touch and hold a widget to move it to a Home screen pane. Keep holding the widget as you move to step 4. This example uses the Hangouts widget.

Tap to see all widgets in a group.

Scroll left and right to see all widgets.

Widget's size

**4.** Position the widget where you want it on the Home screen pane.

**5.** Drag the widget to different Home screen panes if you want to place it on a different pane, or drag it to the right-most pane to create a new Home screen pane and place the widget on the new pane.

**6.** Release your finger to place the widget. Some widgets might help with the setup by prompting you with a few questions after they are positioned.

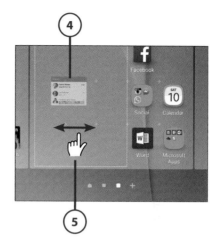

## How Many Widgets Can I Fit?

Each part of the Home screen is divided into a grid of five blocks across and five blocks down. In the figure for step 3, notice that some widgets show their size in blocks across and down (such as 4×3). From that, you can judge if a widget is going to fit on the screen you want it to be on, but it also helps you position it in step 4. You can change the grid size of your Home screen panes: Touch and hold on the Home screen and tap Screen Grid. You can change your screen grid to 4×4, 4×5, or 5×5. Bear in mind that the fewer grid positions there are available, the less you can fit onto each Home screen pane.

## Resizing Widgets

Some (not all) widgets can be resized. To resize a widget, touch and hold the widget until you see an outline and then release it. If the widget can be resized, you see the resizing borders. Drag them to resize the widget. Tap anywhere on the screen to stop resizing.

Drag to resize the widget.

## Remove and Move a Widget

Sometimes you want to remove a widget, resize it, or move it around.

1. Touch and hold the widget until the widget zooms out, but continue to hold it.

2. Drag the widget to the word Remove to remove it.

3. Drag the widget around the screen or drag it off the edge of the Home screen panes to reposition it on another screen.

4. Release the widget.

# Setting the Language

If you want to change the language used by your Galaxy Note 5, you can do so with a few taps.

1. Pull down the Notification bar and tap the Settings icon.

2. Tap Language and Input under the System section.

3. Tap Language.

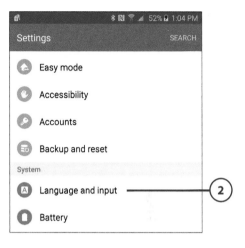

Tap to set the
handwriting
language.

4. Tap the language you want to switch to. The language is changed, and you are returned to the previous screen automatically.

## What Obeys the Language Setting?

When you switch your Galaxy Note 5 to use a different language, you immediately notice that all standard applications and the Galaxy Note 5 menus switch to the new language. Even some third-party applications honor the language switch. However, many third-party applications ignore the language setting on the Galaxy Note 5. Therefore, you might open a third-party application and find that all its menus are still in English.

← Language

○ Deutsch

◉ English

○ Español

○ Français

○ Italiano

○ 한국어

○ 中文 (简体)

○ 中文 (繁體)

○ 中文 (香港)

④

# Changing Accessibility Settings

Your Galaxy Note 5 includes built-in settings to assist people who might otherwise have difficulty using some features of the device. The Galaxy Note 5 has the ability to provide alternative feedback, such as vibration and sound. It can even read menu items aloud to you.

1. Pull down the Notification bar and tap the Settings icon.

2. Tap Accessibility under the Personalization section.

3. Tap one of the categories on the Accessibility screen and use the following sections to change the settings in the different categories.

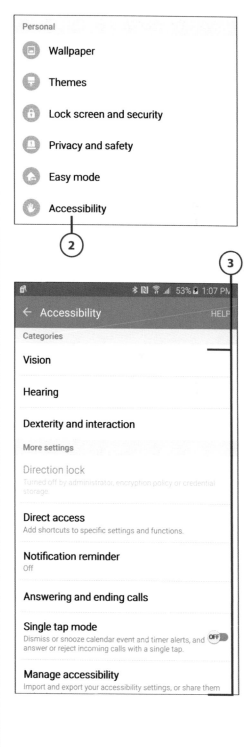

# Vision

1. Tap to enable or disable Voice Assistant. When enabled, Voice Assistant speaks everything, including menus, but it also has other features, such as one that requires that you double-tap something to select it instead of single tapping.

2. Tap to see a tutorial on how Voice Assistant works.

3. Tap to enable the Dark Screen feature. After this feature is enabled, you double-press the Power key to enable and disable it. When you have it enabled, your screen remains off for privacy.

4. Tap to enable the Rapid Key Input feature. When enabled, it overrides the Voice Assistant requirement of having to double-tap each key while typing.

5. Tap to enable Speak Passwords. When this feature is enabled, Voice Assistant speaks each character of your password as you type it.

6. Tap to record voice labels and write them to NFC tags.

## What Is a Voice Label?

Imagine if you could hold your Note 5 near an Near Field Communications (NFC) tag that was close to an object in the room, and a recording played back to tell you about the object? Voice Labels allow you to do just that. When you tap Voice Label in step 6, you can record your voice saying the name of the object, or something relevant about the object (say a refridgerator). After you have recorded what you want to say, you are prompted to hold a new NFC tag against the back of your Note 5 and your recording is written to the NFC tag. You can then stick the NFC tag near the object. When your Note 5 comes close to the NFC tag in the future, what you recorded will be automatically played back.

7.  Tap to set the font size used on your Galaxy Note 5. You can choose sizes ranging from tiny to huge.

8.  Tap to enable or disable magnification gestures, which include the ability to magnify any screen by triple-tapping it. When a screen is magnified, you can pan around it.

9.  Swipe up for more settings.

10. Tap to open a new screen that enables or disables a Magnifier Window that can magnify whatever is under it. You can change the size of the Magnifier Window and how much magnification is applied.

11. Tap to enable or disable the Grayscale feature, which makes everything on the screen grayscale instead of full color.

12. Tap to enable or disable the Negative Colors feature, which makes all colors displayed on your Galaxy Note 5 reversed. (For example, black text on a white background instead appears as white text on a black background.)

13. Tap to enable the Color Adjustment Wizard, which helps you adjust the screen colors if you have difficulty seeing it.

14. Tap to enable or disable the Accessibility Shortcut feature. When it's enabled, you can access accessibility features by performing certain gestures.

15. Tap to change the settings for the Text-to-Speech service provided by Samsung or to switch to the Google Text-to-Speech service.

16. Tap to save your changes and return to the previous screen.

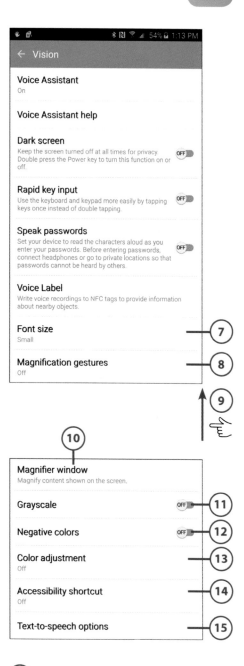

## More About Text-to-Speech

By default, your Galaxy Note 5 uses the Samsung Text-to-Speech service with an option to use the Samsung service to speak any text you need to read. You can install other text-to-speech software by searching for them in the Google Play Store. After you've installed the software, you'll have multiple choices.

# Hearing

1. Tap to enable or disable an option that makes your Note 5 vibrate when it detects a baby crying or a doorbell ringing.

2. Tap to enable or disable making your Note 5 light up the camera flash when you have a new notification.

3. Tap to turn off all sounds.

4. Tap to enable or disable improving the sound quality if you use a hearing aid.

5. Tap to enable video subtitles provided by Samsung, and adjust how the subtitles appear on the screen.

6. Tap to enable or disable video subtitles provided by Google, and adjust how the subtitles appear on the screen.

7. Tap to adjust the balance of audio played when wearing earphones.

8. Swipe up for more settings.

9. Tap to use mono audio when wearing one earphone.

10. Tap to enable or disable a feature that causes your Note 5 to vibrate in time to music being played, a video being watched, or a game being played.

11. Tap to save your changes and return to the previous screen.

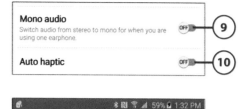

# Dexterity and Interaction

1. Tap to manage using universal switches to control your Note 5. Switches can include tapping on the screen, detecting movement of your head, eyes, or mouth, and can even include buttons being pressed on an externally con-nected accessory.

2. Tap to enable or disable the Assistant menu. Once it is enabled, you can set your domi-nant hand, reorder the menu items, and adjust the level of zoom. The Assistant menu appears as a small gray box on your screen at all times. When you tap it, it provides quick access to common device functions.

3. Tap to enable or disable the Gesture Wake Up feature. When this feature is enabled, you can wave your hand over the front of the device to wake it up as it rests on a flat surface .

4. Tap to adjust the Press and Hold Delay (also known as touch and hold) feature.

5. Tap to enable or disable Interaction control, which includes blocking areas of the screen so they do not respond to taps.

6. Tap to save your changes and return to the previous screen.

## What Is Direction Lock?

Direction Lock is a method of unlocking your Note 5 by drawing a pattern of directions on the screen. When you enable Direction Lock, you are asked to draw a series of directions on the screen (consisting of up, down, left, and right) that can be used as an unlock pattern. If you have enrolled in your company's Mobile Device Management (MDM) system, your administrator might have disabled Direction Lock, which prevents you from using this feature to unlock your Note 5.

## Direct Access

1. Tap to enable or disable direct access to certain accessibility settings. When this feature is enabled, press the Home button three times in quick succession to see the direct access menu.

2. Choose which accessibility settings you want direct access to.

3. Tap to save your changes and return to the previous screen.

**Dexterity and interaction**

Dexterity

**Universal switch**
Control your device with your customized switches.

**Assistant menu**
Turns on functions to improve device accessibility for users with reduced dexterity.

**Gesture wake up**
Turn on the screen without having to press hardkeys.

**Press and hold delay**
Short (0.5 seconds)

Interaction

**Interaction control**
Set options for touch control and other device interactions.

**Direct access**

**On**

Open your accessibility settings by pressing the Home key 3 times in quick succession.

Accessibility settings

**Accessibility** OFF

**Voice Assistant** OFF

**Universal switch** OFF

**Magnifier window** OFF

**Negative colors** OFF

**Grayscale** OFF

**Color adjustment** OFF
Set up to use in Direct access.

**Interaction control** OFF
Interaction control must be turned on before you can select it in Direct access.

# Notification Reminder

1. Tap to enable or disable extra notifications for certain apps.

2. Tap to choose whether to vibrate when one of your chosen apps sends a notification.

3. Tap to choose whether to turn on the indicator light when one of your chosen apps sends a notification.

4. Tap to choose how frequently the reminder occurs if you have not responded to the notification.

5. Choose which apps you want to receive this extra notification for.

6. Tap to save your changes and return to the previous screen.

**⑥**

← Notification reminder

**On** ① ON

Set the device to alert you via vibration, sound, or LED indicator when you have unread notifications.

Notification settings

**Vibrate** OFF ②

**LED indicator** OFF ③
Light up the blue LED when there are missed calls, unread messages, or app notifications while the screen is off. This function is not available while charging, voice recording, and receiving other notifications.

**Reminder interval** ④
1 minute

Select applications

➕ Samsung+ ON
Ⓢ Skype ON ⑤
▶ YouTube ON
G Google App ON

# Answering/Ending Calls

1. Tap to enable or disable answering a call by pressing the Home button.

2. Tap to enable or disable using voice commands to answer or reject calls. When enabled, just say "Answer" or "Reject."

3. Tap to enable or disable ending a call by pressing the Power button.

4. Tap to save your changes and return to the previous screen.

**④**

← Answering and ending calls

Answer calls by

**Pressing the Home key** OFF ①

**Using voice commands** OFF ②
Say "Answer" or "Reject" to answer or reject calls with your voice.

End calls by

**Pressing the Power key** OFF ③

## Manage Accessibility

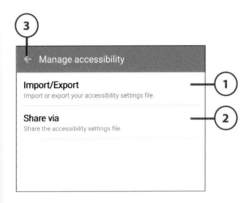

1. Tap to import accessibility settings that someone has shared with you or to export your settings.

2. Tap to share your accessibility settings with friends. You must first export your settings as mentioned in step 1.

3. Tap to return to the previous screen.

# Adjusting Sound and Notifications Settings

You can change the volume for games, ringtones, and alarms, change the default ringtone and notification sound, plus control what system sounds are used.

1. Pull down the Notification bar and tap the Settings icon.

2. Tap Sound and Notifications in the Device section.

**3.** Tap to change the sound mode between Sound (play all sounds), Vibrate (vibrate instead of playing sounds), or Mute (silence all sounds and vibrations).

**4.** Tap to change the volume for ringtones, music, video games and other media, notifications, and system alerts.

**5.** Tap to choose the intensity of vibrations for incoming calls, notifications, and haptic feedback. This screen also enables you to create custom vibration patterns. See the "Vibrations" section later in this chapter for more information.

**6.** Tap to choose whether you want to go through a wizard so that your Note 5 can adapt its audio output to your ears, and choose whether you want to enhance the audio using UHQ Upscaler, SoundAlive+, or TubeAmp Pro. See the "Sound Quality and Effects" section later in this chapter for more information.

**7.** Tap to choose whether you want to enable Do Not Disturb, and set any exceptions. See the "Do Not Disturb" section later in this chapter for more information.

**8.** Tap to choose which apps you want to see notifications for, choose whether you want notifications to be displayed on the Lock screen, and also which ones you want to see as priority notifications.

**9.** Tap to enable or disable having the LED indicator light when charging or recording a voice memo, or when you receive a new notification.

**10.** Tap to change the ringtone and sounds of Messages, Calendar, and Email, plus System sounds. See the next section for more on ringtones and sounds.

# Ringtones and Sounds

1. Tap to choose which ringtone plays when you receive an incoming phone call. While choosing the ringtone, you can add any audio file on your Note 5 as your ringtone.

2. Tap to choose the default notification sound that plays when a new notification is displayed.

3. Tap to choose whether you want to be notifiied when you receive a new SMS or MMS message, what ringtone plays when the notification is shown, and whether your Note 5 must also vibrate.

4. Tap to choose whether you want to be notified when you receive a new calendar notification (like an event reminder), what ringotne plays when the notification is shown, and whether your Note 5 must also vibrate.

5. Tap to choose whether you want to be notifiied when you receive a new email, what ringotne plays when the notification is shown, and whether your Note 5 must also vibrate. This alert does not change the Gmail notification setting.

6. Tap to enable or disable playing a sound when you interact with the touch screen, like tapping a menu item.

7. Tap to enable or disable touch tones that play while you type a phone number on the dialpad.

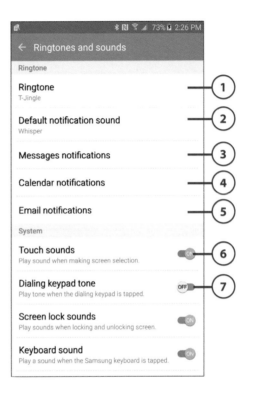

**8.** Tap to enable or disable playing a sound when you lock or unlock your Note 5.

**9.** Tap to enable or disable playing a sound for each key that you tap on the on-screen keyboard.

**10.** Tap to save your changes and return to the previous screen.

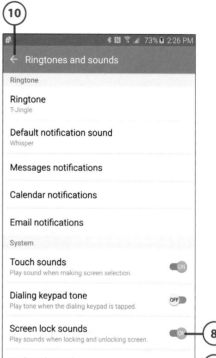

# Vibrations

**1.** Tap to choose the vibration intensity for incoming calls, notifications, and vibration feedback.

**2.** Tap to choose a default vibration pattern for notifications. You can also create your own custom vibration pattern that can later be assigned to contacts.

**3.** Tap to choose whether you want your Note 5 to also vibrate when receiving an incoming call.

**4.** Tap to choose whether you want vibration feedback when you tap the Recent apps and Back buttons.

**5.** Tap to choose whether you want to feel a vibration as you type on the on-screen keyboard.

**6.** Tap to save your changes and return to the previous screen.

## Creating Your Own Vibration Patterns

In step 2, you can choose the vibration pattern to be used when you are notified, but you can also create your own. Tap Create. On the next screen, tap in the
area where it reads Tap to Create, and then tap out your vibration pattern on the
screen using short taps for short vibrations and long taps for longer vibrations.
The example in the figure uses Morse Code for SOS. You can create any vibration
pattern you want. You can create more than one custom vibration pattern and
can then use those custom patterns to distinguish between incoming calls from
certain people in your Contacts. To do that, open the Contacts app, tap a contact, tap Edit, tap Add Another Field, and choose Vibration Pattern. You can then
change the Vibration Pattern from Default to one of your custom patterns.

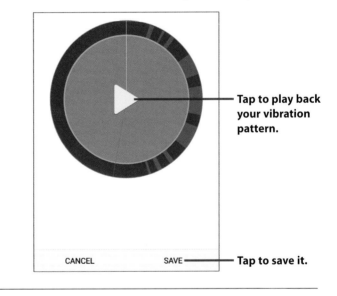

**Tap to play back
your vibration
pattern.**

CANCEL  SAVE ——— **Tap to save it.**

# Sound Quality and Effects

1. Tap to run through an audio test to determine your exact audotory range, and have your Note 5 customize the sound to best suit your hearing abilities.

2. Tap to enable or disable the UHQ Upscaler feature that enhances the sound resolution of audio to make the sound clearer.

3. Tap to enable or disable the SoundAlive+ feature that simulates surround sound. You can only enable this feature if you have a wired or Bluetooth headset connected.

4. Tap to enable or disable the Tube Amp feature that simulates a tube amplifier. You can only enable this feature if you have a wired or Bluetooth headset connected.

5. Tap to save your changes and return to the previous screen.

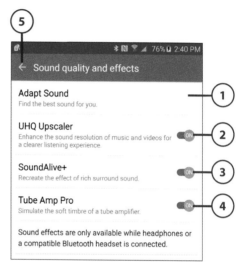

# Do Not Disturb

1. Tap to enable or disable the Do Not Disturb feature. When enabled, you receive no notifications unless you have specified exceptions.

2. Tap to allow exceptions to the Do Not Disturb rule. For example, you probably want to allow the alarm to still wake you up in the morning, and you might want to allow incoming calls from certain people.

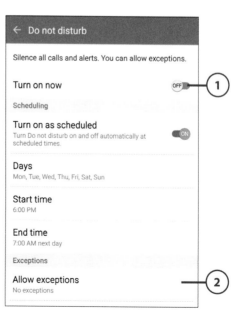

3. Tap to set a schedule when Do Not Disturb is automatically enabled and disabled. For example you might want to set it to be enabled when you go to sleep and disabled when you wake up.

4. Set the Do Not Disturb schedule.

5. Tap to save your changes and return to the previous screen.

# Modifying Display Settings

You can change many display settings, the screen mode, the wait time before your Galaxy Note 5 goes to sleep, the size of the font used, and the Pulse notification light settings.

1. Pull down the Notification bar and tap the Settings icon.

**2.** Tap Display in the Device section.

**3.** Hold and move your finger along the slider to change the screen brightness manually or use the check box to set it to automatic. When on Auto, your Galaxy Note 5 uses the built-in light sensor to adjust the brightness based on the light levels in the room.

**4.** Tap to change the system font and how large the font style is. The system font is used for all menus, notifications, alerts, and warnings on your Note 5.

**5.** Tap to choose whether you want to enable the one-handed keyboard or have the ability to press the Home button three times in quick succession to reduce the screen size.

**6.** Tap to choose how many minutes of inactivity must pass before your Galaxy Note 5 puts the screen to sleep.

**7.** Tap to enable Smart Stay. When this feature is enabled, your Note 5 uses the front-facing camera to look for your eyes. It keeps the screen on as long as it detects that you are looking at the screen.

**8.** Tap to choose the Screen mode, which is how the screen represents colors. You can manually choose AMOLED Cinema, AMOLED Photo, and Basic, or leave it set to Adapt Display, which means your Note 5 chooses the best settings based on usage.

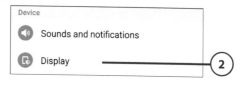

Device

🔊 Sounds and notifications

📱 Display ——————————— ②

---

⟵ Display

Brightness ——————————┐ ③
🔅A ——————————●————— ✓ Auto

Font
Small, Default ————————————— ④

One-handed operation ———————— ⑤

Screen timeout
After 30 seconds of inactivity. ————— ⑥

Smart stay
Off ————————————————— ⑦

Screen mode
Adaptive display ——————————— ⑧

Daydream
Off

9. Tap to enable or disable Daydream mode, decide what must be displayed when daydreaming, and when to daydream. Daydream mode is essentially a screensaver.

10. Tap to save your changes and return to the previous screen.

## What Is One-Handed Operation?

In step 5, you can choose to enable two features that allow you to use your Note 5 with one hand. The Note 5 is a large phone, and using it with one hand without special settings can be tricky. To help you achieve one-handed operation, you can choose to turn on reducing the screen size and/or turning on the one-handed keyboard. After you enable one-handed typing, your regular keyboard shrinks, which makes it easier to type with one hand. You can switch the shrunken keyboard to the bottom left or bottom right of the screen. When you enable the Reduce Screen Size feature, you can press the Home button three times in quick succession to make the screen shrink, which makes it easier to reach items near the top of the screen with one hand.

## Is Adaptive Display Mode Good?

If you leave your screen mode set to Adaptive Display, you should know that your Note 5 adjusts the color range, saturation, and sharpness of the screen for the Gallery, Camera, Internet Web Browser, Samsung Video, Samsung Smart Remote, and Google Play Books apps only. All other system apps and apps that you install are not optimized. With this in mind, you might prefer to manually select an appropriate screen mode in step 7.

## Aren't Screensaver's Obsolete?

Step 8 explains how to enable and manage the Daydream mode, which is essentially a screensaver as you might remember them from desktop computers. For many years now, screen savers have not been needed because we no longer use Cathode Ray Tube (CRT) monitors and screens. In the days when we used CRTs, if an image remained in one spot for a long time, it would be burned into the front of the screen. Having a screensaver on a CRT monitor made sense because the images were moving and changing constantly. Screen savers continued to be used because people liked seeing the patterns and images in the screensavers. This is why Daydream mode is on your Note 5. Once activated, it can display your photos or cool color patterns after a period of inactivity, when you plug your Note 5 into a dock, or when it is charging.

# Easy Home Screen Mode

Home Screen mode changes which widgets are placed on your Home screen and how many you have on the Home screen. When Easy mode is enabled, it makes available a lot of widgets that have shortcuts to many apps, and it makes the icons larger.

1. Tap Easy Mode in the Personal section.

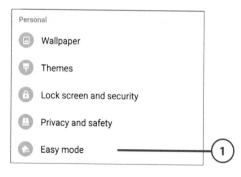

2. Tap to enable Easy Mode.

3. Swipe up to select which apps you want to have shortcuts to on your Home screen.

4. Tap Done to save your changes. You return to the Easy Mode Home screen.

# Privacy And Safety

You use Privacy and Safety to set whether you want to allow your geographic location to be available to Google and apps running on your phone, to manage Private Mode, and to set up a feature that allows your phone to send information to people when you are in an emergency situation.

1. Tap Privacy And Safety in the Personal section.

2. Tap to manage whether Google or apps running on your phone have access to your geographic location.

3. Tap to enable or disable allowing your phone to report diagnostic information to Google.

4. Tap to manage how SOS messages are handled. See the "Send SOS Messages" section later in this chapter for more information.

5. Tap to manage Private Mode, which is covered in the next section.

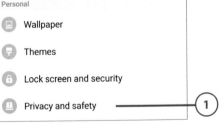

# Private Mode

Private mode is a bit confusing at first. While it is enabled, you can move content from certain apps to a secret area on your Galaxy Note 5. When Private mode is disabled, the content is invisible unless you come back into Settings and enable it again.

**④**

← Private mode

On                                              **①**

Private mode access type                        **②**
PIN

Auto off                                         **③**
Automatically turn off Private mode when the screen turns off.

Use Private mode to hide content that you want to keep private. While you are using the following apps, select items you want to move to Private, then tap MORE and select Move to Private.

- Gallery
- Video
- Music
- Voice Recorder
- My Files
- Internet
- S Note

1. Tap to enable or disable Private mode.

2. Choose a method for securing Private mode. The method you use here is in addition to the method you already use for unlocking your Note 5. You need to make this choice only one time when you first enable Private mode.

3. Tap to enable or disable automatically disabling Private mode when the screen turns off. This is recommended.

4. Tap to save your changes and return to the previous screen.

## >>>Go Further
## USING PRIVATE MODE

Private mode is a confusing feature. Essentially when Private mode is enabled, you can move content from certain apps to a secret, hidden area on your Note 5. You are also able to see content that you previously moved to this secret area. When Private mode is disabled, anything in the secret area becomes unavailable and invisible. When you enable Private mode again, you have to use a password, PIN, pattern, or your fingerprint. Private mode works only with the following apps (that Samsung has heavily modified): Gallery, Video, Music, Voice Recorder, My Files, and Internet (not the Chrome browser). When Private mode is enabled, you tap the Menu icon to reveal a new menu item called Move to Private.

**Move selected items to the Private area.**

# Send SOS Messages

When you have this feature enabled, if you find yourself in an emergency situation where you need help, you can press the Power button on your Note 5 three times in quick succession, and your phone starts taking note of your geographic location, recording audio, taking pictures, and sending it all to one or more contacts that you have previously set up.

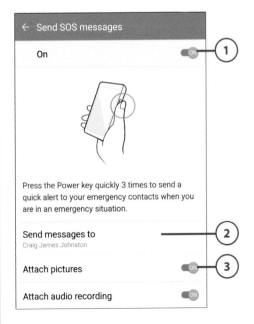

1. Tap to enable the Send SOS messages feature. The first time you enable it, you are asked to choose at least one person from your contacts or to enter a new mobile phone number to be used by the feature.

2. Tap to manage which contacts will be sent your location, audio, and pictures when you trigger this feature. You can have more than one contact.

3. Tap to enable or disable including pictures with the SOS messages.

4. Tap to enable or disable including audio recordings with the SOS messages.

5. Tap to save your changes and return to the previous screen.

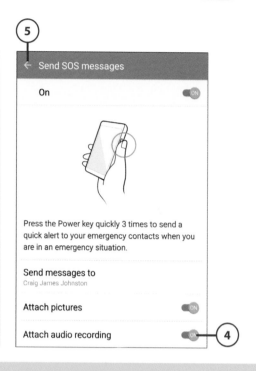

# >>>Go Further
## USING THE SEND SOS MESSAGES FEATURE

If you find yourself in an emergency situation, press the Power button three times in quick succession. You phone immediately starts sending Save Our Souls (SOS) text messages to the people you have previously indicated should received them. If you have chosen to, your phone also starts taking pictures and sending them. Finally, if you have chosen to, your phone starts recording audio and sending it to your chosen contacts. This continues until you stop it. To stop sending SOS messages, again press the Power button three times in quick succession.

## Themes

Themes are packaged changes that, once chosen, change the look and feel of your Note 5. Themes have ability to change the system sounds, wallpaper, icons, fonts used, and colors used in phone menus and including the Notification screen. The themes can also modify the look and feel of some core Samsung apps, such as the Phone app.

1. Pull down the Notifications bar and tap the Settings icon.

2. Tap Themes in the Personal section or in the Quick Settings section.

>>>*Go Further*

## CHANGE THEMES MORE QUICKLY

A faster way to get to the Theme screen is to touch and hold on the Home screen and tap Themes.

**Applied theme**

3. Tap a theme to download it and make it active. If you have previously downloaded and installed the theme, skip to step 5.

4. Tap Download to download and install the theme.

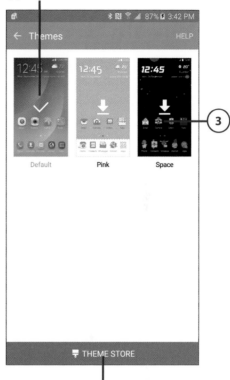

**Download or purchase new themes.**

**5.** Tap Apply.

Tap to delete
the theme.

## Lock Screen and Security

These settings screens allow to
control what is shown on the Lock
screen, how your device is unlocked,
whether you want non-Google Play
apps to be installed, and many other
security-related options.

**1.** Pull down the Notification bar
and tap the Settings icon.

2. Tap Lock Screen and Security.

3. Tap to change what must be done to unlock your phone's screen. You can choose to do nothing, or require a swipe across the screen, or you can use a security method like a numeric PIN, trace a pattern, type a password, or use your fingerprint.

4. Tap to choose what information is shown on the Lock screen. You can choose to show the clock, weather, and even your name.

5. Tap to choose whether notifications appear on the Lock screen, and if they do, whether they show the content of the notification or just the notification itself. You can also choose which apps can send notifications to the Lock screen.

6. Tap to manage your Secure Lock settings. Secure Lock settings include the setting for automatically locking the screen after a specified time, allowing you to press the Power button to lock the screen, and Smart Lock settings that allow you to keep your Note 5 unlocked under certain situations. See the "More About Smart Lock" margin note later in this section for more information.

7. Tap to manage your fingerprints. This includes adding or removing fingerprints, choosing when to use your fingerprint, and changing the backup password that you use when your fingerprint cannot be detected.

8. Tap to choose whether you want to enabled Samsung's KNOX Active Protection (KAP) or install and use Samsung's My KNOX, which is a secure container for your company apps and data.

# >>>Go Further
## WHAT IS KNOX?

Samsung KNOX is a feature that, once enabled, creates a "container" on your Note 5 where your company information is kept seperate from your personal information. You might want to use KNOX if you want to reduce the possibility that an app you install on your Note 5 might compromise or steal your company information. Read more about KNOX at https://www.samsungknox.com.

9. Tap to enable and manage Samsung's Find My Mobile service. When it's enabled, you can log in to the Find My Mobile website to track your stolen phone and send a remote wipe command to it. For more information, see the "More About Find My Mobile" note at the end of this chapter.

10. Swipe up for more settings.

11. Tap to be allowed to install Android apps that are not found in the Google Play Store. This is not recommended because apps that aren't in the official app store might contain viruses and malware. Proceed with caution if you enable this feature. If you have enrolled your device in your company's Mobile Device Management (MDM) system, you might be required to enable this option.

12. Tap to see other security settings.

13. Tap to encrypt your phone's file system. When the system is encrypted, if you power off your phone and then power it back on, you need to enter a numeric PIN to unencrypt your device before it starts up. In this example, the Note 5 is already encrypted.

14. Tap to set and manage a PIN to unlock your SIM card. If you use a PIN to lock your SIM card, you need to enter it in addition to entering any security measures you set for your phone.

15. Tap to enable or disable briefly showing each character of a password as you type it.

16. Tap to manage how your phone gets security policy updates from Samsung. You can choose to have them automatically download and installed, and you can choose to have them download only when you're connected to Wi-Fi.

17. Tap to enable or disable automatically sending security reports to Samsung.

18. Tap to manage device administrators. See the nearby margin note "More About Device Adiministrators" for more information.

19. Swipe up for more settings.

## More About Device Administrators

Device Administrators are apps that you have given permission to administer your phone. One of the Device Administrators is the Android Device Manager. This enables you to log in to www.google.com/android/devicemanager on a desktop computer and reset your device password or erase all your device's data (in the event your phone has been stolen). If you enroll your phone in your company Enterprise Mobile Management (EMM) system, like those made by AirWatch or MobileIron, those systems also add a Device Administrator.

## More About Smart Lock

Smart Lock is an Android security service that allows your device to automatically lock and unlock based on certain criteria and situations. For example, you can have your Note 5 unlock if it detects a trusted device, such as a smartwatch or other paired Bluetooth device. You can have your Note 5 unlock when it detects that it is within a certain geographical area. Finally, you can have your Note 5 unlock when it detects that it is on your body, either in your pocket or in your hand. To set up Smart Lock, open Settings, Lock Screen and Security, Secure Lock Settings, and tap Smart Lock.

**20.** The Storage type item is for information only. It indicates whether your phone supports storing your private encryption keys in the hardware (Hardware-backed) or stored in software only.

**21.** Tap to view and select or deselect trusted certificates that the Android system uses and the ones you may be using.

**22.** Tap to install certificates from your phone's storage. This assumes you previously saved the certificate to storage.

**23.** Tap to remove all trusted user certificates (if you are using any).

**24.** Tap to manage Trust Agents. Trust Agents are trusted agents or services that you trust to manage your phone's security. Today there is only one Trust Agent called Smart Lock, which is provided by Google. Smart Lock is discussed in more detail in a previous margin note.

**25.** Tap to enable or disable Screen Pinning, which allows you to "pin" an app so that the person using it cannot exit the app. See the "More About Pinning an App" margin note for more information.

**26.** Tap to manage which apps running on your phone are allowed to collect app usage information about all apps you have installed. This usage information includes how often each app is run, how long it sits in the foreground (active on your screen), and how long it sits in the background (still running but not visible).

**27.** Tap to manage which apps have access to notifications that appear on your phone. Typically if you use an Android Wear Smartwatch, the Android Wear app is listed in this screen.

**28.** Tap to save your changes and return to the previous screen.

**28**

**⬡**      ✳ ℕ 🛜 📶 90% 🔋 3:58 PM

←   Other security settings

View or turn off device administrators.

Credential storage

**Storage type**
Back up to hardware.

**View security certificates**
Display trusted CA certificates.

**Install from device storage**
Install certificates from storage.

Clear credentials
Remove all certificates

Advanced

**Trust agents**
Perform selected actions when trusted devices are connected.

**Pin windows**                    **25**
Off

**Usage data access**          **26**
View which applications can access your device's usage history.

**Notification access**         **27**
1 application is allowed to read notifications.

## More About Pinning an App

When you enable screen pinning in step 24, you are enabling a feature that allows you to "pin" an app to the screen. When an app is pinned to the screen, you cannot exit the app, go back to the Home screen, pull down the Notification or Quick Settings bars, or do anything other than interact with the app. You can only pin the app you ran most recently. To pin an app to the screen, first run the app so that it is the most recently used app. Tap the Recent Apps button, and slide the app up so that you can see the pin icon. Tap the pin icon to pin the app to the screen. To exit pinned mode, touch and hold the Back and Recent Apps buttons at the same time. Pinning an app to the screen is a quick way to allow someone to use your phone without letting them access anything else other than the app they should be using.

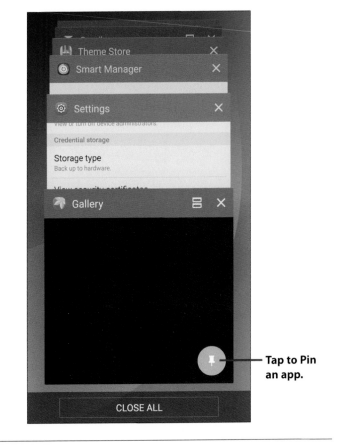

Tap to Pin an app.

## More About Fingerprints

You can store one or more thumb- or fingerprints on your Galaxy Note 5, and choose to use them to unlock your phone, sign in to websites, and verify your Samsung account. To manage your fingerprints, tap Settings, Lock Screen and Security, Fingerprints. Use this screen to add fingerprints. As you add a new fingerprint, your phone walks you through the process of capturing your fingerprint via the fingerprint sensor in the Home button. You can also choose or change your backup password. You use your backup password if the fingerprint sensor cannot detect your fingerprint.

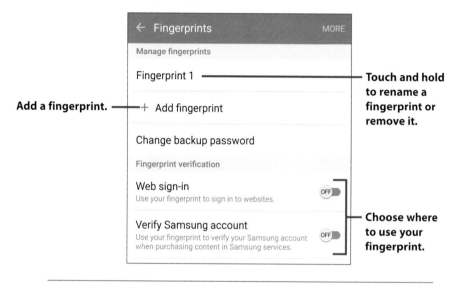

**Add a fingerprint.**

**Touch and hold to rename a fingerprint or remove it.**

**Choose where to use your fingerprint.**

## More About Find My Mobile

If you have a Samsung account, and you have enabled Find My Mobile in step 8, you can locate and remotely wipe your phone if it ever gets lost. To do this, open a desktop web browser on a computer, and browse to https://findmymobile.samsung.com to log in with your Samsung account. Once logged in, click Registered Device to select the device you want to work with (if you have more than one device registered). You can then locate your device, make the device play a ringtone (if you lost it in the couch and need to find it), enable Emergency mode, and enable Ultra Power Saving mode to conserve the battery. You can also remotely lock your device's screen, or send a wipe command that wipes your device and sets it back to factory condition. You would do this last step in a situation where your device has been stolen and you want to make sure that the thief doesn't get to your data.

Browse without leaving traces using the Incognito feature.

In this chapter, you discover how to browse the World Wide Web using the Chrome browser app that comes with your Galaxy Note 5. Topics include the following:

→ Bookmarking websites
→ Using tricks to browse quickly
→ Keeping track of websites you have visited
→ Configuring Chrome to work your way

# Browsing the Web

Your Galaxy Note 5 comes with not one but two web browsers to enable you to explore the Web on its large screen. This chapter shows you how to use Chrome, a browser developed by Google. Your Galaxy Note 5 also includes the browser usually called simply Internet, but sometimes called (arguably even more simply) Browser, which is developed by Samsung.

Chrome is fast and easy to use. You can bookmark sites you want to revisit, hold your Galaxy Note 5 in landscape orientation so you can see more on the screen, and optionally share your GPS location with sites.

## Navigating with Chrome

The Chrome browser app enables you to access sites quickly, bookmark them for future use, and return instantly to the sites you visit most frequently. You can even sync your open Chrome tabs among your Galaxy Note 5, your other portable devices, and your computer.

## Should You Sign In to Chrome?

When you first launch Chrome on your Galaxy Note 5, the app might display the Set Up Chrome screen, which prompts you to select an account and sign in so that you can share your bookmarks, history, passwords, and other settings on all your devices. Signing in is usually helpful, because it enables you to start browsing on one device (such as your desktop computer) and then, on your Galaxy Note 5, to pick up where you left off.

So normally, you would want to select the right Google account (if there's a choice) and tap the Sign In button. The Hi screen appears, telling you that your data will be synced. From this screen, you can tap Settings to change your settings or tap Done to start browsing with Chrome.

## Go to a Web Page by Typing Its Address

1. Tap the Chrome icon on the Apps screen. Alternatively, if the Chrome icon appears on the Home screen, tap it there, or it might be in the Google folder on the Home screen. Chrome opens and displays either your home page (as in the example shown here) or the last page you visited.

2. Tap the omnibox—a combined address box and search box—to select its contents. If the website has moved the previous page up so that the omnibox is hidden, drag the web page down so that the omnibox appears again.

3. Type the web address, such as **android.com**. Chrome displays any matching results.

4. Tap the result for the web page you want to display. The web page appears.

5. Tap Home to go back to your home page.

6. Tap the Menu button to display the menu, which contains many commands. The next section explains these commands.

7. If the square green icon bearing a white padlock appears, tap it to display the security information for the website. See the nearby note for more details.

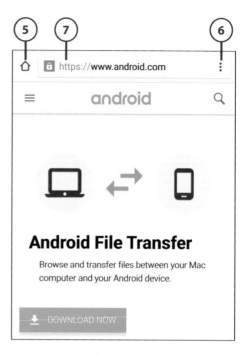

## What Does the Green Icon with the White Padlock Mean?

The green icon with the white padlock appears when Chrome has established a secure connection to the website. The omnibox shows the address here starting with https:// to indicate that the connection uses Hypertext Transfer Protocol Secure (HTTPS) instead of regular Hypertext Transfer Protocol (HTTP), which is not secure. Chrome uses technologies called Secure Sockets Layer (SSL) and Transport Layer Security (TLS) to secure the connection using encryption.

**Tap Details to view the details of the connection.**

When you connect to any site with which you will exchange private or sensitive information, it is best to make sure that the padlock icon appears. But because of the recent furor over government surveillance of the Internet, more and more websites are using encryption as a matter of course, so don't be surprised to see the padlock icon for "regular" websites.

You can tap the padlock icon to display a pop-up window containing details about the website's identity and the security of your connection to it.

| | |
|---|---|
| 🔒 **www.android.com** | **Look here to see whether the website's identity has been verified.** |
| The identity of this website has been verified by Google Internet Authority G2. Valid Certificate Transparency information was supplied by the server. | |
| Certificate information | |
| 🔒 Your connection to www.android.com is encrypted using a modern cipher suite. | **Look here to confirm that the connection to the website is encrypted.** |
| The connection uses TLS 1.2. | |
| The connection is encrypted and authenticated using AES_128_GCM and uses ECDHE_RSA as the key exchange mechanism. | |
| What do these mean? | |

# Web Page Options

While a web page is open, you have a number of options, such as opening a new tab, creating a bookmark for the page, and finding text on the page.

1. Tap the Menu button to display the menu.

2. Tap the Forward button to return to the previous web page from which you have gone back on this tab. The Forward button is available only when you have visited multiple pages on this tab and have gone back from at least the last page, by tapping the Back button (the soft button below the screen), to an earlier page.

3. Tap the Bookmark star to add a bookmark for this page.

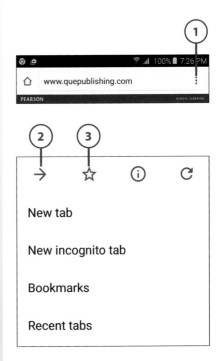

4. Tap the Information icon to display information about the connection to the website on this page. See the first image in the nearby note titled "What Does the Green Icon with the White Padlock Mean?" for an example of the information window that appears. Tap outside the information window to close it.

5. Tap the Refresh icon to refresh the display of the current web page. You'd normally do this either if a page failed to load completely or to load updated information, such as fresh news.

6. Tap New Tab to open a new tab.

7. Tap New Incognito Tab to open a new Incognito tab for private browsing. Incognito tabs are covered later in this chapter.

8. Tap Bookmarks to display your bookmarks.

9. Tap Recent Tabs to display your Recent Tabs list. This list includes the Other Devices list, which gives you access to recent tabs on other devices with which you sign in to the same Chrome account.

10. Tap History to display the History screen, which contains a list of the pages you have visited on your Galaxy Note 5.

11. Tap Share to share this web page with other people using apps such as Email, Gmail, Facebook, Messaging, and Twitter. The Share Via dialog shows all the apps you can use to share the web page.

12. Tap Print to start the process of printing the current page.

13. Tap Find in Page to search this page for specific text you type.

14. Tap Add to Home Screen to display the Add to Home Screen dialog. You can then type the name to give the icon that Android adds to the Home screen. You can then tap this icon to go straight to the website in your default browser, such as Chrome.

15. Tap Request Desktop Site to enable or disable forcing websites to show the regular view of a web page designed for full-size screens instead of a mobile view designed for small screens. When you change this setting, Chrome reloads the page, displaying the desktop version if it is available.

16. Tap Settings to change the settings for the Chrome browser.

17. Tap Help & Feedback to get help or to vent your frustrations with Chrome.

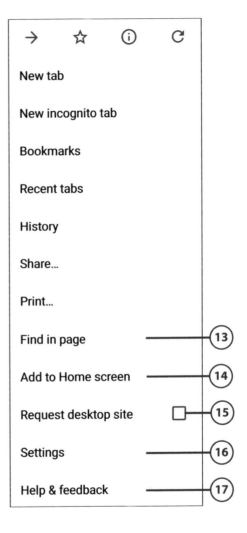

## Browser Tricks

The Chrome browser app has some neat tricks to help you browse regular websites comfortably on your Galaxy Note 5's screen.

1. Rotate your Galaxy Note 5 so that its long edge is sideways. This puts the screen into what's called *landscape orientation*. Your Galaxy Note 5 automatically switches the screen to Landscape mode.

### Why Won't My Screen Rotate?

If Chrome does not switch to landscape mode when you rotate the Galaxy Note 5, you need to turn on screen rotation. Pull down the Notification panel and tap the Screen Rotation icon in the Quick Settings bar, turning the arrow green.

2. If necessary, double-tap the screen to zoom in and out. You can also place your thumb and forefinger on the screen and spread them apart to zoom in or pinch them together to zoom out.

**Portrait**

> **What Exactly Is a Smart Home?**
>
> The IoT-connected home is being dubbed a *smart home*, although experienced techie might know it from its older moniker of *home automation*. Home automation has been around for a few decades now, in terms of automating lighting, heating and cooling, and the like, typically in high-end full-house systems created by suppliers such as Crestron and Control4, but also in lower-priced DIY systems, such as the X10.
>
> The concept of home automation is a simple one. You take a given task or operation, typically performed when you manually turn on a device, and somehow make that device turn on and work automatically, without your manual intervention. Simple home automation uses timers and clocks, and sometimes smartphones and tablets, to enable the operations. More advanced smart home technology can handle more sophistication operating scenarios and trigger devices based on input from other devices.

**Landscape**

## Using Bookmarks, Recent Tabs, and History

Chrome enables you to bookmark your favorite websites for quick access, but it also keeps a list of the sites you visit most often so you can return to them at the tap of an icon. Chrome also syncs your recent tabs among your devices that run Chrome and sign in to the same Google account, so you can quickly pick up browsing on your Galaxy Note 5 exactly where you left it on your desktop computer, laptop, or tablet—or vice versa.

# Manage Bookmarks

1. Tap the Menu button.

2. Tap Bookmarks. Normally, the Mobile Bookmarks folder opens. If not, you can navigate to it manually.

3. Tap Bookmarks to display the main Bookmarks folder. From there, you can tap a bookmark it contains or another bookmarks folder.

4. Tap a bookmarks folder to display the bookmarks it contains.

5. Tap a bookmark to display the web page it marks.

6. Tap and hold a bookmark to display a menu of extra actions you can take with it.

7. Tap Open in New Tab to open the bookmarked web page in a new tab.

8. Tap Open in Incognito Tab to open the bookmark in an Incognito tab.

9. Tap Edit Bookmark to edit the bookmark. For example, you can change the bookmark's name or move it to a different folder.

10. Tap Delete Bookmark to delete the bookmark.

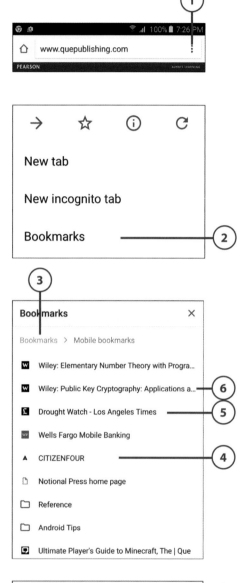

# Create a Bookmark

1. Navigate to the page you want to bookmark.

2. Tap the Menu button to open the menu.

3. Tap the Bookmark star to start creating a new bookmark.

4. Change the bookmark name if you want to. The default is the web page's title; you might prefer a shorter name.

5. Edit the address if necessary. If you went to the right page in step 1, you do not need to change the address.

6. Select the folder in which to save the bookmark. You can create new folders as needed by tapping New Folder on the Choose a Folder screen.

7. Tap Save to save the bookmark.

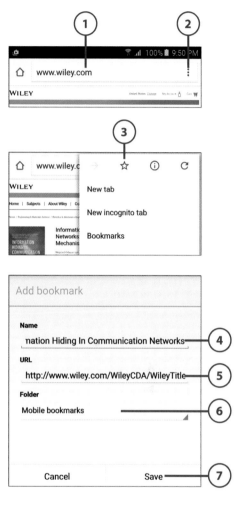

# Go to a Web Page Using the Recent Tabs List

Chrome's Recent Tabs list enables you to go back to web pages that you have opened recently on either your Galaxy Note 5 or any other device on which you log Chrome in to the same Google account, such as your Android tablet or your PC or Mac.

1. Tap the Menu button.

2. Tap Recent Tabs to display the Recent Tabs screen.

3. Look at the This Device list to see tabs that are currently open on your Galaxy Note 5.

4. Look at the Recently Closed list to see tabs you've recently closed on your Galaxy Note 5.

5. Tap a downward caret on a heading to expand the list of tabs the computer or device contains.

6. Tap an upward caret on a heading to collapse the list of tabs.

7. Tap Show Full History to display the full history of Chrome browsing on your Galaxy Note 5.

8. Tap a tab name to display the web page.

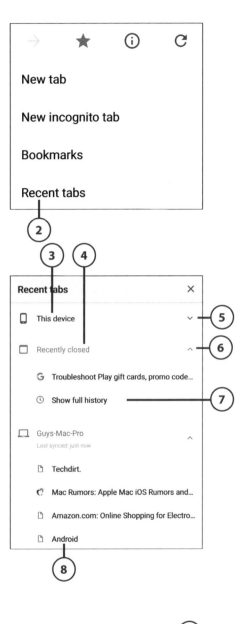

# Go to a Web Page Using Your History

Chrome's History list enables you to go back to web pages that you have opened in Chrome on your Galaxy Note 5. The History list contains both pages you have bookmarked and pages you have not bookmarked.

1. Tap the Menu button.

2. Tap History to display the History screen.

3. Tap Search History to search through your history using keywords.

4. Tap the name of the page you want to display.

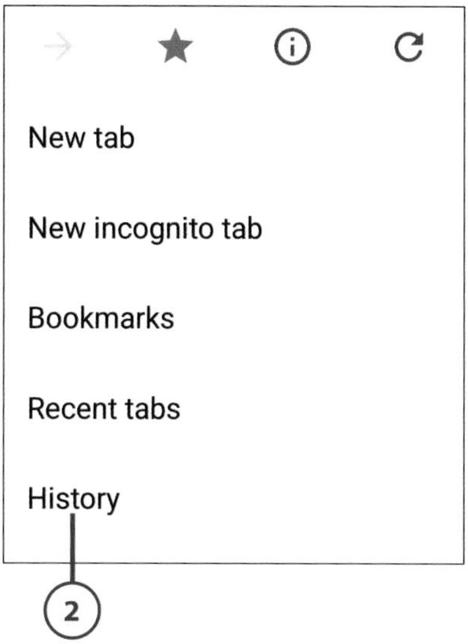

→  ★  ⓘ  C

New tab

New incognito tab

Bookmarks

Recent tabs

History

②

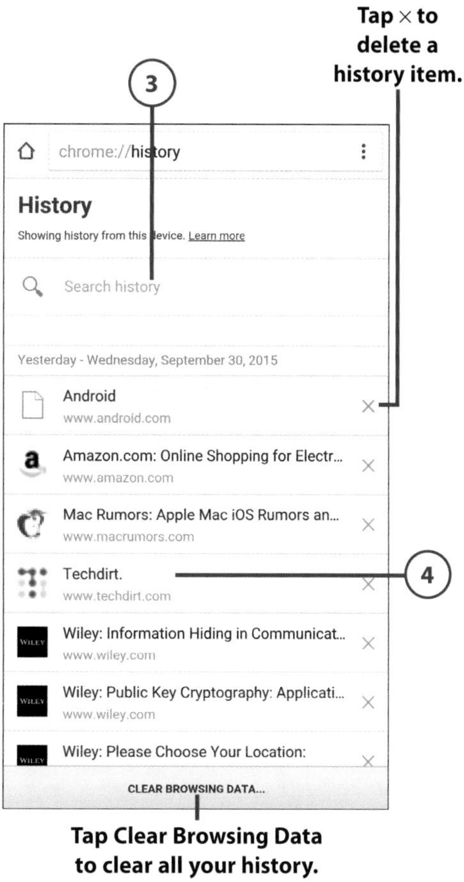

**Tap × to delete a history item.**

③

⌂  chrome://history  ⋮

**History**

Showing history from this device. Learn more

🔍  Search history

Yesterday - Wednesday, September 30, 2015

▢  Android
   www.android.com  ×

a  Amazon.com: Online Shopping for Electr...
   www.amazon.com  ×

🌀  Mac Rumors: Apple Mac iOS Rumors an...
   www.macrumors.com  ×

⋮⋮⋮  Techdirt.
   www.techdirt.com  ×  ④

WILEY  Wiley: Information Hiding in Communicat...
       www.wiley.com  ×

WILEY  Wiley: Public Key Cryptography: Applicati...
       www.wiley.com  ×

WILEY  Wiley: Please Choose Your Location:  ×

CLEAR BROWSING DATA...

**Tap Clear Browsing Data to clear all your history.**

## Delete Individual History Items—or All History Items

Given the nature of the Web, it's easy enough to browse to a site that you don't want to keep in your history. When this happens, tap the Menu button, tap History, and then tap the × icon on the right side of the button for the item you want to remove.

**Check the Clear Browsing History box.**

### Clear browsing data

Browsing history ☑

Cache ☑

Cookies, site data ☑

Saved passwords ☐

Autofill data ☐

You won't be signed out of your Google Accounts

CANCEL    CLEAR ——— **Then tap Clear.**

If you want to get rid of all your history items, tap the Clear Browsing Data button at the bottom of the History screen to open the Clear Browsing Data screen. Check the Clear Browsing History box and tap Clear to delete your history. From the Clear Browsing Data screen, you can also clear other browsing data than your history; we'll look at your options later in this chapter.

# Browsing with Multiple Tabs

Chrome can have multiple web pages open at the same time, each in a different tab. This enables you to open multiple web pages at once and switch between them without having to reload pages.

You can switch among your open web pages in two ways:

- **By using the Recents feature**—As you know, the Recents feature (which is called Overview in standard versions of Android) shows you a thumbnail for each app or window you have open. When you have multiple Chrome tabs open, each appears as a separate thumbnail on the Recents screen. So you can tap the Recents button to display the Recents screen, and then tap the window containing the tab you want to view. This is Android's new method of switching among Chrome tabs, but it's not necessarily better, faster, or easier than the old method.

- **By switching directly within Chrome**—If you don't find it convenient to switch tabs via the Recents screen, you can turn off the Merge Tabs and Apps setting in Chrome. Doing this activates the tab switcher inside Chrome, and you can switch tabs without leaving Chrome. You might find this method of browsing easier, so this chapter shows you how to use it as well as the new method.

## Open a New Tab

To make sure that you have multiple tabs among which to switch, open one or more extra tabs by following these steps in Chrome:

1. In Chrome, tap and hold a link on the page that is currently displayed. The pop-up menu of actions appears.

2. Tap Open in New Tab. Chrome opens a new tab and displays the web page in it. Repeat these steps one or more times to open other tabs.

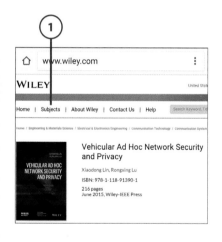

## What If the Current Page Has No Links?

If the current page contains no links, tap the Menu button, and then tap New Tab to open a new tab. The new tab normally displays your Most Visited list by default. Tap a page thumbnail to display that page, or tap the Search box, type a web address or search terms, and then tap the search result you want to view.

**Tap the Search box and type a web address or search terms.**

**Tap a thumbnail to display that web page.**

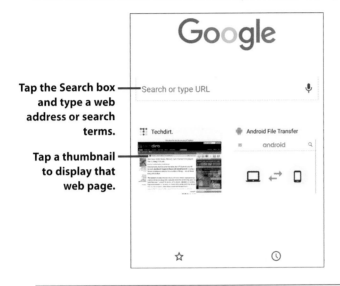

# Browse with Multiple Tabs Using the Recents Screen

By default, Chrome normally has the Merge Tabs and Apps setting enabled, so you use the Recents screen to switch from one tab to another within Chrome.

1. After opening multiple tabs, as explained in the previous section, tap the Recents button below the screen. The Recents screen appears, showing a thumbnail for each open app or window, including the Chrome tabs. The most recent items are at the bottom.

2. Scroll down as needed to display the thumbnail for the tab you want, and then tap the thumbnail. Chrome appears full screen showing that page.

**Tap Multi Window to display the tab's page in the upper half of the screen.**

②

**Tap × to close a tab.**

# Browse with Multiple Tabs Within Chrome

If you find the Recents screen an awkward way to navigate among the tabs you have opened in Chrome, you can enable Chrome's built-in tab switcher by turning off the Merge Tabs and Apps setting.

## Disable the Merge Tabs and Apps Setting

In Chrome, follow these steps to turn off the Merge Tabs and Apps setting and enable the built-in tab switcher:

1. Tap the Menu button.

2. Tap Settings to display the Settings screen.

3. Tap the Merge Tabs and Apps button to display the Merge Tabs and Apps screen.

4. Set the Merge Tabs and Apps switch to Off. The Separate Tabs and Apps dialog opens.

5. Tap OK to close the Separate Tabs and Apps dialog. The Recents screen appears briefly, and then Chrome appears again, showing the web page from where you started—but with the Tabs icon now displayed. The Tabs icon shows the number of open tabs in Chrome.

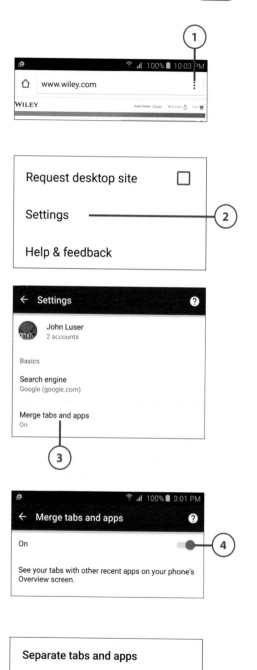

# Browse Multiple Tabs Using Chrome's Built-In Tab Switcher

After enabling Chrome's built-in tab switcher, you can browse multiple tabs by following these steps:

1. Tap the Tabs icon to display the Tabs screen.

2. Tap New Tab (+) to open a new tab displaying the New Tab screen. You can then navigate to a web page by entering an address, searching, or tapping a thumbnail or bookmark.

3. Tap the Menu button to navigate to a web page via the menu. For example, you may want to tap History on the menu so that you can navigate to a web page you visited earlier.

4. Tap the Tabs button (the button showing the number of tabs) if you want to go back to the page you were viewing before you displayed the Tabs screen. You can also tap the Back button to go back to that page.

5. Tap × to close a tab.

6. Swipe a tab left or right off the list to close it.

7. Tap the tab you want to display.

# Browsing in Secret with Incognito Tabs

If you want to visit a website in secret, you can use Incognito tabs. Incognito is a special mode that means that the web pages you visit don't appear in your browser history or search history and do not leave traces on your Galaxy Note 5 unless you create bookmarks for the pages or download files from them.

1. Tap the Menu button.

2. Tap New Incognito Tab. Chrome displays the Incognito screen for new tabs, which shows the "You've gone incognito" message.

3. Navigate to the web page using normal means. For example, tap Search or Type URL and type your search terms; then tap the appropriate search result.

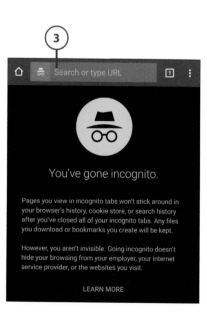

4. When you want to switch tabs, tap the Tabs icon to display the Tabs screen if you have turned off the Merge Tabs and Apps setting. (If Merge Tabs and Apps is on, tap the Recents button to display the Recents screen, as usual.)

5. Tap and drag the border between the gray Incognito tabs and the light-shaded regular tabs to switch from your Incognito tabs to your regular tabs.

**The Incognito icon and dark control area show you are using Incognito mode.**

## It's Not All Good

### Incognito Mode Doesn't Make You Anonymous

If you use Incognito mode, it's important you understand its limitations. Incognito mode keeps the web pages you visit out of your browser history and search history so they don't appear either on your Galaxy Note 5 or on other devices on which you use Chrome with the same Google account.

However, Incognito mode doesn't make you anonymous on the Web. Your ISP can still see, and may well store, the details of your web browsing in Incognito mode. Worse, government agencies may be able to extract this information from your ISP.

# Customizing Browser Settings

You can customize Chrome to make it behave the way you want. Chrome has a wide range of settings, which it breaks up into the categories Basics and Advanced. Chrome also enables you to choose settings for syncing your data among the computers and devices that log in to your Google account.

## Choose Sync Settings

1. In Chrome, tap the Menu button.

2. Tap Settings to display the Settings screen.

3. Tap your Google account name to display the screen for configuring your account.

4. Move the Accounts switch to On if you want to sign in to your account or to Off if you don't want to sign in.

5. Tap your Google account's email address to display the Sync screen.

6. Move the Sync switch to On or Off, as needed. To get the most out of Chrome, set the switch to On, as in this example, and then choose which items to sync.

7. Move the Sync Everything switch to On if you want to sync all the available items. Otherwise, check the Autofill box, the Bookmarks box, the History box, the Passwords box, the Open Tabs box, and the Settings box as needed.

8. Tap Encryption to display the Encryption dialog.

9. Tap the Encrypt All with Passphrase radio button and then enter the passphrase when prompted. Make sure your password is strong enough by using at least eight characters (preferably 12 to 20), combining uppercase and lowercase letters with numbers and symbols (such as $ or %), and avoiding any word or misspelling of a word in any language.

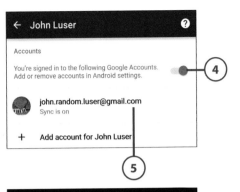

You can tap Manage Synced Data to display the Chrome Sync page of configuration options.

## Why (and How) You Should Encrypt Your Chrome Sync Data

Browsing the Web often involves private or sensitive data, even when you don't buy anything or do anything embarrassing. So it is a good idea to encrypt your Chrome sync data to prevent others from being able to read it if they intercept it.

The Encryption dialog contains two options: the Encrypt Passwords with Google Credentials radio button and the Encrypt All with Passphrase radio button. Normally, you should choose the Encrypt All with Passphrase radio button, because it encrypts all the data that Chrome syncs instead of encrypting only the passwords.

**10.** Tap the arrow or the Back button to return to the account screen.

**11.** Tap the arrow or the Back button to return to the Settings screen.

## Choose Basics Settings

Chrome's basic settings include choosing your search engine and home page, deciding whether to use the Autofill Forms feature, and managing your saved passwords.

**1.** From the Settings screen, tap Search Engine to display the Search Engine dialog.

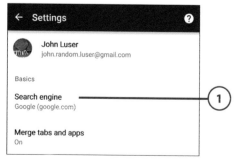

2. Tap the search engine you want to use.

3. Tap Close to close the Search Engine dialog and return to the Settings screen.

## Choosing Whether the Search Engine Can Access Your Location

If, when you tap the search engine you want in the Search Engine dialog, you see blue text saying "Location is blocked," you might want to enable location access so that the search engine can give you more targeted search results. To enable location access, tap the Location Is Blocked message. Android displays a screen on which you can enable location access for the search engine.

4. Tap Merge Tabs and Apps to control whether Chrome tabs appear on the Recents screen (when the Merge Tabs and Apps setting is enabled) or within the app (when the setting is disabled).

5. Tap Autofill Forms to display the Autofill Forms screen.

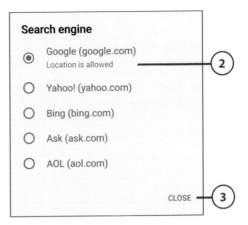

6. Set the Autofill Forms switch to On to enable the use of Autofill Forms.

7. Check the Show Addresses and Credit Cards from Google Payments box if you want this screen to show your details and cards from Google Payments.

8. Tap Add (+) on the Addresses heading to display the Add Address screen, where you enter the name and address details you want Autofill Forms to use.

9. Tap an existing address if you need to edit it.

10. Tap Add (+) on the Credit Cards heading to display the Add Credit Card screen, where you enter the details of the credit cards you want to use.

11. Tap an existing credit card if you need to edit its details. For example, you might need to update the expiration date when you receive a replacement card.

12. Tap the arrow or the Back button to return to the Settings screen.

13. Tap Save Passwords to display the Save Passwords screen. Here, you can move the Save Passwords switch to On or Off to enable or disable Chrome's ability to save your passwords so it can enter them for you. You can also manage the passwords on the Saved Passwords list and the Never Saved List.

14. Tap Home Page to display the Home Page screen.

---

**12**

← Autofill forms                              ❓

On                                              ⚪  **6**

Show addresses and credit cards from Google    ☑  **7**
Payments

Addresses                                       +  **8**

John R. Luser
Notional Press, 2573 Main St. Suite 274    ——    **9**

Credit cards                                    +  **10**

MasterCard ···5118
07/2017                          Google Payments

**11**

---

← Settings                                     ❓

John Luser
john.random.luser@gmail.com

Basics

Search engine
Yahoo! (yahoo.com)

Merge tabs and apps
On

Autofill forms
On

Save passwords
On

Home page
On

**14**  **13**

15. Set the Home Page switch to On if you want to use a home page. If you don't want a home page, set this switch to Off; this makes Chrome remove the Home Page icon from the area to the left of the omnibox.

16. Tap Open This Page to display the Edit Home Page screen. You can then type or paste the address of the page you want to use as your home page, and then tap Save.

17. Tap the arrow button or the Back button to return to the Settings screen.

## Choose Advanced Settings

In the Advanced section of the Settings screen in Chrome, you can choose settings in three categories: Privacy, Accessibility, and Site Settings. You can also turn on or off the Data Saver feature and view the About Chrome information, which may be useful for troubleshooting problems.

1. On the Settings screen, tap Privacy to display the Privacy screen.

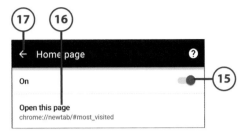

2. Check or uncheck the Navigation Error Suggestions box to enable or disable showing suggestions for web addresses that you enter incorrectly or that Chrome cannot locate.

3. Check or uncheck the Search and URL Suggestions box to enable or disable showing related queries and popular websites similar to those you type in the omnibox.

4. Tap Touch to Search to display the Touch to Search screen.

5. Set the Touch to Search switch to On if you want to be able to search by tapping and holding a word on a web page. If you don't need this capability, set the switch to Off.

6. Tap the arrow button or the Back button to return to the Privacy screen.

7. Tap Prefetch Page Resources to display the Prefetch Page Resources dialog.

8. Tap the Always radio button, the Only on Wi-Fi radio button, or the Never radio button, as needed. See the "What Does Prefetch Page Resources Do?" sidebar for details.

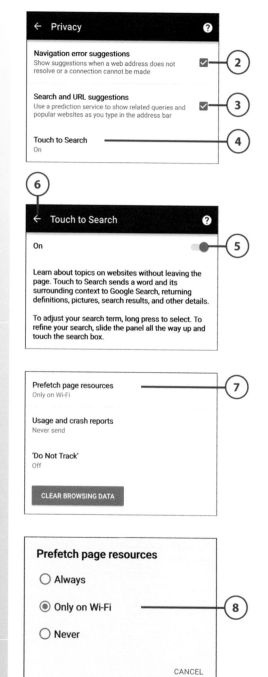

# >>>*Go Further*

## WHAT DOES PREFETCH PAGE RESOURCES DO?

Prefetch Page Resources is a feature that allows the Chrome app to preload web pages you are likely to want to load. The app does this in two ways. First, when you start typing an address in the omnibox, the Chrome app preloads a matching web page if it has high confidence that you will want it—for example, because you have visited that page before. Second, when you are on a particular web page, the app might preload the pages whose links you are most likely to click—for example, the top few search results.

If Chrome has predicted correctly and loaded the correct pages into memory, when you tap a link, that page renders straight from your Galaxy Note 5's memory instead of first loading over the network. Although this can be a timesaver, it means that your Galaxy Note 5 might preload pages that you will not look at, which can lead to wasted data usage. If you decide to use Prefetch Page Resources, it is normally best to choose the Only on Wi-Fi radio button to allow the Chrome app to preload pages only when your Galaxy Note 5 is connected to Wi-Fi, not when it's connected via a cellular data connection (as it does if you select the Always radio button).

**9.** Tap Usage and Crash Reports to display the Usage and Crash Reports dialog.

**10.** Tap the Always Send radio button, the Only Send on Wi-Fi radio button, or the Never Send radio button. If you are happy to provide usage and crash data, choosing Only Send on Wi-Fi is usually the best choice because it prevents the reports from consuming your cellular data allowance.

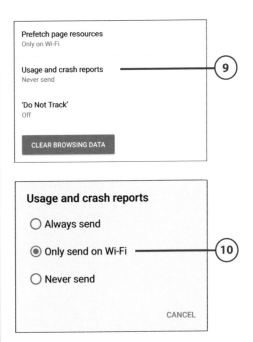

11. Tap 'Do Not Track' to display the Do Not Track screen, where you can choose whether to turn on the Do Not Track feature. This feature requests that the websites you visit not track you, but websites are not bound to honor the request.

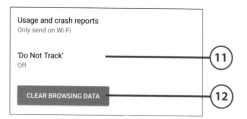

Usage and crash reports
Only send on Wi-Fi

'Do Not Track'
Off                                                    ⑪

CLEAR BROWSING DATA                                    ⑫

12. Tap Clear Browsing Data to display the Clear Browsing Data dialog.

13. Check the Browsing History box if you want to clear your browsing history. This clears the history of websites you have visited using the Chrome app on your Galaxy Note 5.

14. Check the Cache box to clear the cache. The cache contains data that Chrome stores so that it can redisplay web pages more quickly when you visit them again.

**Clear browsing data**

Browsing history                    ☑   ⑬

Cache                               ☑   ⑭

Cookies, site data                 ☑   ⑮

Saved passwords                    ☐   ⑯

Autofill data                      ☐   ⑰

You won't be signed out of your Google Accounts

CANCEL    CLEAR   ⑱

15. Check the Cookies, Site Data box if you want to clear your cookies and website data. Browser cookies are used by websites to personalize your visit by storing information specific to you in the cookies.

16. Check the Saved Passwords box if you want to clear your saved passwords.

17. Check the Autofill Data box if you want to clear your Autofill data.

18. Tap Clear to clear the items whose boxes you checked in the Clear Browsing Data dialog.

19. Tap the arrow button or the Back button to return to the Settings screen.

20. Tap Accessibility to display the Accessibility screen.

21. Drag the Text Scaling slider to make the text in the Preview box appear at a comfortable size for reading. This is the minimum size to which the Chrome app zooms the text when you double-tap a paragraph.

## What Is Text Scaling?

When you use text scaling, you instruct your Galaxy Note 5 to always increase or decrease the font sizes used on a web page by a specific percentage. For example, you can automatically make all text 150% larger than was originally intended.

22. Tap Force Enable Zoom to turn on or off Chrome's ability to zoom in on a website that prevents zooming. Some websites turn off zooming because their creators consider design to be more important than readability.

23. Tap the arrow button or the Back button to return to the Settings screen.

24. Tap Site Settings to display the Site Settings screen.

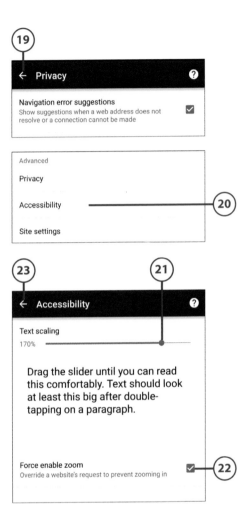

**25.** Tap All Sites if you want to review the list of sites that have stored data on your Galaxy Note 5 via Chrome. From there, you can tap a site to display the Site Settings screen, on which you can see how much data the site has stored; you can also clear and reset the data if you want.

**26.** Tap Cookies to display the Cookies screen. Here, you can set the Cookies switch to On or Off to control whether Chrome accepts cookies (see the nearby Note). If you set the Cookies switch to On, you can check or uncheck the Allow Third-Party Cookies box to control whether Chrome accepts cookies from third-party sites as well as from the sites you actually visit.

**27.** Tap Location to display the Location screen. Here, you can set the Location switch to On to make Chrome prompt you before it supplies your location to a website that requests it.

**28.** Tap Camera to display the Camera screen. Here, you can set the Camera switch to On to make Chrome prompt you before it lets a website use the camera. You'll almost certainly want to know when a website is trying to use the camera.

| | Site settings | ? |
|---|---|---|
| ≡ | All sites | **25** |
| ⊛ | Cookies — Allowed | **26** |
| ● | Location — Ask first | **27** |
| ◼ | Camera — Ask first | **28** |
| ⬇ | Microphone — Ask first | |
| ⊡ | JavaScript — Allowed | |
| ⬈ | Pop-ups — Blocked | |
| :: | Fullscreen — Ask first | |
| 🔔 | Notifications — Ask first | |

## Which Cookies Should You Accept?

Browser cookies are used by websites to personalize your visit by storing information specific to you in the cookies. Normally, you want to set the Cookies switch on the Cookies screen to On, because if you set your browser to refuse all cookies, many websites do not work correctly. But it is best to uncheck the Allow Third-Party Cookies check box on the Cookies screen to prevent third-party cookies, which are often used for advertising, for tracking your movements from site to site, or both.

**29.** Tap Microphone to display the Microphone screen. Here, you can set the Microphone switch to on to make Chrome prompt you before it lets a website use the microphone. Like the camera, the microphone is something over which you'll want to keep control.

**30.** Tap JavaScript to display the JavaScript screen. Here, you can set the JavaScript switch to On or Off to enable or disable JavaScript. JavaScript is used on many web pages for formatting and other functions, so you might want to leave this enabled.

**31.** Tap Pop-Ups to display the Pop-Ups screen. Here, you can set the Pop-Ups switch to On if you want to enable pop-up windows or to Off if you want to block them. Pop-up windows are almost always advertisements, so usually you would want to block them; however, some websites might not work correctly if pop-up blocking is on.

**32.** Tap Fullscreen to display the Fullscreen screen. Here, you can set the Fullscreen switch to Off if you want Chrome to get your permission before allowing an app to switch to full-screen mode. Set the Fullscreen switch to On if you want apps to be able to switch to full-screen mode without your approval.

**33.** Tap Notifications to display the Notifications screen. Here, you can set the Notifications switch to On to make Chrome prompt you before allowing websites to send notifications. Reviewing requests to send notifications is almost always a good idea, so normally you wouldn't want to set the Notifications switch to Off.

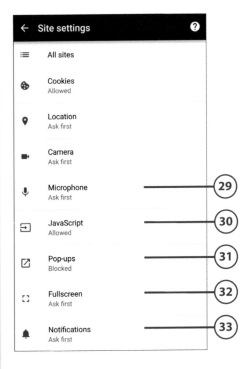

**34.** Tap Protected Content to display the Protected Content screen. Here, you can set the Protected Content switch to On or Off, as needed, to control whether Chrome asks your permission when a website wants to authenticate your Galaxy Note 5 to verify it is authorized to play premium videos. Tap the Learn More link if you want to learn more about protected content.

**35.** Tap Google Translate to display the Google Translate page, where you can enable or disable the Google Translate service for translating web pages. You can tap Reset Translate Settings if you need to reset your settings for Google Translate.

**36.** Tap Storage to display the Storage screen. Here, you can view the list of websites that are storing data on your Galaxy Note 5. You can then clear the data for a specific website if necessary.

**37.** Tap the arrow button or the Back button to return to the Settings screen.

**38.** Tap Data Saver to display the Data Saver screen.

**39.** Set the Data Saver switch to On if you want Chrome to use Google's servers to compress web pages other than pages you load via secure HTTP or in Incognito tabs.

**40.** After turning on Reduce Data Usage and doing some browsing, you can look at the Data Savings histogram to see how much data the compression has saved you.

**41.** Tap the arrow button or the Back button to return to the Settings screen.

← Site settings

Camera
Blocked

Microphone
Ask first

JavaScript
Allowed

Pop-ups
Blocked

Fullscreen
Ask first

Notifications
Ask first

Protected content
Ask first

Google Translate
Ask first

Storage

Accessibility

Site settings

Data Saver
Off

About Chrome

← Data Saver

On

Data savings

September 1     October 1

43%     Original size     4.00MB
        After compression     2.29MB

Gmail and other personal email

Personal and company email

Text messages

In this chapter, you discover your Galaxy Note 5's email applications for Gmail and other accounts, such as POP3, IMAP, and even Microsoft Exchange. In addition, you discover how to use the Messages app for text messaging. Topics include the following:

→ Sending and receiving email
→ Setting up the Gmail and Email apps
→ Sending and receiving text messages
→ Sending and receiving multimedia messages

# Email and Text Messages

Your Galaxy Note 5 has two email programs: the Gmail app, which works with Gmail and POP3 and IMAP email accounts, and the Email app that works with POP3, IMAP, and Microsoft Exchange (corporate email) accounts. In addition, you can use the Messages app to send and receive text messages

## Gmail

When you first set up your Galaxy Note 5, you set up a Gmail account. The Gmail application enables you to have multiple Gmail accounts, which is useful if you have a business account and a personal account. If you don't want to add a second Gmail account, you can skip this section.

# Add a Google Account

When you first set up your Galaxy Note 5, you added your primary Google (Gmail) account, but you might have other Gmail accounts that you'd also like to access through your Galaxy Note 5. The following steps describe how to add a second account.

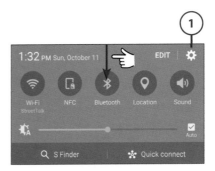

1. Pull down the Notification bar and tap the Settings icon.

2. Tap Accounts under the Personal section.

3. Tap Add Account.

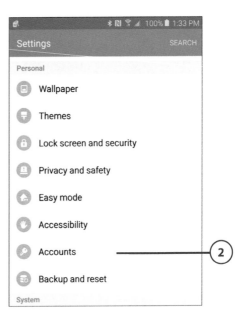

4. Tap Google.

5. Enter your existing Google account name. This is your Gmail address.

## What If I Don't Have a Second Google Account?

If you don't already have a second Google account but want to set one up, in step 5, tap New. Your Galaxy Note 5 walks you through the steps of creating a new Google account.

6. Tap Next.

7. Enter your existing Google password.

8. Tap Next.

9. Tap Accept.

**Tap to get a new Google account.**

10. Select Remind Me Later and tap Next to bypass setting up payment information for Google Wallet for this Google account. Right now you just want to set up the email account.

## Why Multiple Google Accounts?

You are probably wondering why you would want multiple Google accounts. Isn't one good enough? Actually, it is not that uncommon to have multiple Google accounts. It can be a way to compartmentalize your life between work and play. You might run a small business using one account, but email only friends with another. Your Galaxy Note 5 supports multiple accounts, but still enables you to interact with them in one place.

# Add a POP3/IMAP Account

Unlike previous versions of the Gmail app, the latest version supports the non-Gmail account types of POP3 and IMAP. If you don't want to add a POP3 or IMAP account to the Gmail app, you can skip this section.

1. Pull down the Notification bar and tap the Settings icon.

2. Tap Accounts under the Personal section.

3. Tap Add Account.

4. Tap Personal (IMAP) or Personal (POP3). This example uses an IMAP account type. However, the steps are the same for a POP3 account type.

5. Enter your IMAP account's email address.

6. Tap Next.

## What Is Manual Setup?

If you are using an email service provider that is not well known, or you are using email from your personal domain, the Gmail app may not be able to automatically work out the server settings. In that situation you might want to tap Manual Setup, which enables you to enter all information manually.

7. Enter the password for the email account you are adding.

8. Tap Next.

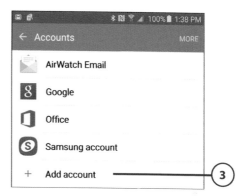

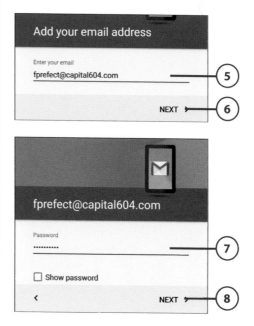

**Carried over from previous screens.**

9. Verify the incoming server name and change if needed.

10. Verify the port number and change if needed.

11. Verify the security type and change if needed.

12. Tap Next.

13. Verify the outgoing server name and change if needed.

14. Verify the port number and change if needed.

15. Verify the security type and change if needed.

16. Check the box if your email provider requires that you use your username and password when sending email. This is almost always the case.

17. Tap Next.

**Carried over from previous screens.**

18. Tap to choose how often the Gmail app automatically looks for and downloads new email in this account. You can also set it to Never, which means that email from this account is only downloaded when you open the Gmail app.

19. Check the box to be notified when new email arrives in this account.

20. Check the box if you want to synchronize mail from this account. Unchecking this box means that you don't want email to synchronize (not common).

21. Check the box if you want the Gmail app to automatically download email attachments when it detects that your Note 5 is connected to a Wi-Fi network.

22. Tap Next.

23. Enter a friendly name for this account.

24. Enter the name you want to use when sending email from this account.

25. Tap Next to complete the setup of the email account.

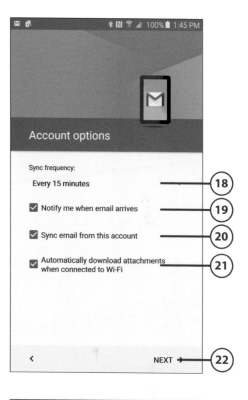

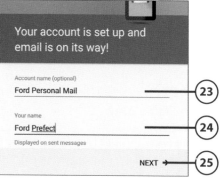

## Be Secure If You Can

If your mail provider supports email security such as SSL or TLS, you should strongly consider using it. If you don't, emails you send and receive go over the Internet in plain readable text. Using SSL or TLS encrypts the emails as they travel across the Internet so that nobody can read them. Set this under the Advanced settings for the Incoming and Outgoing Servers.

# Navigate the Gmail App

Let's take a quick look at the Gmail app and find out how to navigate the main screen.

Gmail

1. Tap the Gmail icon to launch the app. Your initial view will be of the Inbox of your primary Google (Gmail) account, which is the account you used when setting up your tablet.

2. Tap to search the current folder for an email.

3. Tap to compose a new email.

4. Tap to see only new messages received from your social net-working sites such as Facebook and Google+. When you have tapped it once, the Social option disappears until new social media emails arrive.

5. Tap to see any new emails that are promotions for products. When you have tapped it once, the Promotions option disappears until more promotional emails arrive.

6. Tap to see any new updates. Updates include messages about updating an app, but can also include email relating to things you have purchased, bills you need to pay, and even updates to meeting invites. After you have tapped Updates once, this option disappears until there are more new updates.

7. Swipe in from the left to reveal the menu.

8. Tap to switch between your email accounts, if you have more than one.

9. Tap to view Social, Promotions, or Updates. These are only visible when viewing Google (Gmail) accounts.

10. Tap to view messages in any forums you are participating in. This is only visible when viewing Google (Gmail) accounts.

11. Tap to switch between your different folders (or *labels,* as the Gmail app calls them).

12. Scroll down to see all of your labels.

13. Swipe the vertical action bar to the left to close the menu.

**Tap to see Inboxes from all of your accounts on one screen**

es Johnston
editor.ford.prefect@gmail.com

| | All inboxes | 77 |
| | Primary | 60 |
| | Social | 99+ new |
| | Promotions | 99+ new |
| | Updates | 11 new |
| | Forums | |
| | All labels | |
| | Starred | 1 |
| | Important | 74 |
| | Sent | |
| | Outbox | |

# >>>Go Further
## STARS AND LABELS

In the Gmail app, you use stars and labels to help organize your email. In most email clients you can create folders in your mailbox to help you organize your emails. For example, you might create a folder called "emails from the boss" and move any emails you receive from your boss to that folder. The Gmail app doesn't use the term *folders;* it uses the term *labels* instead. You can create labels in Gmail and choose an email to label. When you label the email, it is actually moved to a folder with that label. Any email that you mark with a star is actually just getting a label called "starred." However, when viewing your Gmail, you see the yellow star next to the email. People normally add a star to an email as a reminder of something important.

# Compose an Email

1. Tap the compose icon.

2. Tap to change the email account from which the message is being sent (if you have multiple accounts).

3. Type names in the To field. If the name matches someone in your Contacts, a list of choices is displayed and you can tap a name to select it. If you only know the email address, type it here.

4. Tap to add Carbon Copy (CC) or Blind Carbon Copy (BCC) recipients.

5. Tap the paperclip icon to add one or more attachments or insert links to one or more Google Drive files. See the next section for more information.

6. Type a subject for your email.

7. Type the body of the email.

8. Tap to save the email as a draft or discard it.

9. Tap to send the email.

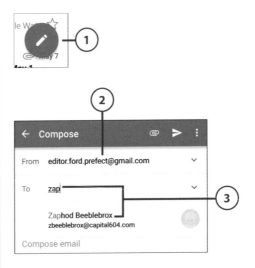

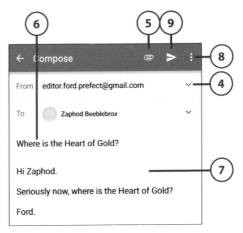

# Add Attachments or Insert Drive Links

Before sending an email, you can add one or more attachments or insert links to files you have in your Google Drive account. The Gmail app can attach files that you've saved on your tablet and in your Google Drive account. Here is how to add attachments and link Drive documents.

1. After filling in the fields as described in the "Compose an Email" task, tap the paperclip icon.

2. Tap either Attach File or Insert from Drive. This example uses the Attach File option.

---

## What Is the Difference Between Attaching and Inserting?

When you choose to attach a file to an email, you can choose a file located on your tablet, in the Photos app, or in your Google Drive account. The file is then copied from that location and attached to the email. If you choose to insert a file from Google Drive, the file you choose is not actually copied out of Google Drive and attached to the email. Instead, a link to that file is placed in the body of the email. The link enables the recipients to tap the link and open the document right in your Google Drive account.

---

3. Choose where you want to search for the file. This can include your recent downloads, your Google Drive account, the Downloads folder, internal tablet storage, or the Photos app.

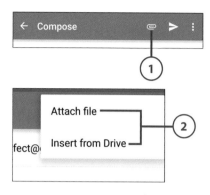

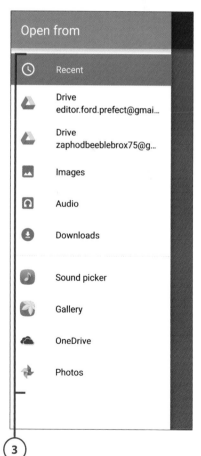

**4.** Tap the file to attach it. In this example, the attachment is a document in my Google Drive account.

**5.** Tap Send.

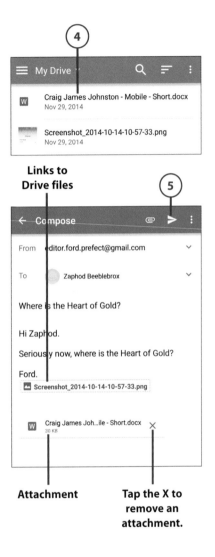

Links to
Drive files

Attachment

Tap the X to
remove an
attachment.

## Read an Email

**1.** Tap an email to open it. The sender name and subject for unread emails are in bold; those same items for emails that you have already read are not bold.

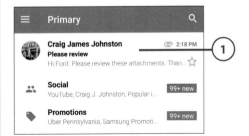

2. Tap to mark the email as unread and return to the email list view.

3. Tap to reply to the sender of the email. This does not reply to anyone in the CC field.

4. Tap the Menu icon to reply to the sender of the email and any recipients in the To and CC fields (Reply All). You can also choose to forward the email or print it.

5. Tap to expand the email header to see all recipients and all other email header information.

6. Tap to "star" the message, or move it to the "starred" label.

7. Tap the sender's contact picture to see more contact information about them.

8. Tap to move the email to the Trash folder.

9. Tap to move the email to a different label.

10. Swipe up to see the rest of the email and extra actions you can take.

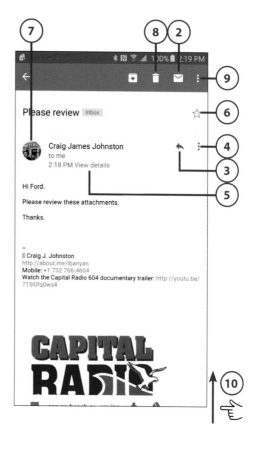

## Rich Text Formatting

A Rich Text Formatting (RTF) message is a message formatted with anything that is not plain text. RTF includes bulleted lists, different fonts, font colors, font sizes, and styles such as bold, italic, and underline. Although you cannot type an email on your tablet with the standard keyboard using RTF, when you receive an RTF email, your tablet preserves the formatting and displays it correctly.

## What Are Conversations?

Conversations are Gmail's version of email threads. When you look at the main view of the Gmail app, you are seeing a list of email conversations. The conversation might have only one email in it, but to Gmail that's a conversation. As you and others reply to that original email, Gmail groups those messages in a thread, or conversation.

11. Tap to reply to the email and all recipients (Reply All).

12. Tap to forward the email.

13. Tap attachments to open them.

14. Tap the download icon to download the attachment to your Note 5. It will be saved in the Download folder on your Note 5. Use the My Files app to view and manage your downloaded files.

15. Tap the Google Drive icon to save the attachment to your Google Drive.

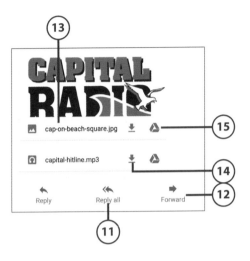

# >>>Go Further
## GMAILS HAVE EXTRA OPTIONS

If you are receiving email in your Gmail Inbox, you will have a few extra options that are specific to Gmail. You will be able to archive an email as well as send it to Trash. You will also be able to mark an email as important, mute the email conversation, report an email as spam, and report an email as a phishing scam. When you mute a conversation, you will no longer see any emails in that conversation (or email thread). For more information on printing emails, and an explanation on what an important email is, see the Go Further sidebars later in the chapter.

Archive email. ———  ——— Tap for more options.

# >>>*Go Further*

## HOW DO I PRINT EMAILS?

When you choose to print an email, the print dialog enables you to choose to print the email to a PDF, which turns the email into a Portable Document Format (PDF) file, or to print the email to any printers you have previously connected to Google Cloud Print using your desktop Chrome web browser. To learn more about how to connect your printers to your Google Cloud Print account, look at the instructions at https://support.google.com/chrome/answer/1069693?hl=en.

## What Is Important?

Gmail tries to automatically figure out which of the emails you receive are important. As it learns, it might sometimes be wrong. If an email is marked as important but it is not important, you can manually change the status to "not important." Important emails have a yellow arrow whereas emails that are not important have a clear arrow. All emails marked as "important" are also given the Priority Inbox label.

## What Happens to Your Spam or Phishing Emails?

When you mark an email in Gmail as spam or as a phishing scam, two things happen. First, it gets a label called Spam. Second, a copy of that email is sent to Gmail's spam servers so that they are now aware of a possible new spam email that is circulating around the Internet. Based on what the servers see for all Gmail users, they block the emails that have been marked as spam and phishing emails from reaching other Gmail users. So the bottom line is that you should always mark spam emails because it helps all of us.

# Customize Gmail App Settings

You can customize the way the Gmail app works, and you can also customize how each independent email account functions.

1. Swipe in from the left and tap the current email account to reveal its folders.

2. Tap Settings.

3. Tap General Settings.

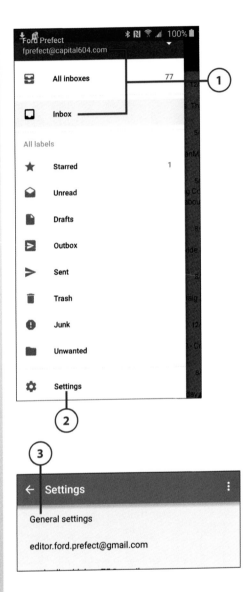

4. Tap to choose what the default action is when you choose to archive or delete a message in Gmail accounts. The choices are Archive and Delete.

5. Check the box to enable the feature where emails with the same subject line are grouped together. Emails with the same subject line are normally in the same conversation.

6. Check the box to enable the ability to swipe an email left or right to archive it.

7. Check the box to enable showing the email sender's contact image in the conversation list.

8. Check the box to enable making Reply All the default reply action.

9. Tap to enable automatically shrinking the emails to fit on the screen.

10. Tap to choose what happens when you archive or delete a message. Your choices are to show newer messages, older messages, or the conversation list.

11. Choose which actions you want to show a confirmation screen for.

12. Tap to save your changes and return to the main Settings screen.

13. Tap one of your accounts to change settings specific to that account, and then follow the steps in the following sections.

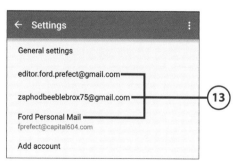

## Additional Options in General Settings

While in the General Settings screen, if you tap the Menu icon, you can clear your email search history or your picture approvals. When you clear picture approvals, you are clearing your previous decisions on which emails you wanted to automatically load the images for.

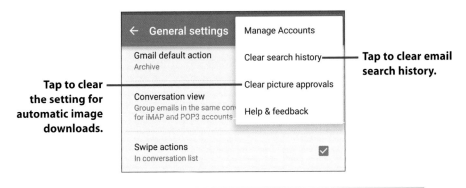

Tap to clear the setting for automatic image downloads.

Tap to clear email search history.

## Customize Google Account Settings

1. Tap to choose whether you want to see your Priority Inbox instead of your regular Inbox (Default Inbox) when opening the Gmail app.

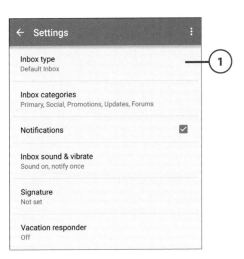

### What Is the Priority Inbox?

Google introduced the Priority Inbox as a way to sort emails that are important to you into a folder called Priority Inbox. It does this by analyzing which emails you open and reply to. If it makes a mistake, you can mark a message as less important or more important. Over time, Google's handle on which emails are important to you gets more accurate. Because the Priority Inbox probably has the most-important emails, you might want to open it first and then go to the regular Inbox later to handle less-important emails. Learn more about the Priority Inbox at https://youtu.be/5nt3gE9dGHQ.

2. Tap to choose what Inbox categories will be shown. As shown earlier in the chapter, by default the Social and Promotions categories are displayed. You can also show Updates and Forums.

3. Tap to enable or disable notifications when new email arrives for this Gmail account.

4. Tap to select how to get notified when new email arrives for this account. You can choose a different notification for each label and also decide which labels in addition to the Primary label you will be notified for.

5. Tap to enter a signature to be included at the end of all emails composed using this account.

## Email Signature

An email signature is a bit of text that is automatically added to the bottom of any email you send from your Galaxy Note 5. It is added when you compose a new email, reply to an email, or forward an email. A typical use for a signature is to automatically add your name and some contact information at the end of your emails. Email signatures are sometimes referred to as email footers.

6. Tap to set your Vacation Responder. This is a message that is automatically sent to people when you are on vacation.

7. Swipe up for more settings.

### Settings

| ← Settings | ⋮ |
|---|---|
| **Inbox type**<br>Default Inbox | |
| **Inbox categories**<br>Primary, Social, Promotions, Updates, Forums | 2 |
| **Notifications** | ☑ 3 |
| **Inbox sound & vibrate**<br>Sound on, notify once | 4 |
| **Signature**<br>Not set | 5 |
| **Vacation responder**<br>Off | 6 |
| | 7 |

8. Tap to choose whether to synchronize Gmail to this device. Turning this off stops Gmail from arriving on your Note 5.

9. Tap to choose how many days' worth of email to synchronize to your Note 5.

10. Touch to manage labels. Labels are like folders. You can choose which labels synchronize to your Note 5, how much email synchronizes, and what ringtone to play when new email arrives in that label.

11. Check the box to automatically download attachments to recently received emails while connected to a Wi-Fi network.

12. Tap to choose how images embedded in emails are handled. They can be automatically downloaded, or you can be prompted before they are downloaded for each email.

13. Tap to save your changes and return to the main Settings screen.

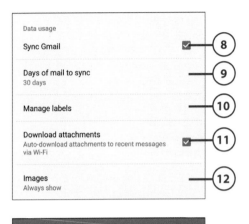

# Customize POP/IMAP Account Settings

1. Tap to change the name of your account. This is the friendly name you may have typed when you originally set it up on your Galaxy Note 5.

2. Tap to change the full name you want people to see when you reply to emails using this account.

3. Tap to enter a signature to be included at the end of all emails composed using this account.

4. Tap to choose how images in emails are handled. You can choose to ask you before showing them, or always show them.

5. Tap to change the frequency with which your Note 5 checks for new email for this account. You can set it to Never, which means that your phone checks for email only when you open the Gmail app, or you can set it to automatically check between every 15 minutes to every hour.

6. Check the box to automatically download attachments to recently received emails while connected to a Wi-Fi network.

7. Swipe up for more settings.

8. Tap to enable or disable notifications when new email arrives for this email account.

9. Tap to select the ringtone to play when you are notified of new email for this account.

10. Check the box if you also want to feel a vibration when new email arrives for this account.

11. Tap to change the incoming email server settings for this account.

12. Tap to change the outgoing email server settings for this account.

13. Tap to save your changes and return to the main Settings screen.

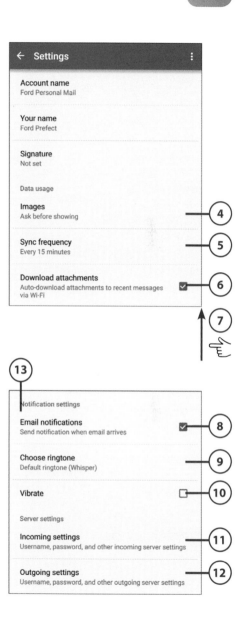

# Email Application

The Email application supports all email accounts with the exception of Gmail. This includes any corporate email accounts that use Microsoft Exchange or corporate email systems, such as Lotus Domino/Notes, that have an ActiveSync gateway. In addition to corporate email accounts, the Email application also supports POP3 and IMAP accounts. POP3 and IMAP accounts are also supported by the Gmail app, so this is a duplication of functionality.

## Add a Work Email Account

Your Galaxy Note 5 can synchronize your contacts from your work email account as long as your company uses Microsoft Exchange or an email gateway that supports Microsoft ActiveSync (such as Lotus Traveler for Lotus Domino/Notes email systems). It might be useful to be able to keep your work and personal contacts on one mobile device instead of carrying two phones around all day.

1. From the Home screen, pull down the Notification bar and tap the Settings icon.

2. Tap Accounts under the Personal section.

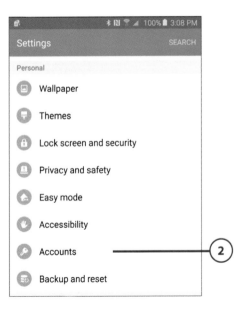

3.  Tap Add Account.

4.  Tap Microsoft Exchange ActiveSync.

5.  Enter your full corporate email address.

6.  Enter your corporate network password.

7.  Tap Next.

## Error Adding Account? Guess the Server.

Your Galaxy Note 5 tries to work out some information about your company's ActiveSync setup. If it can't, you are prompted to enter the ActiveSync server name manually. If you don't know what it is, you can try guessing it. If, for example, your email address is dsimons@allhitradio.com, the ActiveSync server is most probably webmail.allhitradio.com or autodiscover.allhitradio.com. If options like these don't work, ask your email administrator.

Add POP3 or IMAP accounts in the Email app instead of the Gmail app.

8. Tap to agree that your mail administrator may impose security restrictions on your Galaxy Note 5 if you proceed.

9. Tap to choose how many days' worth of email to synchronize to your Note 5.

10. Tap to choose how often your corporate email is delivered to your Galaxy Note 5. Auto means that as it arrives in your Inbox at work, it is delivered to your phone. You can set it to Manual, which means that your work email is only delivered when you open the Email app on your phone. You can also set the delivery frequency from every 5 minutes to every hour.

11. Tap to choose how much of each email is retrieved. You can also set this to have no size limit so that the entire email is downloaded.

12. Tap to choose how many days in the past calendar items are synchronized to your Galaxy Note 5.

13. Swipe up to see more settings.

14. Tap to enable or disable being notified when new email arrives from your corporate Inbox.

15. Tap to enable or disable synchronizing your corporate contacts to your Galaxy Note 5.

16. Tap to enable or disable synchronizing your corporate calendar to your Galaxy Note 5.

17. Tap to enable or disable synchronizing your corporate tasks to your Galaxy Note 5.

18. Tap to enable or disable synchronizing SMS (text) messages you receive on your Galaxy Note 5 to your corporate Inbox.

19. Tap Next.

**20.** Tap Activate to allow your company's mail server to act as a device administrator for your Note 5.

**21.** Enter a name for this email account. Use something meaningful that describes the purpose of the account, such as Work Email.

**22.** Tap Done to complete the setup.

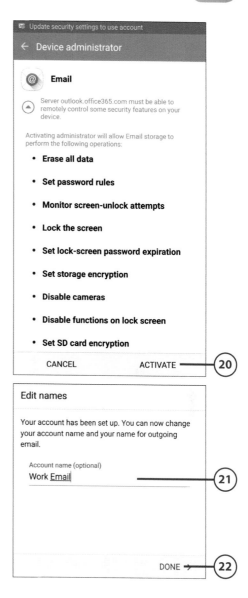

# Add a New POP3 or IMAP Account

Remember that the Gmail app also supports POP3 and IMAP accounts, so you might not want to use the Email app for this type of account. It is up to you.

**1.** Pull down the Notification bar and tap the Settings icon.

2. Tap Accounts under the User and Backup section.

3. Tap Add Account.

4. Tap Email.

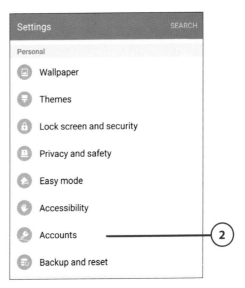

5. Enter your email address.

6. Enter your password.

7. Tap Next.

## Why Manual Setup?

Your Galaxy Note 5 tries to figure out the settings to set up your email account. This works most of the time when you are using common email providers such as Yahoo! and Hotmail. It also works with large ISPs such as Comcast, Road Runner, Optimum Online, and so on. It might not work for smaller ISPs, in smaller countries, or if you have created your own website and set up your own email. In these cases, you need to set up your email manually.

8. Tap POP3 or IMAP. IMAP has more intelligence to it, so select that option when possible.

9. Ensure that the information on the incoming server screen is accurate.

10. Tap Next.

## Where Can I Find This Information?

If you need to manually set up your email account, you must have a few pieces of information. Always check your ISP's (or email service provider's) website, and look for instructions on how to set up your email on a computer or smartphone. This is normally under the Support section of the website.

## Username and Password

On the Incoming Server and Outgoing Server screens, your username and password should already be filled out because you typed them in earlier. If not, enter them.

Enter sign-in details

fordprefect@capital604.com — 5

·········· — 6

☐ Show password

☐ Set this account as the default for sending emails.

MANUAL SETUP                    NEXT › — 7

← Select account type

POP3 ACCOUNT

IMAP ACCOUNT — 8

MICROSOFT EXCHANGE ACTIVESYNC

← Incoming server settings

Email address
fordprefect@capital604.com

User name
fordprefect

Password
··········

☐ Show password

IMAP server
imap.capital604.com

Security type
None ▼

Port
143

IMAP path prefix
Optional — 9

NEXT › — 10

11. Ensure that the information on the outgoing server screen is accurate.

12. Tap Next.

13. Tap to change how far back in the past email must synchronize.

14. Tap to change the frequency with which email from this account synchronizes to your Galaxy Note 5.

15. Tap to check the box if you want to be notified when new email arrives into this account.

16. Tap Next.

17. Enter a friendly name for this account, such as Home Email.

18. Enter your full name or the name you want to be displayed when people receive emails sent from this account.

19. Tap Done to save the settings for this account and return to the Add Accounts screen.

## Be Secure If You Can

If your mail provider supports email security, such as Secure Sockets Layer (SSL) or Transport Layer Security (TLS), you should strongly consider using it. If you don't, emails you send and receive go over the Internet in plain readable text. Using SSL or TLS encrypts the emails as they travel across the Internet so nobody can read them. Set this under the Advanced settings for the incoming and outgoing servers.

← Outgoing server settings

SMTP server
smtp.capital604.com

Security type
None ▼

Port
587

☑ Require sign-in

User name
fordprefect@capital604.com

Password
··········

☐ Show password

NEXT >

← Sync settings

Period to sync Email
2 weeks ▼

Sync schedule
Every 15 minutes ▼

☑ Notify me when email arrives

NEXT →

Edit names

Your account has been set up. You can now change your account name and your name for outgoing email.

Account name (optional)
Home Email

Your name (for outgoing email)
Ford Prefect

DONE →

# Working with the Email App

Now that you have added two new accounts, you can start using the Email application. Everything you do in the Email application is the same for every email account. The Email app enables you to work with email accounts either separately or in a combined view.

## Navigate the Email Application

Before you learn how to compose or read emails, you should become familiar with the Email application.

Email

1. Tap to launch the Email app.

2. Tap to switch between email accounts or select Combined Inbox, which shows all emails from all accounts.

3. Tap the star to mark a personal account (POP3/IMAP) email as flagged.

4. Each color represents a specific email account.

5. Tap to compose a new email.

**Message has an attachment.**    **Tap to flag a corporate message.**

Combined ▼          SEARCH    MORE

Craig Johnston                                    3/4
Canceled: Performance review

Craig James Johnston                      12/28/14
Please review
Hi Ford. Please review these attachments. Thanks. ...

Craig James Johnston                      11/30/14
Please review
Hi Ford. Please review these attachments.

Craig Johnston                                   8/26/14
Canceled: Kick off MDM Pilot

**Read message**

Craig James Johnston                        5/11/14
**Check out the latest Digg videos**
- Craig J. Johnston http://about.me/ibanyan My Boo...

Craig James Johnston                        5/11/14
Fwd: USB Flash Drive with Apple Lightning Con...
Check this out. - Craig J. Johnston http://about.me/...

Craig James Johnston                        8/27/13
Please review this jingle
Hi Ford. Please review this jingle and provide me wit...

Craig James Johnston                        8/27/13
Testing
Hi Ford. Is this new account working? - Craig J. Jo...

Craig Johnston
Accepted: Brown Bag Lunch

**Unread message**

# Compose an Email

1. Tap to compose a new email.

2. Enter one or more recipients. As you type, your Galaxy Note 5 tries to guess who you want to address the message to. If you see the correct name, tap it to select it. This includes names stored on your Galaxy Note 5 and in your company's corporate address book.

3. Enter a subject.

4. Type the body of the email.

5. Tap to send the message.

## Enable Rich Text

If you want to format your email using different fonts and formatting (bold and italic) or you want to embed images, you can do this by tapping on More, and tapping Turn On Rich Text. You will then see a bar that has formatting options. Scroll left and right over the formatting bar to see all formatting options. To change the formatting of a specific work, touch and hold the word, drag the end markers to select more words if needed, and then change the formatting using the formatting bar.

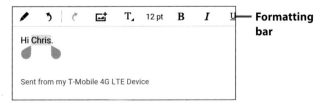

# Add Attachments to a Message

Before you send your message, you might want to add one or more attachments. You can attach any type of file, including pictures, video, audio, contacts, and location.

1. Tap Attach.

2. Choose the type of attachment. If you choose My Files, you will be able to browse your Note 5 and attach any file type, including documents, presentations, and spreadsheets.

3. Tap the red minus symbol to the right of each attachment to remove it from the email.

4. Tap to send your email.

**Attach any file on your Note 5.**

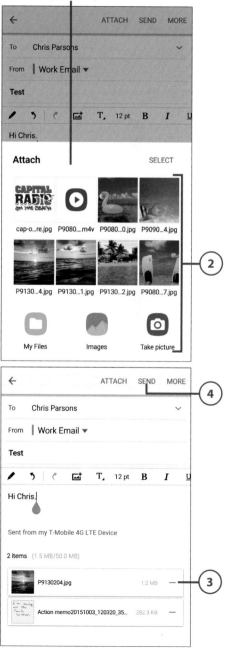

## Other Options Before Sending

Before you send your email, you can change a few additional options. To see these additional options, tap More. Tap Priority to change the priority of the email to high, normal, or low. Tap Security Options to Encrypt the email, or digitally sign it. To encrypt or sign an email, you need certificates installed on your Note 5. When you are sending an email using your company's Exchange email system, tap Permissions to set the permissions for the sent email. These permissions can include preventing it from being forwarded and setting an expiration date on the email. The permissions options are set by your email administrator.

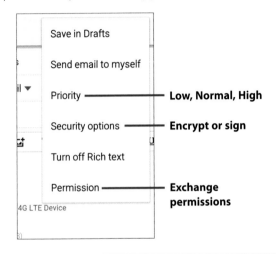

## Read Email

Reading messages in the Email application is the same regardless of which account the email has come to.

1. Tap an email to open it.

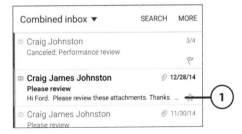

2. Tap to reply to the sender of the email. This does not reply to anyone in the Cc field.

3. Tap to forward the email.

4. Tap to expand the email header to see all recipients and all other email header information.

5. Tap to mark the message as flagged.

6. Tap to delete the message.

7. Tap to see the attachments on a separate screen.

8. Tap to preview the attachment. In this example it is an audio file.

9. Tap to save the attachment to your phone.

10. Tap to return to the email view.

11. Tap More to see more options (not shown).

12. Tap to mark the message as unread.

13. Tap to move the message to a different folder.

14. Tap to save the email as a file on your phone (outside the Email app).

15. Tap to set yourself a reminder to respond to this email.

16. Tap to mark the message as spam or junk mail.

17. Tap to add the sender to the Priority Sender list. Email from people in the Priority Sender list are displayed in the Priority Sender view.

18. Tap to compose a new email.

19. Tap to print the email on a Samsung printer available on the Wi-Fi network, or save the email as a Portable Document Format (PDF) file.

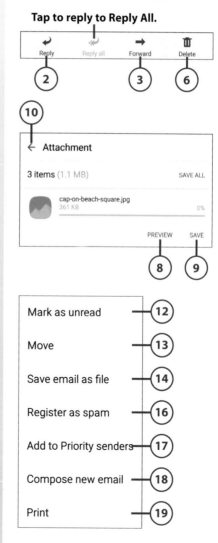

**Tap to see more options.**

**Tap to reply to Reply All.**

Craig James Johnston  DETAILS

To  FordPrefect@Capital604.com

cap-on-beach-square.jpg and 2 more

**Please review**

December 28, 2014  12:49 PM

Reply  Reply all  Forward  Delete

Attachment

3 items (1.1 MB)  SAVE ALL

cap-on-beach-square.jpg
361 KB  0%

PREVIEW  SAVE

Mark as unread

Move

Save email as file

Register as spam

Add to Priority senders

Compose new email

Print

# Change Email App Settings

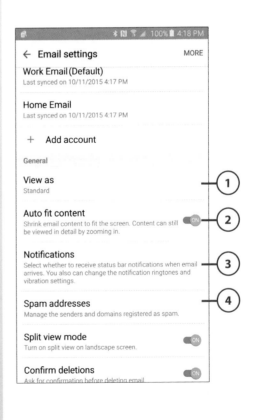

1. Tap More on the top-right of the main Email app screen (not shown).

2. Tap Settings.

## General Settings

General settings are settings that take effect no matter what type of email account you are working with.

1. Tap to choose whether you want your email shown in the standard way, where each received email is on its own line, or in Conversation mode, where emails are grouped together based on the email subject line, to form an email conversation.

2. Tap to enable or disable auto-fit. When Auto Fit Content is enabled, your Note 5 adjusts emails so they fit on the screen properly when you read them.

3. Tap to manage when you receive notifications of new emails. You can choose to receive notifications when senders you have placed on the Priority Senders list send you email, and you can choose which email accounts to receive notifications from.

4. Tap to manage your spam address list. This includes manually adding email addresses and removing ones already on the Spam list.

5. Tap to choose whether you want to use the split screen view when you rotate your Note 5 sideways. Split screen view shows the list of emails on the left and the contents of the selected email on the right.

6. Tap to choose whether you want to see a confirmation screen when you delete emails.

## What Is the Priority Sender List?

Emails received from people who you have listed in the Priority Sender list are shown in the Priority Sender Inbox as well as in the regular Inbox. Opening the Priority Sender Inbox folder shows only emails from these people, which can be a way of filtering email so that you respond to the important people first and then switch to the regular Inbox and respond to everyone else.

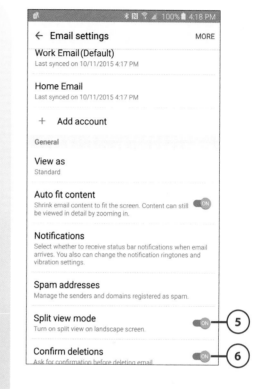

## Corporate Account Settings

You are able to change your email signature as well as control what components are synchronized and how often they are synchronized.

1. Tap your corporate email account.

**Tap to choose which is the default account.**

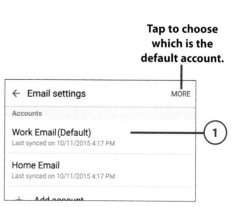

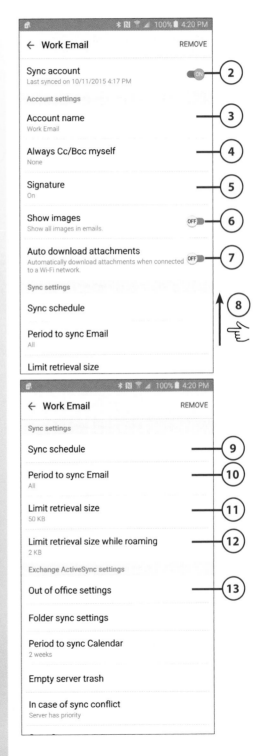

2. Tap to choose whether you want this account to synchronize with your Note 5.

3. Tap to change the friendly name for this account.

4. Tap to choose whether to always Bcc or Cc yourself on emails you send.

5. Tap to enable or disable using an email signature, add an email signature, or edit a signature.

6. Tap to enable or disable automatically loading embedded images in emails sent to you on this account.

7. Choose whether you want email attachments to automatically download when your Note 5 is connected to a Wi-Fi network.

8. Swipe up for more settings.

9. Tap to manage the synchronization settings for this account. This includes choosing different synchronization options depending on peak and off-peak times.

10. Tap to choose how far back in the past your email synchronizes.

11. Tap to choose how much of each email is retrieved.

12. Tap to choose how much of each email is retrieved when you are roaming outside your home cellular provider network.

13. Tap to set whether you are out of the office and your out-of-office message. This synchronizes to the out-of-office feature on your corporate mailbox so your out-of-office messages will be sent by your mail server.

14. Tap to choose which folders (excluding Inbox and Outbox) you want to synchronize from your office email account and when they synchronize based on the peak and off-peak schedule.

15. Tap to choose how far back in the past your calendar synchronizes.

16. Tap to empty your Trash folder on the email server back in the office.

## Why Empty the Office Trash Folder?

Step 16 describes how you can choose to empty your Trash folder back in the office. This feature is useful because sometimes your email administrator sets a limit on the size of your mailbox, and when you reach that limit, you are unable to send emails. By emptying your Trash folder back at the office, you might be able to clear a little bit of space in your mailbox so you can send that important email.

17. Swipe up for more settings.

---

| 🖻 | ⚹ 🔃 📶 100% 🔋 4:20 PM |
|---|---|
| ← **Work Email** | REMOVE |

Sync settings

Sync schedule

Period to sync Email
All

Limit retrieval size
50 KB

Limit retrieval size while roaming
2 KB

Exchange ActiveSync settings

Out of office settings

Folder sync settings ⎯⎯⎯ (14)

Period to sync Calendar ⎯⎯⎯ (15)
2 weeks

Empty server trash ⎯⎯⎯ (16)

In case of sync conflict (17)
Server has priority

18. Tap to change which device wins if there is a conflict between your phone and your email account back at the office.

## How Are There Conflicts?

A conflict can occur if you or someone who has delegate access on your email account makes a change in your mailbox using a desktop email client such as Outlook (for example, your delegate moves an email to a folder) and you then make a change on your Galaxy Note 5 (say, you delete that same email). Now there is a conflict because an email has been both moved and deleted at the same time. If you set the server to have priority, then the conflict is resolved using your rule that the server wins. In this example, the email is not deleted but rather is moved to a folder.

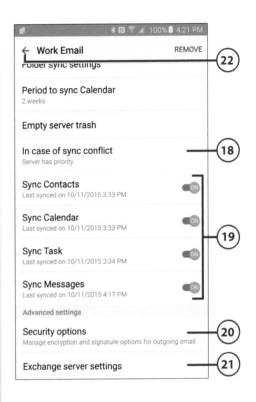

19. Select what to synchronize between your Note 5 and your office email account.

20. Tap to set advanced security options, including whether you want to encrypt your emails, sign emails with an electronic signature, and email certificates to use with S/MIME (if your company supports it).

21. Tap to change the Exchange mail server settings for this account. This includes your account username and password if these have changed.

22. Tap to return to the previous screen.

# POP/IMAP Account Settings

1. Tap your POP3 or IMAP email account.

2. Tap to choose whether you want this email account to synchronize with your Note 5.

3. Tap to change the friendly name for this account.

4. Tap to edit the name that is displayed when you send email to others.

5. Tap to choose whether to always Bcc or Cc yourself on emails you send.

6. Tap to enable or disable using an email signature, add an email signature, or edit a signature.

7. Tap to enable or disable automatically loading embedded images in emails sent to you on this account.

8. Tap to enable or disable automatically downloading email attachments when your Note 5 is connected to Wi-Fi.

9. Swipe up for more settings.

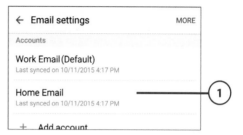

10. Tap to manage the synchronization settings for this account. This includes choosing different synchronization options depending on peak and off-peak times.

11. Tap to choose how far back in the past your email synchronizes.

12. Tap to choose how much of each email is retrieved.

13. Tap to choose how much of each email is retrieved when you are roaming outside your home cellular provider network.

14. Tap to set advanced security settings for this account, including choosing to encrypt emails, sign them with a digital signature, and manage encryption keys on your phone for use with encrypting emails.

15. Tap to change the incoming server settings for this account.

16. Tap to change the outgoing server settings for this account.

17. Tap to return to the Settings main screen.

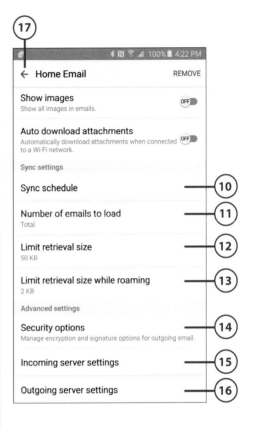

# SMS and MMS

Short Message Service (SMS), also known as text messaging, has been around for a long time. Multimedia Message Service (MMS) is a newer form of text messaging that can contain pictures, audio, and video as well as text. Your Galaxy Note 5 can send and receive both SMS and MMS messages.

# Get to Know the Messages App

The Messages app is what you use to send and receive text messages. This app has all the features you need to compose, send, receive, and manage these messages.

1. Tap the Messages icon.

2. Tap to compose a new text message.

3. Tap the picture of someone who has sent you a message to show their contact card. You can then contact the person using email, phone, and other methods.

4. Tap a message thread to open it.

5. Tap More to see more options.

6. Tap to select one or more message threads and delete them or mark them as spam.

7. Tap to open the Locked Messages folder. Locked messages are messages that you have chosen to lock so they are not accidentally deleted. See the "How Do I Lock Messages?" margin note for more information.

8. Tap to select from a list of Quick Responses to send and manage the current Quick Responses. When you select a Quick Response, a new message opens with that Quick Response added to the text field.

9. Tap to choose to use your Note 5's built-in font size, or select a smaller or larger size while you have the Messages app open.

10. Tap to open the Settings screen. See the next section for more on Settings.

## How Do I Lock a Message?

You might want to lock a message so that it does not get accidentally deleted when you delete the message thread. To lock a message, touch and hold on the message and choose Lock when the menu pops up. The lock symbol displays just below the locked message. To unlock the message, touch and hold on the message and choose Unlock.

# >>>*Go Further*

## SWIPE TO CALL

If you would like to call the sender of an SMS or MMS message, swipe the message from left to right to dial that person's number.

**Swipe to call.**

## Manage Settings for the Messages App

You use the settings of the Messages app to manage how the app handles your SMS and MMS messages. Before you actually start working with SMS and MMS, let's take a look at the settings.

1. Tap More on the top-right of the main Messages app screen (as shown in Step 5 of the previous task).

2. Tap Settings.

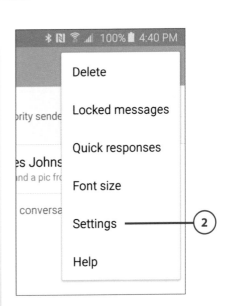

3. Tap to manage how you are notified when new messages arrive. This includes choosing the notification sound, whether you want to feel a vibration, whether you want to see the new message in a pop-up display, and whether you want a preview of the message in the status bar.

4. Tap to manage how the Messages app looks. You can choose what kind of bubble style is used for text message display and which background the app uses for messages.

5. Tap to manage the settings for blocking messages and viewing previously blocked messages, if there are any. You can block messages based on phrases, or simply block messages from certain phone numbers.

6. Tap to manage chat settings. This includes choosing to receive a delivery report for text messages you send, choosing to limit the size of incoming MMS messages, whether you want to automatically download messages when you are roaming, and whether you want to send an indication to others when you are typing.

7. Tap to manage which emergency alerts you want to receive. These alerts are sent out by your government or law enforcement (for example, AMBER alerts).

8. Tap to see more settings.

← Messages settings

Notifications
On — 3

Backgrounds and bubbles — 4

Block messages — 5

Chat settings — 6

More settings — 8

Emergency alert settings — 7

9. Tap to control and manage text messages. This includes choosing to receive a delivery report for text messages you send, choosing the input mode (leaving it set to Automatic is recommended), and managing text messages that may still be on your old SIM card.

10. Tap to control how the Messages app handles multimedia messages. Settings include the ability to request delivery and read reports and as well as to control whether to automatically retrieve multimedia messages while roaming outside your wireless carrier's home area.

11. Tap to enable or disable receiving messages "pushed" from the server. Push messages arrive at your Galaxy Note 5 shortly after they arrive at the server, which is usually faster than waiting until the Galaxy Note 5 checks for messages. You can also choose how to handle remote requests to load services. Your choices are Always, Prompt, and Never.

12. Tap to enable or disable automatically deleting old text or multimedia messages when the limit you set is reached. When the limit is reached, messages within the thread or conversation are deleted using the FIFO method.

13. Tap to enable or disable split view when in landscape mode. This controls whether your Note 5 goes into split screen mode when you rotate it on its side. In split screen mode, the conversation lists are on the left while the selected conversation is shown on the right.

14. Tap to save your changes and return to the previous screen.

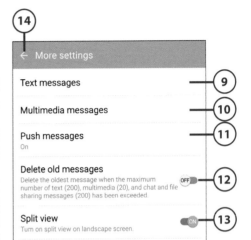

## What Does the Manage SIM Card Messages Option Do?

Many old cell phones store text messages on the SIM card and not in the phone's memory. If you have just upgraded from an older phone, you might still have text messages on the SIM card that you would like to retrieve. If you choose the option to manage text messages on your SIM card, as mentioned in step 9, you can then copy the messages to your Galaxy Note 5's memory and copy the senders to your contacts in the Contacts app.

## Don't Auto-Retrieve MMS While Roaming

Disable the automatic retrieval of multimedia messages when you travel to other countries because automatically retrieving these messages when you're roaming can result in a big bill from your provider. International carriers love to charge large amounts of money for people traveling to their countries and using their networks. The only time it is a good idea to leave this enabled is if your carrier offers an international SMS or MMS bundle, where you pay a flat rate up front before leaving. When you have the auto-retrieve feature disabled, you see a Download button next to a multimedia message. You have to tap it to manually download the message.

## What's the Difference Between a Delivery Report and a Read Report?

A delivery report indicates that the message has reached the destination device. A read report indicates that the message has been opened for viewing. There is still no guarantee that whoever opened the message has actually read it, let alone understood it.

## It's Not All Good

### What Setting Should I Choose for Service Loading?

Samsung's Service Loading feature has been used for attacks that remotely wipe smartphones without the owner's consent. Because of this danger, never choose Always as the Service Loading setting. Choose Prompt if you want your Galaxy Note 5 to let you decide about service-loading requests. Choose Never if you prefer to suppress service-loading requests.

## Compose Messages

When you compose a new message, you do not need to make a conscious decision whether it is an SMS message or an MMS message. As soon as you add a subject line or attach a file to your message, your Galaxy Note 5 automatically treats the message as an MMS message.

Here is how to compose and send messages:

1. Tap the pencil compose icon to compose a new message.

2. Start typing the recipient's name or phone number, or if the person is in your contacts, type the name. If a match is found, tap the mobile number.

3. Tap and start typing your message.

4. Tap to send your message.

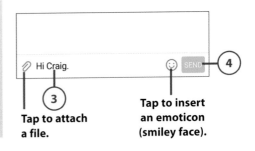

**Tap to attach a file.**

**Tap to insert an emoticon (smiley face).**

## It's Not All Good

**Inserting Smiley Icons**

By tapping the smiling face icon, you can insert emoticons (also known as smiley faces). Just be aware that the very first emoticon you insert into a new text message counts as 92 characters. Each additional emoticon counts only one character each. Each text message is limited to 160 characters, so after inserting your first emoticon, you'll only have 68 characters left.

## Delay Sending the Message

You might decide that you want a text message to be sent automatically at a later time. To do this, before sending the message, tap More and choose Schedule Message. Choose the date and time you want your message to be sent and tap Done. Then tap the Send button, and your message sends when you set it to.

# >>>Go Further
## MESSAGE LIMITS AND MESSAGES

Text messages can be only 160 characters long. To get around this limit, most modern phones simply break up text messages you type into 160-character chunks. The Galaxy Note used to display a readout showing the number of characters remaining and the number of messages it would be sending: The readout started at 160/1 when you began a new message and ran down to 1/1; then it started at 145/2 (fewer characters because there is some overhead in linking the messages). The phone receiving the message simply combines them into one message. This is important to know if your wireless plan has a text message limit. When you create one text message, your Galaxy Note 5 might actually break the message into two or more. The screen show shows how the message screen looked on *previous* Galaxy Notes when the number of characters were displayed. The Note 5 no longer shows this information, so if your plan has a text-message limit, you need to bear in mind that your messages might be broken into two or more individual messages.

This is a long text message to see how it is broken up automatically into multiple text messages so as not to go over the SMS character limits and although this is good it will cost more.

119/2 —— **Message count indicator**

## Attach Files to Messages

If you want to send a picture, audio file, or video along with your text message, all you need to do is attach the file. Be aware that attaching a file turns your SMS text message into an MMS multimedia message and might be subject to additional charges.

1. Tap the paperclip icon to attach a file.

2. Choose a picture that you recently took on your Note 5 *or...*

3. Choose other attachment types, including the option to take a picture or record a video and attach it directly.

4. Tap to send your MMS.

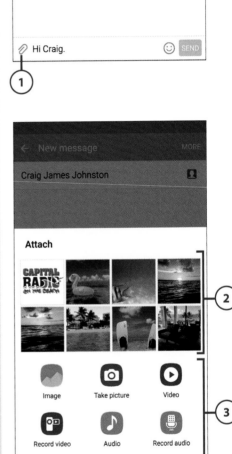

## It's Not All Good

### Is It Worth Attaching Files?

Attaching files to text messages is not as useful as you might desire. Most carriers limit the attachment size to around 300KB. This means that you can attach only about 60 seconds of very low-quality video; pictures with low resolution, high compression, or both; and very short audio files. The Messaging app automatically compresses larger picture files to make them small enough to send, but you will often find that it simply refuses to send video files because they are too large. Choosing the option of capturing pictures, capturing video, or recording audio when you choose to attach is the only way you can guarantee that the files are small enough. This is because when you do this, the camera and audio recorder apps are set to a mode that makes them record low-quality audio and take low-quality pictures.

## Receive Messages

When you receive a new SMS or MMS message, you can read it, view its attachments, and even save those attachments to your Galaxy Note 5.

1. When a new SMS or MMS message arrives, your Galaxy Note 5 plays a ringtone and displays a notification in the status bar.

2. Pull down the notification shade to see newly arrived messages.

3. Tap a message alert to display the message and reply to it.

**Tap to call the sender.**

4. Tap an attachment to open it for viewing.

5. Tap to write a reply to the message.

6. Touch and hold a message to display the Message Options dialog.

7. Tap to delete the message. This deletes just the message and not the entire thread.

8. Tap to copy the message text so you can paste it elsewhere.

9. Tap to forward the message and attachment to someone else.

10. Tap to share the message via social media or other methods.

11. Tap to lock the message against deletion if you later decide to delete the message thread.

12. Tap to save the attachment to your Galaxy Note 5.

13. Tap to view a slideshow of attached images.

14. Tap to view the message details, such as its size and the date and time it was sent.

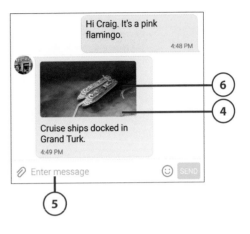

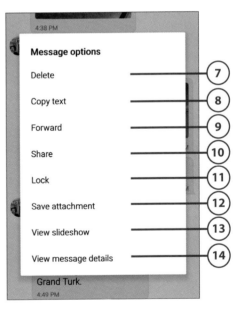

## Usable Content

If a text message contains links to websites, phone numbers, or email addresses, tapping those links makes the Galaxy Note 5 take the appropriate action. For example, when you tap a phone number, your Galaxy Note 5 calls the number; when you tap a web link, the Galaxy Note 5 opens the page in Chrome or your other default browser.

# >>>Go Further

## USING GOOGLE HANGOUTS FOR SMS AND MMS

You might decide that because you already use Google Hangouts to instant message your friends and family, as well as to video chat with them, it makes sense to set the Google Hangouts app to handle text messages (SMS) and multimedia messages (MMS) so that all communications with your friends and family are in one place. To set this, open the Google Hangouts app. Swipe in from the left of the screen and tap Settings. Tap SMS. Under General tap SMS disabled and tap Yes when prompted. The way in which you interact with SMS and MMS while using the Hangouts app is very similar to the way it works in the Messages app, so the steps in this chapter should help you. Even the settings for handling SMS and MMS are similar. When one of your contacts has signed up for a Google account and has started using Google Hangouts, you can switch from sending and receiving SMS and MMS messages with them and start using Hangouts messages instead. Doing this saves you from costly SMS and MMS charges and just uses your data plan.

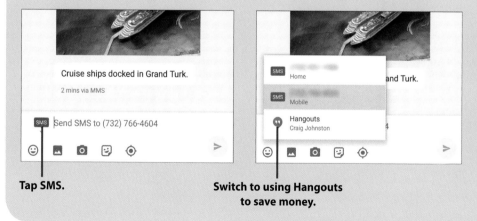

Tap SMS.

Switch to using Hangouts
to save money.

Search or command
Google

See stocks

In this chapter, you find out how to use Google Maps, Navigation, and Google Now. Topics include

→ Google Now
→ Google Maps
→ Navigation
→ Taking map data offline

**5**

# Google Now and Navigation

You can use your Samsung Galaxy Note 5 as a GPS navigation device while you walk or drive around. Your phone also includes an app called Google Now that provides all the information you need when you need it.

## Google Now

You can access Google Now from any screen (except the Lock screen), which enables you to search the Internet. Google Now provides you with information such as how long it takes to drive to work and the scores from your favorite teams.

### Access Google Now

You can access Google Now from any app or the Home screen pane by pressing and holding the Home button.

Press and hold

1. Cards automatically appear based on your settings. Examples of these cards are scores for the sports teams you follow, upcoming meetings, weather in the location where you work, and traffic on the way to work.

2. Say "OK Google" to speak a search, or to command Google Now to do something. You can also type your search terms.

3. Information relevant to your search appears.

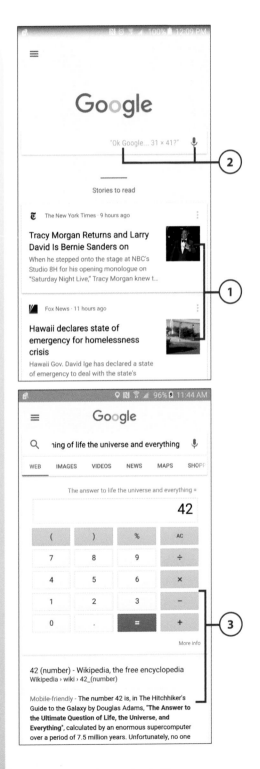

## Commanding Google Now

In addition to searching the Internet using Google Now, you can command Google to do things for you using the "OK Google" feature. For example, you can tell Google to set an alarm for you, compose a text message, or even send an email. This is just a small list of the types of things you can have Google do for you. You do not need to have the Google Now app open to use the "OK Google" feature. You can say "OK Google" from any screen. To see a comprehensive list of commands, visit http://trend-blog.net/list-of-google-now-voice-commands-infographic/.

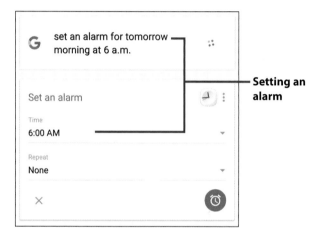

**Setting an alarm**

## Set Up Google Now

For Google Now to work for you, you need to set it up correctly. This also means sharing your location information with Google.

1. Swipe in from the left bezel to reveal the menu.

2. Tap to add and manage reminders. After adding a reminder, Google Now will ensure you are reminded of the activity.

3. Tap to customize what kinds of Google Now cards are displayed. This includes choosing the sports teams, stocks, places, and TV and video.

4. Tap Settings.

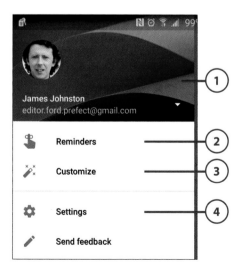

5. Tap to manage what Google Now can search for on your Note 5. This can include apps you have installed, bookmarks and web history in the Chrome web browser, your contacts, Google Play Books, Movies & TV, and Music.

6. Tap Voice to manage how and when Google Now responds to your voice.

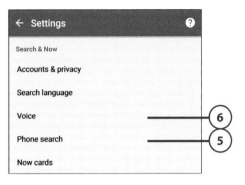

7. Tap to choose the languages that Google Now responds to.

8. Tap to choose whether Google Now should be listening for you to say "OK Google."

9. Tap to choose whether Google Now works when your phone is locked, and how it should listen for your commands. You can choose to let Google Now use a paired Bluetooth device, or a headset connected by a cable, or both.

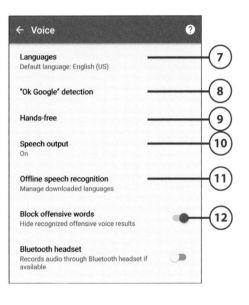

10. Tap to choose when Google Now speaks back to you. Your choices are On (which means Always), Off (which means never), or only when you are using a hands-free device (such as a Bluetooth headset or your car's built-in Bluetooth connection).

11. Tap to manage whether Google Now speech recognition can work even when there is no Internet connection. This is achieved by downloading one or more languages to your phone.

12. Tap to block offensive words being spoken when search results are returned by voice.

13. Tap to allow Google Now to record your voice using your Bluetooth headset or built-in car Bluetooth.

14. Tap to save your changes and return to the main Google Now settings screen.

15. Tap Accounts & Privacy.

16. Tap to choose which of your Google accounts (if you have more than one) you want to use for Google Now.

17. Tap to manage any nicknames that you are using for people in your contacts.

18. Tap to manage whether apps can share your data with Google and clear any data that apps on your phone have shared with Google.

19. Tap to enable or disable the SafeSearch Filter that blocks offensive content.

20. Tap to choose whether you want to share your commute status, such as when you leave for home or leave for work. People need to be in your Google+ Circles to receive your Commute updates.

21. Tap to enable or disable high contrast text if you have a vision disability.

22. Tap to save your changes and return to the main Google Now settings screen.

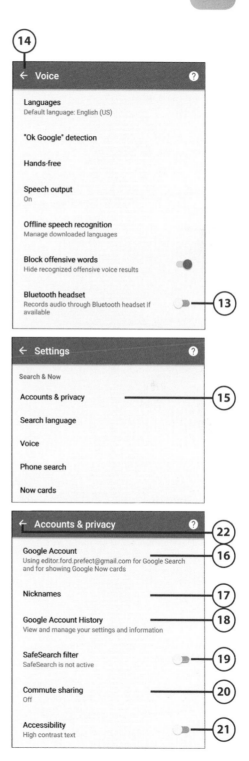

**23.** Tap to manage how Google Now alerts you when new cards are ready, and choose the ringtone that plays when they are ready to view.

**24.** Tap to save your changes and return to Google Now.

## Tell Google Maps Where You Live and Work

Google Now can be even more effective if you configure your work and home addresses in Google Maps. Google Now uses that information to tell you things like how long your commute to work will be, whether there is heavy traffic on the route, and so on. See step 3 in the "Configure Google Maps Settings" task later in this chapter for information on how to configure your addresses.

<br>

(24)

← Settings                                    ❓

Search & Now

Accounts & privacy

Search language

Voice

Phone search

Now cards ——————————— (23)

# Google Maps

Google Maps enables you to see where you are on a map, find points of interest close to you, get driving or walking directions, and review extra layers of information, such as a satellite view.

**1.** Tap to launch Google Maps.

Maps — (1)

2. Tap to type a search term, the name of a business, or an address.

3. Tap to speak a search term, the name of a business, or an address.

4. Tap to get walking or driving directions from one location to another. You can also choose to use public transit or biking paths to get to your destination.

5. Tap to switch between the top-down view that always points North, and the 3D view that follows the direction your phone is pointing.

6. Tap to explore what's around your current location.

7. Swipe in from the left of the screen to reveal the menu.

8. Tap to switch to a different Google account for use with Google Maps.

9. Tap to see your work and home address, plus addresses you have recently searched for.

10. Tap to toggle between the map view and the satellite.

11. Tap to show the current traffic conditions on the map or satellite view.

12. Tap to show all public transport locations on the map view or satellite view.

13. Tap to show all bicycling routes on the map view or satellite view.

14. Tap to see the terrain view.

15. Tap to launch the Google Earth app.

16. Touch to change the settings for Google Maps.

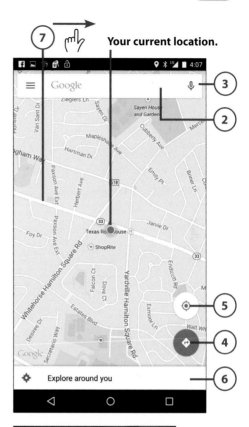

Your current location.

## Changing Google Maps Settings

See the "Configure Google Maps Settings" task later in this chapter for more information about customizing Google Maps.

# Get Directions

You can use Google Maps to get directions to where you want to go.

1. Tap the Directions icon.

2. Tap to set the starting point or leave it as My Location (which is where you are now).

3. Tap to flip the start and end points.

4. Tap to use driving directions.

5. Tap to use public transportation.

### Public Transportation

If you choose to use public transportation to get to your destination, you have two extra options to use. You can choose the type of public transportation to use, including bus, subway, train, or tram/light rail. You can also choose the best route (fewer transfers and less walking).

6. Tap to use bike paths (if available).

7. Tap to walk to your destination.

8. Tap to choose a previous destination. If you need to type the address of your destination, skip to step 9; if not, skip to step 10.

9. Type or speak the destination address.

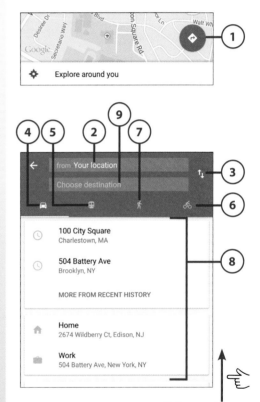

**Swipe up to see more previous destinations.**

10. Tap to adjust how the map appears, and to modify options like avoiding toll roads. If you are happy with the route as-is, skip to step 14.

11. Tap to share your directions with someone via email, text message, and many other methods.

12. Choose how your map appears. You determine whether it should include traffic information, satellite images, or terrain.

13. Tap to adjust the route options. You can choose to avoid highways, avoid tolls, or avoid ferries.

14. Tap to start the navigation.

15. Tap to see and select alternative routes as they appear on the map.

16. Tap the Menu icon to mute the voice guidance, show traffic conditions, choose the satellite view, and show the entire route alternatives.

17. Tap to speak commands like "Show alternative route", "How's traffic ahead?", or "What time will I get there?"

18. Tap to cancel the route.

# Configure Google Maps Settings

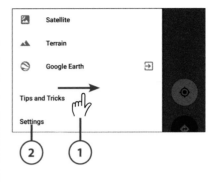

1. Swipe in from the left side of the screen.

2. Tap Settings.

3. Tap to edit your work and home addresses. Telling Maps your home and work addresses is important for Google Now to work more effieciently, but it also helps you quickly plan new routes to work and home.

4. Tap to enable or disable the capability for your phone to report its location. You can also choose the accuracy of your location by changing the mode.

5. Tap to improve your location accuracy if you think that your phone is not reporting it correctly.

6. Tap to see addresses you have looked up and received directions to. You can also delete items in this list.

7. Tap to choose whether you want to see location-specific information such as schedules in transit stations.

8. Tap to set the distance unit of measure. You can either set it to automatic so that Google Maps adjusts it based on where you are on the planet, or you can manually set it.

9. Tap to choose when to see the scale on the map. Your choices are when zooming in and out, or always.

10. Tap to change the volume level for the voice that speaks the turn-by-turn directions, and choose whether you want to always start navigation using the Tilt Map. The Tilt Map is a view as if looking ahead from behind the navigation arrow.

11. Check the box if you want to be able to shake your Note 5 to send feedback about your experiences with Google Maps to Google.

12. Tap to save your changes and return to the main Google Maps screen.

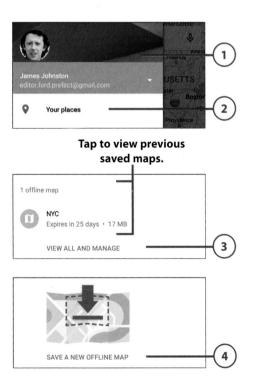

## Use Offline Google Maps

Google Maps enables you to download small parts of the global map to your phone. This is useful if you are traveling and need an electronic map but cannot connect to a network to download it in real time.

1. Swipe in from the left of the screen.

2. Tap Your Places.

3. Scroll down to the bottom of the Your Places screen, and tap View All and Manage.

4. Tap Save a New Offline Map.

5. Pan around to find the area of the map you want to save offline.

6. Pinch to zoom out or unpinch to zoom in to the area of the map you want to save offline.

7. Tap Save when the area of the map fills the screen.

8. Type a name for the offline map and tap save.

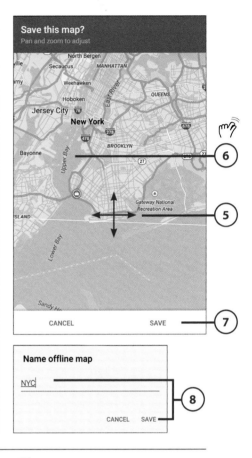

## How Much Map Can I Take Offline?

When selecting the area of the map to take offline, you are limited to approximately 100 Mb of map data. You don't need to worry about the size of the data because if you have selected an area that is too large, Google Maps gives you a warning.

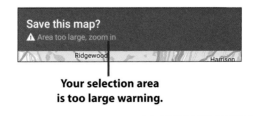

**Your selection area
is too large warning.**

## *It's Not All Good*

**Offline Maps Have Limited Use**

If you download some map data to your phone, you can use it to zoom in and out of the area you downloaded and also see where you are on the map in real time even though you have no network coverage. You cannot, however, get directions within the downloaded map area or use the Navigation app to get turn-by-turn directions. You also cannot search for things in the downloaded map area or see points of interest.

So how useful is having map data already downloaded to your phone? Because offline maps are already downloaded, they help when you have a network connection and are getting driving directions because Google Maps does not need to download the map data in real time, which could save you a lot of money in data roaming charges.

Use the World Clock
feature to track the time
around the world.

In this chapter, you find out how to set the time, use the Clock application, and use the S Planner calendaring application. Topics include the following:

→ Synchronizing to the correct time
→ Working with the Clock application
→ Setting alarms
→ Waking up with the latest weather, news, and your schedule
→ Working with S Planner

6

# Working with Date, Time, and S Planner

Your Galaxy Note 5 has a Clock application you can use as a bedside alarm, stopwatch, timer, and world clock. The S Planner application synchronizes with your Google or Microsoft Exchange calendars and enables you to create events and meetings while on the road and to always know where your next meeting is.

## Setting the Date and Time

Before you start working with the Clock and S Planner applications, make sure your Galaxy Note 5 has the correct date and time.

1. Pull down the Notifications panel.

2. Tap the Settings icon to display the Settings screen.

3. In the System section, tap Date and Time to display the Date and Time screen.

4. Set the Automatic Date and Time switch to On or Off to enable or disable synchronizing time and date with the wireless carrier. It is best to leave time and date synchronization enabled so that your Galaxy Note 5 automatically sets date and time based on where you are traveling.

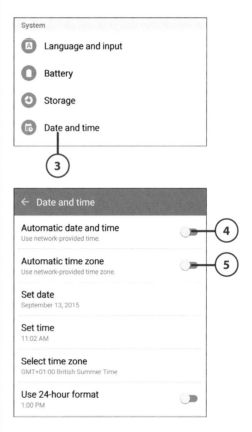

## Does Network Time Sync Always Work?

In some countries, on some carriers, time synchronization does not work. This means that when you get off the plane and turn Airplane mode off (see the Prologue for information on Airplane mode), after a reasonable amount of time your time, date, and time zone will still be incorrect. In these instances, it is best to disable Automatic Date and Time and manually set the time, date, and time zone yourself. You can then try it on automatic in the next country you visit or when you are back in your home country.

5. Set the Automatic Time Zone switch to On or Off to enable or disable synchronizing the time zone with the wireless carrier. It is best to leave this enabled so that your Galaxy Note 5 automatically sets the time zone based on where you are traveling.

6. Tap Set Date to set the date if you choose to disable network synchronization.

7. Tap Set Time to set the time if you choose to disable network synchronization.

8. Tap Select Time Zone to set the time zone manually if you choose to disable network synchronization.

9. Set the Use 24-Hour Format switch to On or Off to enable or disable the use of 24-hour time format. This format makes your Galaxy Note 5 represent time without a.m. or p.m. For example, 1:00 p.m. becomes 13:00 in 24-hour format.

| ← Date and time | |
| --- | --- |
| **Automatic date and time** | |
| Use network-provided time. | |
| **Automatic time zone** | |
| Use network-provided time zone. | |
| **Set date** | 6 |
| September 13, 2015 | |
| **Set time** | 7 |
| 11:02 AM | |
| **Select time zone** | 8 |
| GMT+01:00 British Summer Time | |
| **Use 24-hour format** | 9 |
| 1:00 PM | |

# Clock Application

The Clock application is preinstalled on your Galaxy Note 5 and provides the functionality of a bedside clock and alarm clock.

## Navigate the Clock Application

1. Tap the Clock icon on the Apps screen.

2. Tap the Alarm tab to view and edit your alarms. Read more about setting alarms in the next section.

3. Tap the World Clock tab to see the World Clock and manage the clocks on that screen. Read more about using the World Clock in the "Use the World Clock" section later in this chapter.

4. Tap the Stopwatch tab to use the Stopwatch.

5. Tap the Timer tab to use the Timer.

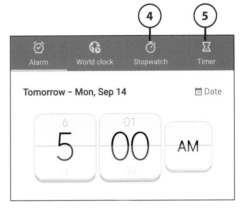

## Manage Alarms

The Clock application enables you to set multiple alarms. These can be one-time alarms or recurring alarms. Even if you exit the Clock application, the alarms you set still trigger.

1. Tap the Alarm tab to display the Alarm screen.

2. By default, the Clock application sets the alarm for tomorrow. If you want to set the alarm for a particular date, tap Date. In the Date panel that appears in the lower half of the screen, tap the appropriate date, and then tap the Done button to close the Date panel.

3. Scroll the time buttons up or down to set the hours and minutes. You can also tap the top of a button to increase the value by one or tap the bottom of a button to decrease the value by one.

4. Tap the AM/PM button to toggle between a.m. and p.m.

5. To set up a weekly alarm schedule, tap the Repeat Weekly button. The Repeat Weekly screen appears.

**Tap Keypad to display a keypad for setting the alarm time quickly.**

6. Check the box for each day of the week when you want the alarm to trigger. You can tap the Every Day box to check or uncheck all the other boxes quickly.

7. Tap the arrow button or the Back button to return to the Alarm screen.

8. Tap the Options button to display the remaining options for the alarm.

9. Tap the Alarm Type button. A pop-up menu opens.

10. Tap the alarm type you want: Sound, Vibrate, or Sound & Vibrate. This example uses Sound & Vibrate.

11. Drag the Volume slider to set the volume for a Sound alarm or a Sound & Vibrate alarm.

12. Set the Snooze switch to On or Off to enable or disable the Snooze feature. Snooze makes the alarm sound three times at five-minute intervals.

13. Set the Increasing Volume switch to On if you want the alarm volume to increase gradually for the first 60 seconds. Set this switch to Off if you want the alarm to play at a constant volume.

14. Tap the Save button to save the alarm. The alarm appears at the bottom of the Alarm screen (not shown).

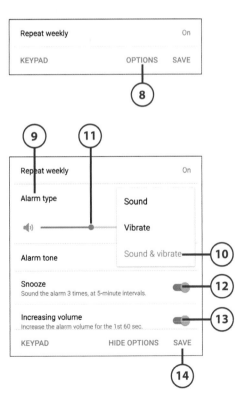

## Stopping or Snoozing an Alarm

When the alarm goes off, you can turn it off by tapping the red circled × and dragging it to either side.

If you enabled the Snooze feature for the alarm, you can tap the Snooze button to give yourself five minutes of peace.

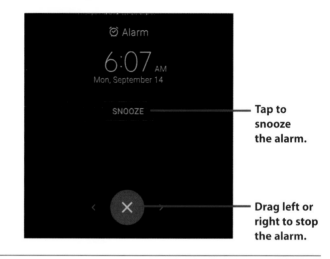

**Tap to snooze the alarm.**

**Drag left or right to stop the alarm.**

## Turning an Alarm On or Off—or Deleting It

After setting up an alarm, you can turn it off so that it doesn't ring. Tap the alarm on the Alarm screen, making its alarm-clock icon (and the days for which it is set) change from green to gray.

To delete an alarm, simply tap the × icon on the alarm's button. Clock deletes the alarm without confirmation.

**The alarm icon indicates one or more alarms is on.**

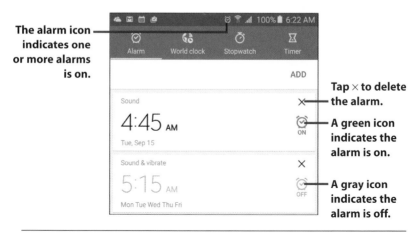

**Tap × to delete the alarm.**

**A green icon indicates the alarm is on.**

**A gray icon indicates the alarm is off.**

## Editing an Alarm

To edit an alarm, go to the Alarm screen in the Clock app and tap the alarm you want to edit. On the alarm's screen, change the alarm as needed—for example, change the time, enable Snooze, or pick a livelier tone—and then tap Save.

← Alarm tone

○ Beep-Beep

○ Beginning

◉ Bunny Hopping

**On the Alarm Tone screen, select a tone that suits the alarm's purpose.**

# Use the World Clock

The World Clock enables you to keep track of time in multiple cities around the world.

1. Tap the World Clock tab to display the World Clock screen.

2. Tap the Search box. The list of cities appears.

## Adding Cities by Exploring the World

Instead of searching for the cities you want to add to World Clock, you can explore the world and locate the cities visually. Tap and drag the map to display the area you want, and then zoom in by either double-tapping or pinching outward. Tap the city you want to add, and then tap the Add (+) button on the pop-up information window that appears.

**Tap to view your current location and the surrounding area.**

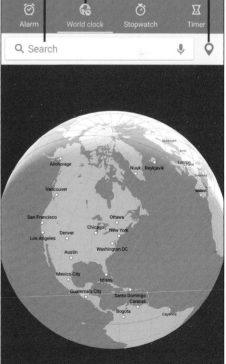

3. Start typing the name of the city you want to add. The list of matches appears.

4. Tap the appropriate match. The map displays the area in which the city is located, and a pop-up window displays the city's time, date, and time difference from the time zone you're currently using.

5. Tap the Add (+) button to add the city to your World Clock list. The city appears on a rectangle at the bottom of the screen.

6. Repeat steps 3–5 to add other cities as needed. You can then tap a city to display its location.

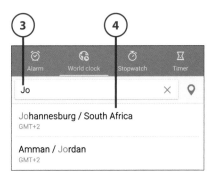

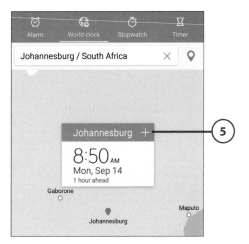

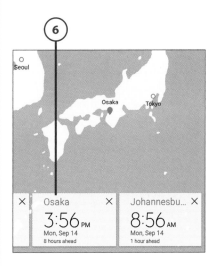

## Managing Cities

From the World Clock screen, you can easily remove a city or rearrange the cities you've saved. To remove a city, tap the × icon on the city's rectangle. To rearrange the cities, tap and hold a city's rectangle until it becomes mobile, and then drag it to where you want it in the list.

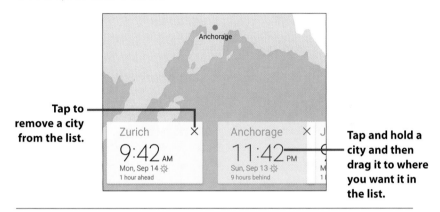

**Tap to remove a city from the list.**

**Tap and hold a city and then drag it to where you want it in the list.**

# Using the S Planner Calendaring Application

The S Planner calendaring application enables you to synchronize all your Google Calendars under your primary Google account to your Galaxy Note 5. You can accept appointments and create and modify appointments right on your phone. Any changes are automatically synchronized wirelessly back to your Google Calendar.

## Navigate the S Planner Main Screen

The main screen of the S Planner app shows a one-day, one-week, or one-month view of your appointments; a full-year view to enable you to navigate quickly among dates; or a list of the tasks you've added. S Planner also shows events from multiple calendars at the same time.

1.  Tap the S Planner icon on the Apps screen.

2. Swipe left to go backward in time.

3. Swipe right to go forward in time.

4. Tap the Today button to show today's date.

5. Tap + to create a new event.

6. Tap the button in the upper-left corner to display the navigation panel.

7. Tap the view you want to see: Year, Month, Week, Day, or Tasks.

## Using Colors to Distinguish Different Calendars

S Planner can display one calendar or many calendars at the same time. If you choose to display multiple calendars, events from each calendar are color coded so you can tell which events are from which calendar. In Google Calendar, you can also assign your choice of color to any event; S Planner preserves these colors.

# Choose Which Calendars and Task Lists to View

If you have set up multiple accounts, which might each have multiple calendars or task lists, you can choose which calendars S Planner shows at the same time.

1. Tap the More button to open the menu.

2. Tap Manage Calendars to display the Manage Calendars screen.

3. Set the All Calendars switch to On to quickly display all calendars and task lists from all accounts.

4. Set a switch to On to display the calendar or task list.

5. Set a switch to Off to hide a calendar or task list.

6. Change the color for a calendar by tapping the Calendar Color icon. The Calendar Color dialog opens.

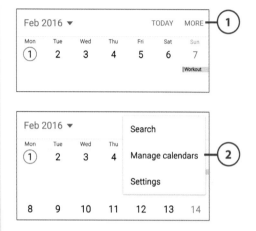

**Tap Add Account to add a new account.**

7. Tap the color you want to assign to the calendar.

8. Tap the arrow button or the Back button to return to the main S Planner screen.

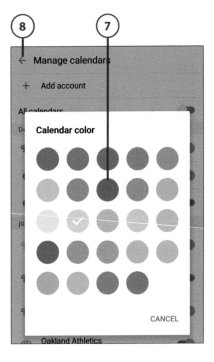

## Change S Planner Settings

1. Tap the More button to open the menu.

2. Tap Settings to display the S Planner Settings screen.

**3.** Specify which day to use as the first day in the week by tapping First Day of Week and then tapping the appropriate item in the pop-up menu. Your choices are Locale Default, Saturday, Sunday, and Monday. Locale Default means the locale determined by the time zone you are in controls what the first day of the week is.

**4.** Set the Show Week Numbers switch to On if you want to display week numbers. For example, March 26th is in week 13.

**5.** Set the Hide Declined Events switch to On if you want to hide events you have declined.

**6.** Display the weather on your calendar by tapping 7-Day Weather Forecast and then setting the switch on the 7-Day Weather Forecast screen to On.

**7.** Tap Notifications to configure how you receive notifications for calendar events, such as appointments or meetings. The Notifications screen appears.

**8.** Set the Notifications switch to On if you want to receive notifications from S Planner. Notifications are usually helpful unless you receive too many of them.

**9.** Tap Notification Sound to display the Notification Sound screen, tap the sound you want to hear for notifications, and then tap the arrow button or the Back button to return to the Notifications screen.

**10.** Set the Vibration switch to On if you want your Galaxy Note 5 to vibrate to alert you to notifications.

**11.** Tap the arrow button or the Back button to return to the S Planner Settings screen.

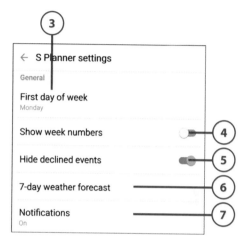

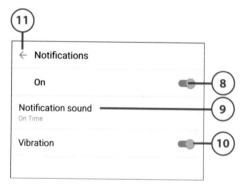

12. Tap Set Default Reminders to display the Set Default Reminders screen.

13. Tap Events to display the Events screen, and then tap the radio button for the reminder you want for regular events, such as 30 Min Before or 1 Hour Before.

14. Tap All-Day Events to display the All-Day Events screen, and then tap the radio button for the reminder you want for all-day events, such as Day Before Event at 5:00 PM or 1 Week Before Event at 9:00 AM.

15. Tap the arrow button or the Back button to return to the S Planner Settings screen.

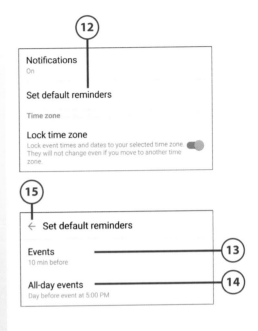

## Setting Custom Default Reminders

The Events screen and the All-Day Events screen give you a fair choice of timings for your default reminders, but you can customize them if necessary. Tap the Customize option button to display the Reminder dialog, specify the timing for your custom reminders, and then tap Done.

**Tap Customize to set custom timing.**

**Set the timing for your custom default reminders in the Reminder dialog.**

**16.** Set the Lock Time Zone switch to On when you want to force S Planner to use your home time zone or another time zone you choose when displaying the calendar and event times. You would do this when you travel but you want to keep your calendar on your home time zone (or another time zone you select) instead of letting S Planner change it to whichever time zone you find yourself in.

**17.** Tap Select Time Zone and select your home time zone if you enabled Lock Time Zone in step 16.

**18.** Tap the View Today According To button to display the View Today According To pop-up menu, and then tap Locked Time Zone or Local Time Zone, as needed.

**19.** Tap the arrow button or the Back button to return to the main S Planner screen.

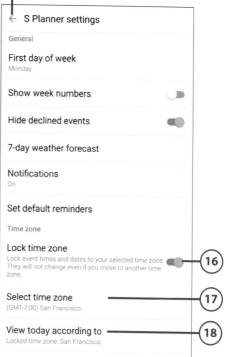

## Add a New Event

Using your Galaxy Note 5, you can add a new appointment or event—and even invite people to it. Events you add synchronize to your Google and corporate calendars in real time.

**1.** Tap + to add a new event.

### A Quicker Way to Add an Event

You can quickly add a new event by tapping and holding on the day on which you want to create the event. This technique works best in Day view, because you can tap and hold the time of day at which you want to create the event.

2. Tap the Title field and type the title for the event.

3. Tap the color swatch to choose the color to assign to the event. You can use colors to make important events more conspicuous.

4. Set the All Day switch to On if the event will be an all-day event.

5. Tap the Start button to display the Start tab of the Start and End dialog, in which you set the start date and time of the event. Tap Done when you finish.

6. Tap the End button to display the End tab of the Start and End dialog, in which you set the end date and time of the event. Again, tap Done when you finish.

7. Tap your account name to display the Calendar dialog, and then tap the calendar you want to add the event to.

8. Tap the Reminder button (which shows the details of the current default reminder) to display the Reminder screen.

9. On the Alert Type line, you can tap the current alert type (either Notification or Email) and then tap the other alert type on the pop-up menu.

10. Tap the radio button for the timing of the reminder. The New Event screen appears again.

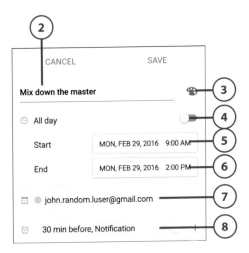

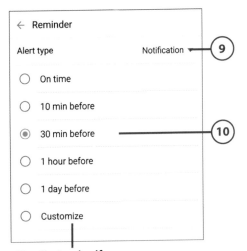

**Tap Customize if you want to create a custom reminder for this event.**

**11.** Tap the + to the right of Reminder if you want to configure another reminder. For example, you might want to receive an email message the day before an event as well as a notification a few minutes before the event.

**12.** Tap the – if you need to remove the existing reminder.

**13.** If you need to change the time zone, tap the current time zone to display the Time Zone screen, and then tap the appropriate time zone.

**14.** Specify the location for the event by tapping the Location box and typing the location.

**15.** Add a map showing the location by tapping Map. A map of the location appears.

**16.** Adjust the map to show what you need. You can move the map by dragging it, zoom in by pinching outward, or zoom out by pinching inward.

**17.** Tap Done. The New Event screen appears again, now showing a section of the map.

**18.** If you need to make the event a repeating event, tap Repeat and choose the schedule on the Repeat screen.

**19.** Tap Invitees to invite people to the event. The Invitees box appears.

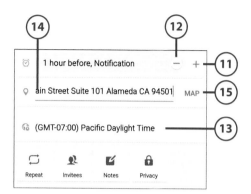

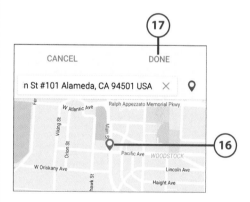

**20.** Enter each invitee's email address by either tapping Enter Name/Email Address and typing the address or by clicking the Contacts icon on the right and then tapping the contact in the Contacts list.

**21.** If necessary, tap the – button to remove an invitee you've added.

**22.** Add notes to the event by tapping Notes and typing the notes in the box that appears.

**23.** Tap Privacy to choose the privacy of the event. You can then tap the Show Me As pop-up menu and choose Busy or Available, as needed. You can also tap the Visibility pop-up menu and choose Calendar Default, Public, or Private to determine who can see details of the event. If the event is being created on your corporate calendar, setting the event to Private means that people can see you are busy, but they cannot see the event details.

**24.** Tap Save to save the event. Any attendees you have added are automatically sent an event invitation.

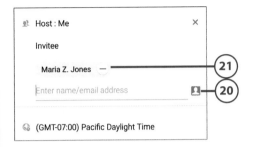

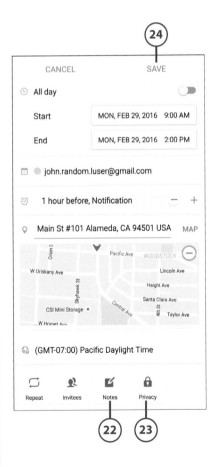

## Editing and Deleting an Event

To edit an event, you must first open it for editing. In Week view or in Day view, simply tap the event to display the event details. In Month view, tap the day to display its events, and then tap the event you want to edit or delete.

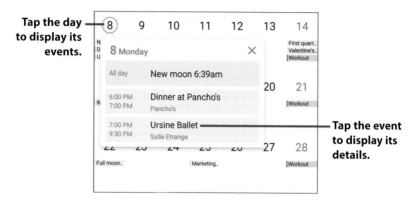

**Tap the day to display its events.**

**Tap the event to display its details.**

To edit the event, use the techniques you learned in the previous list, and then tap the Save button to save your changes. To delete the event, tap the Delete button at the top.

## Respond to a Google Event Invitation

When you are invited to an event, you can choose your response right in the invitation email itself.

1. Tap to open the event invitation email.

2. Tap Yes, Maybe, or No to indicate whether you will attend.

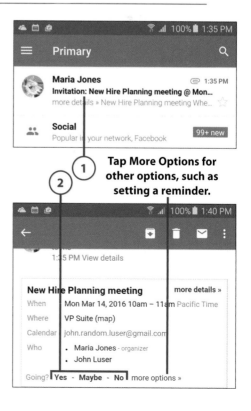

**Tap More Options for other options, such as setting a reminder.**

# Respond to an Event Invitation in the Email App

When you receive an invitation to an event in the Email app, you can choose your response in the invitation email. The process is a little different from that in the Gmail app.

1. Tap to open the event invitation email.

2. Tap Accept, Tentative, or Decline to display a dialog showing options for that type of response. This example uses Accept, so the Accept dialog opens.

3. Tap the appropriate button in the dialog. For example, you can tap Edit Response Before Sending to include custom text, tap Send Response Now to send an unvarnished acceptance, or tap Do Not Send Response to accept the invitation (and add it to your schedule as accepted) but not send a response to the organizer.

## What Happens If You Tap Other in Response to an Invitation?

If you tap Other on an invitation in the Email app, the Other dialog opens. You can then tap Suggest New Time to suggest a new time for the event, or you can tap View in S Planner to view the event in S Planner to see how it fits with your other commitments.

**Tap to propose a different time for the event.** ——

**Other**

Suggest new time

**Tap to see the event in your calendar.** ——

View in S Planner

This event overlaps with another event in S Planner. ——

**S Planner warns you if the event conflicts with an existing event in your calendar.**

## Should You Send a Response to an Invitation?

Usually, it is not only good manners but also helpful to send a response to an invitation. For most events, the organizer will need to know how many people are attending and who they are, so the organizer will find even a Maybe response more useful than no response. For huge public events, however, you may choose not to send a response.

## Add a Task

In addition to calendar events, you can add tasks you need to complete.

1. In S Planner, tap the pop-up menu button in the upper-left corner. The pop-up menu opens.

2. Tap Tasks to switch to the Tasks list.

3. Tap Enter New Task to start adding a new item.

4. Type the text for the task.

5. Tap the Today button if you want to assign the task to today, or tap the Tomorrow button if you want to assign it to tomorrow.

6. Tap the Expand button if you want to enter more details. (If not, tap the Save button to save the task now.)

Feb 2016 ▼                 TODAY   MORE

| Mon | Tue | Wed | Thu | Fri | Sat | Sun |
|-----|-----|-----|-----|-----|-----|-----|
| ① | 2 | 3 | 4 | 5 | 6 | 7 |

| | | | | TODAY | MORE |
|---|---|---|---|---|---|
| Year | 2016 | | | | |
| | | hu | Fri | Sat | Sun |
| Month | February | 4 | 5 | 6 | 7 |
| | | | | | Workout |
| Week | Feb 1 - 7 | | | | |
| Day | Feb 1 | 1 | 12 | 13 | 14 |
| | | | Fly back fr. | | First quart. Valentine's. Workout |
| Tasks | | | | | |

Tasks ▼                                MORE

Enter new task

**Tap Save whenever you're done entering details.**

Tasks ▼                                MORE

**Develop the finances worksheet**              SAVE

| TODAY | TOMORROW |

7. Set the Due Date switch to On if you want to give the task a due date.

8. Tap the Date button, choose the date for the task, and then tap Done.

9. Tap the Task button and then choose the task list in the Task dialog that opens.

10. Set a reminder by tapping Reminder, using the controls that appear, and then tapping Done.

11. Add a note by tapping Notes and then typing in the Notes box that appears.

12. Assign a priority by tapping Priority, and then tapping the Priority pop-up menu and selecting High, Medium, or Low.

13. Tap Save to save the task.

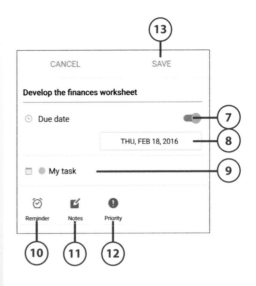

## Marking a Task as Completed

To mark a task as completed, switch to the Task list in S Planner. Check the box to the left of the task to mark it as completed.

Check the box to mark the task as completed.

Add, search, and manage your contacts.

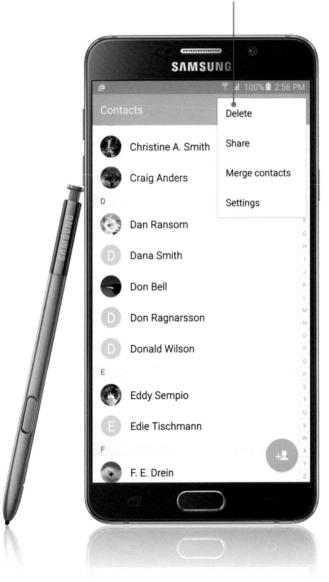

In this chapter, you become familiar with your Galaxy Note 5's contact-management application, which is called Contacts. You find out how to add contacts, synchronize contacts, join duplicate contacts, and add a contact to your Home screen for instant access. Topics include the following:

→ Adding accounts for syncing contacts
→ Navigating the Contacts app
→ Adding and managing contacts
→ Creating contact groups and favorite contacts

# Contacts

On any smartphone, the application for managing contacts is essential because it is where you keep all of your contacts' information. On the Galaxy Note 5, this application is called simply Contacts. It is the central hub for many activities, such as calling and sending text messages (SMS), multimedia messages (MMS), or email. You can also synchronize your contacts from many online sites, such as Facebook and Gmail, so as your friends change their Facebook profile pictures, their pictures on your Galaxy Note 5 change as well.

## Adding Accounts

Before you look around the Contacts app, add some accounts to synchronize contacts from. You already added your Google account when you set up your Galaxy Note 5 in the Prologue.

## Adding Facebook, Twitter, LinkedIn, and Other Accounts

To add accounts for your online services such as Facebook, Twitter, LinkedIn, and so on to your Galaxy Note 5, you might need to install the apps for those services from the Google Play Store. You can see how to install apps in Chapter 11, "Working with Android Apps." After the apps are installed and you have signed in to them, you visit the Accounts settings, as shown in the following sections, to see the accounts for each online service.

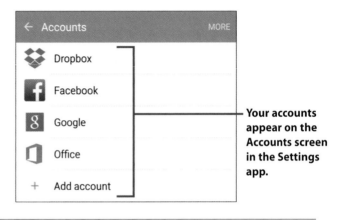

Your accounts appear on the Accounts screen in the Settings app.

1. From the Home screen, pull down to open the Notifications panel.

2. Tap the Settings icon to open the Settings app.

3. In the Personal section, tap Accounts to display the Accounts screen.

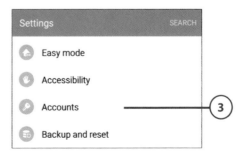

4. Tap Add Account to display the Add Account screen.

5. Tap Microsoft Exchange ActiveSync to display the Exchange ActiveSync screen.

6. Type the email address for the account.

7. Tap Password and type the password.

8. Tap Show Password if you want to see the password rather than the dots the Galaxy Note 5 shows for security. Seeing the password can be helpful when entering complex passwords.

9. Tap Next. The Settings app tries to set up the account with the information you've provided.

**← Accounts**                              MORE

Dropbox

Facebook

Google

Office

+  Add account ————————— 4

**← Add account**

Google                        ●

LDAP                          ○

LinkedIn                      ○

Microsoft Exchange ActiveSync —— 5

**← Exchange ActiveSync**

Configure Exchange account in a few steps.

john@surrealmacs.onmicrosoft.com ——— 6

••••••••••••••æ ——— 7

☐  Show password

MANUAL SETUP                    NEXT → 9

8

**Tap Manual Setup to take full control of setting up Exchange ActiveSync.**

## Dealing with Exchange ActiveSync Setup Problems

Your Galaxy Note 5 tries to work out some information about your company's ActiveSync setup. If it can't, it displays the Setup Could Not Finish screen to explain the problem. Often, you see the "Authentication failed" message. Tap the OK button to dismiss the screen so that you can change the details.

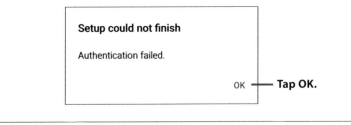

**Setup could not finish**

Authentication failed.

OK —— **Tap OK.**

## Need Domain Name?

On the Exchange Server Settings screen that appears, type the domain name before your username, separating the two with a backslash (for example, CORP\john). Type the Exchange Server's name in the Exchange Server box. Then tap Next to try the credentials again with this extra information.

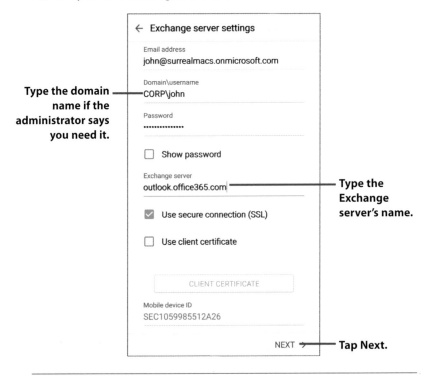

← **Exchange server settings**

Email address
john@surrealmacs.onmicrosoft.com

Domain\username
**Type the domain** —— CORP\john
**name if the**
**administrator says** —— Password
**you need it.** ················

☐ Show password

Exchange server
outlook.office365.com| ——— **Type the**
**Exchange**
**server's name.**

☑ Use secure connection (SSL)

☐ Use client certificate

CLIENT CERTIFICATE

Mobile device ID
SEC1059985512A26

NEXT ⇥ —— **Tap Next.**

10. In the Remote Security Administration dialog, tap OK to agree that your mail administrator may impose security restrictions on your Galaxy Note 5 after you connect to the Exchange Server. The Device Administrator screen appears.

11. Read the details of the powers you're about to assign to the Exchange server. Swipe up to see the full list of horrors.

## What Is Remote Security Administration?

Remote Security Administration says that when you activate your Galaxy Note 5 against your work email servers, your email administrator can add restrictions to your phone. These can include forcing a device password, imposing the need for a very strong password, and requiring how many letters and numbers the password must contain. Your Exchange administrator can also remotely wipe your Galaxy Note 5, restoring it to factory defaults. This is normally done if you lose your phone or it is stolen.

12. Tap Activate. Android finishes setting up the account, and it appears on the Accounts screen.

13. Tap the arrow button or the Back button to display the Settings screen again.

## Removing an Account

To remove an account, open the Settings screen. Tap Accounts to display the Accounts screen and then tap the account you want to remove. On the screen for the account, tap the More button and then tap Remove Account.

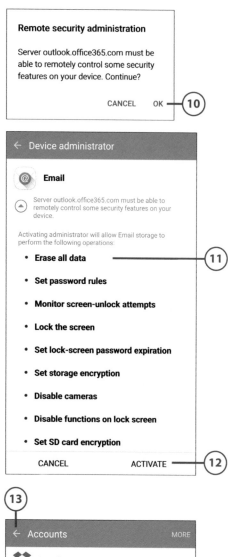

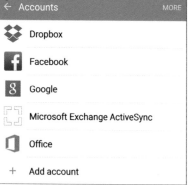

# Navigating Contacts

The Contacts app consists of four screens: Keypad, Logs, Favorites, and Contacts. Normally, the Contacts app displays the Contacts screen first, showing your list of contacts, but you can navigate to any of the other screens by tapping its tab.

1. From the Home screen, tap the Contacts icon. If the Contacts icon doesn't appear on the Home screen, tap it on the Apps screen.

2. Tap the Add (+) icon to add a new contact.

3. Tap Groups to see your contact groups and change which groups appear in the Contacts list. See more information about creating contact groups in the section titled "Create Contact Groups," later in this chapter.

4. Tap More to open the menu, which contains commands for working with contacts.

5. Tap the Search box to search for a contact.

6. Look at the My Profile section to see your phone number. This appears for quick reference in case you haven't memorized it.

7. The Favorites list gives you quick access to the contacts you've designated as favorites.

8. Tap a letter on the right side of the screen to jump to that letter in the contacts list. Jumping to a letter is usually faster than scrolling, especially if you have many contacts. Tap the star at the top to display the Favorites list.

9. Tap a contact to see all information about her.

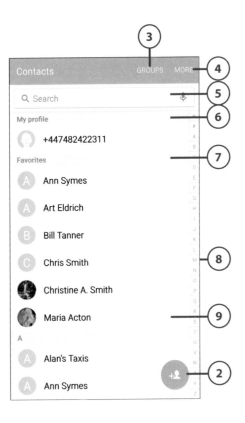

# >>>Go Further

## QUICKLY MESSAGE OR CALL A CONTACT

You can quickly start a new message to a contact by swiping left on the contact's name in the Contacts list. Similarly, you can dial a contact by swiping right on the contact's name.

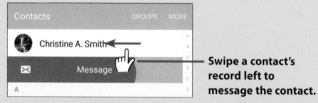

Swipe a contact's record left to message the contact.

If your contact has only one phone number, you get that number—which is fine. But if your contact has multiple numbers, the Galaxy Note 5 uses the default number you have set. This number appears at the top of the list with a blue check mark to the right of the number's type, such as Mobile or Work.

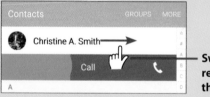

Swipe a contact's record right to call the contact.

If you haven't set a default number for the contact, the Galaxy Note 5 uses the first number in the list. So you should take a few minutes to set default numbers for the contacts you will want to call or message in this way.

To set a default number, open the contact record, tap and hold the appropriate phone number to display the pop-up menu, and then tap Mark as Default.

Maria Acton
Thought Free Co.

Mobile
(212) 555 1238

(212) 555 1238

Copy to clipboard

Mark as default

Tap and hold the phone number.

Tap Mark as Default to set the default number for quick calling and messaging.

## Edit a Contact

When you need to, you can easily change a contact's existing information or add further information to it.

1. Tap the contact you want to edit. The contact record appears.

2. Tap the Edit button to open the contact record for editing.

3. Tap the downward caret to the right of the contact's name to enter a name prefix, middle name, or name suffix.

4. Tap the – icon next to an existing field to delete it.

5. Tap a field subcategory, such as the Mobile subcategory for the phone number, to display a screen with options for changing the field subcategory. For example, you can change a phone number from Mobile to Home or to Work.

6. Tap the + icon to add a new field in a specific category. In this example, tapping + enables you to add a new email address and choose its subcategory, such as Work or Home.

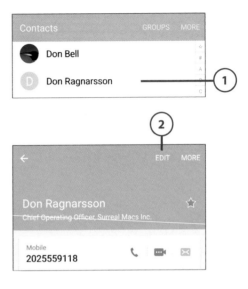

7. Tap Groups to put the contact in a contact group. The Galaxy Note 5 comes with built-in groups, including ICE – Emergency Contacts, Co-Workers, Family, and Friends, but you can also create as many other groups as you need.

8. Tap Add Another Field to add a new field to the contact record. The Add Another Field screen appears, showing a wide range of fields, including Address, Web Address, Event, Nickname, Ringtone, Message Tone, and Vibration Pattern.

9. Tap the field you want to add. For example, tap Ringtone to assign a custom ringtone to the contact so you can easily identify when this person phones you. The contact record appears again, now with the field you added.

10. Tap the new field to display the screen or controls for adding information to it. For example, tap Ringtone to assign a distinctive ringtone to the contact.

11. Tap the ringtone you want to hear.

12. When you have chosen a ring-tone, tap the arrow button or the Back button to return to the con-tact record.

13. Tap Save to save the changes to the contact record.

| Email | | + |
| ragnarsson@surrealmacs.com | Work | – |
| Groups | My contacts, Friends, Seance Circle | |

ADD ANOTHER FIELD

← Add another field

Address

Web address

IM account

Event (e.g., birthday)

Notes

Nickname

Phonetic name

Relationship

Ringtone

Message tone

Vibration pattern

| Groups | My contacts, Friends, Seance Circle |
| Ringtone | Default ringtone |

← Ringtones

○ Ocean Voyage

◉ On the Stage

CANCEL        SAVE

📷   Don Ragnarsson        ⌄

## Using Tones and Vibration to Distinguish Your Contacts

Use the Ringtone field, Message Tone field, and Vibration Pattern field to enable yourself to distinguish your contacts from each other. By assigning a distinctive ringtone to each of your most important contacts, you can easily determine who is calling you and (perhaps) whether you need to answer. Similarly, you can use the Message Tone field to make your Galaxy Note 5 play a distinctive tone when messages from vital contacts arrive.

For times when you mute your Galaxy Note 5's ringer, set a distinctive vibration pattern to enable you to tell one caller from another. In the contact record, tap Add Another Field to display the Add Another Field screen. Tap Vibration Pattern to display the Vibration Pattern screen. You can then tap one of the preset vibrations, such as Waltz or Zig-Zig-Zig; or tap Create Pattern and then create a custom pattern by tapping on the Create Pattern screen.

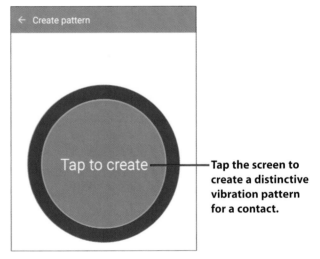

**Tap the screen to create a distinctive vibration pattern for a contact.**

## Add a Contact Photo

A contact record on your Galaxy Note 5 includes a contact photo when you link a social network account to the contact or when you import a contact record that includes a photo (for example, from a vCard file). You can manually add a picture as needed, either from an existing file or by taking a photo.

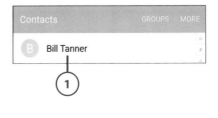

1. Tap the contact to open the contact record.

2.  Tap the Edit button to open the record for editing.

3.  Tap the contact photo (if there is one) or the contact photo icon (if there is not) to open the Contact Photo screen.

4.  Tap the Image icon to add a photo already saved on your Galaxy Note 5.

5.  Navigate to the photo you want to use. In Time view, scroll down as needed. In Albums view, tap the album that contains the photo, and then scroll down if necessary.

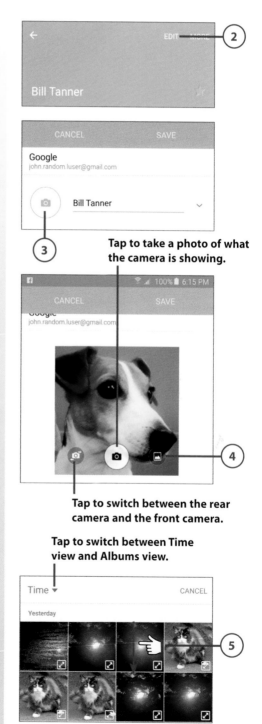

Tap to take a photo of what the camera is showing.

Tap to switch between the rear camera and the front camera.

Tap to switch between Time view and Albums view.

6. Tap the photo you want to use. The photo opens.

7. Drag the cropping box to select the area of the photo you want to use for the contact photo.

8. Drag the outside of the cropping box to expand or contract it, as needed. You can also pinch outward to enlarge the view.

9. Tap Done to add the cropped photo to the contact record.

10. Tap Save to save the contact record.

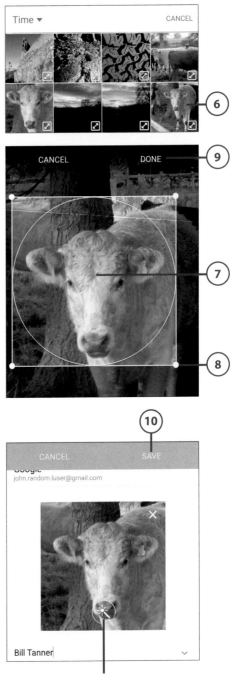

You can tap Filters to apply a filter, such as **Vignette** or **Grayscale**, to the photo.

# Adding and Managing Contacts

As you add contacts to your work email account or Google account, those contacts are synchronized to your Galaxy Note 5 automatically. When you reply to or forward emails on your Galaxy Note 5 to an email address that is not in your Contacts, those email addresses are automatically added to the contact list or merged into an existing contact with the same name. You can also add contacts to your Galaxy Note 5 directly.

## Add a Contact from an Email

To manually add a contact from an email, first open the Email app or the Gmail app and then open a message. See Chapter 4, "Email and Text Messages," for more on how to work with email.

### Add a Contact in the Email App

1. Tap the sender's name to display information about the sender and the message.

2. Tap Create Contact to open the Save Contact To dialog.

3. Tap the account to which you want to save the contact.

Add the email address to an existing contact instead.

---

**What If Android Warns Me Some Contact Information May Be Lost?**

Sometimes, when you go to save a contact, Android displays the Change Save Location dialog, warning you that some contact information may be lost. If this happens, click OK to close the dialog. When the new contact record appears in the Contacts app, you'll be able to see soon enough if anything vital has gone missing.

---

4. Type the contact's name if Contacts has not picked it up from the email message.

5. Tap Save to save the contact.

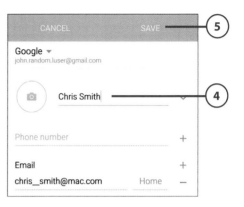

## Add a Contact in the Gmail App

1. Tap the sender image or initial letter to the left of the sender's name to display details about the sender.

2. Tap Add Contact to display the Select Contact screen.

3. Tap Create Contact to create a new contact record containing the contact's information.

Tap an existing contact to add the email address to the contact record.

4. Type the contact's name if Contacts has not derived it from the email message.

5. Tap Save to save the contact.

CANCEL SAVE — 5

Google ▾
john.random.luser@gmail.com

Rikki Nadir — 4

Phone number +

Email +
rickinadir@mac.com          Email —

# Add a Contact Manually

1. Tap the Contacts icon on the Home screen. The Contacts app opens.

Contacts — 1

2. Tap New (+) to add a new contact.

Ⓐ Ann Symes

Ⓐ Art Eldrich          +👤 — 2

3. Tap the pop-up menu to select the account you want to add the new contact to. For example, you might add the new contact to your work email account instead of to your personal account.

5   3          7

4. Type the person's full name, including any middle name. Your Galaxy Note 5 automatically populates the first name, middle name, and last name fields.

5. Tap the photo icon to choose a contact picture.

CANCEL SAVE

Google ▾
john.random.luser@gmail.com

Name — 4

Phone number +

Email +

Groups          My contacts

6. Tap Add Another Field to display the Add Another Field screen, where you can add other fields such as Nickname and Events.

7. Tap Save to save the new contact.

ADD ANOTHER FIELD — 6

# Add a Contact from a vCard

A vCard is a file that contains a virtual business card, which can include a contact's name, job title, email address, physical address, phone numbers, and so on. You can easily exchange vCards with other people by attaching them to email messages or instant messages. When you receive a vCard, you can import it into the Contacts app as a new contact. The procedure is different in the Email app and the Gmail app.

## Add a Contact from a vCard in Email

1. In the Email app, open the message and tap the attachment's button to display the Attachments screen.

2. Tap the Preview button to display a preview of the vCard file.

---

### Choosing the App for vCard Files

If your Galaxy Note 5 displays the Complete Action Using dialog when you tap Preview to open a vCard file, tap Contacts and then tap Always.

---

3. Tap the Save button. The Save Contact To dialog opens.

4. Tap the account you want to add the new contact to. For example, you might want to add the new contact to your work email account instead of to your personal account.

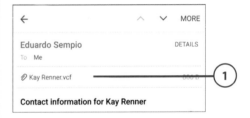

## Add a Contact from a vCard in Gmail

1. In the Gmail app, open the message and tap the attachment icon to display the attachment.

2. Tap the Save button. The Save Contact To dialog opens.

3. Tap the account you want to add the new contact to.

## Add a Contact Using Near Field Communications

Your Galaxy Note 5 has Near Field Communications (NFC) functionality built in. NFC (discussed in Chapter 1, "Working with Different Networks, NFC, and Contactless Payments") enables you to exchange contact cards between NFC-enabled smartphones or to purchase items in a store by holding your Galaxy Note 5 near the NFC reader at the check-out counter. If you encounter someone who has an NFC-enabled smartphone, or she has an NFC tag that contains her business card, follow these steps to import that information:

1. Hold the other person's smartphone back to back with your Galaxy Note 5 and give the command for sharing via NFC, or hold the NFC tag close to the back cover of your Galaxy Note 5. Your Galaxy Note 5's screen dims and the phone plays a tone to indicate that it is reading the NFC information. The Save Contact To dialog then appears.

2. Tap to select the account you want to add the new contact to.

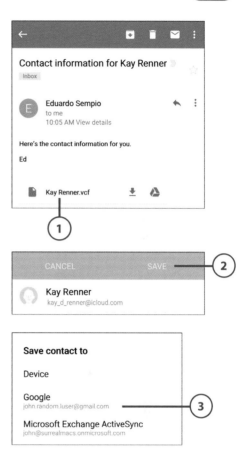

# Manage Contacts Settings

To make the Contacts app display contacts the way you prefer, you can customize it. For example, you can choose the contact list display order and whether to display contacts using their first names first or last names first.

1. Tap the Contacts icon on the Home screen.

2. Tap the More button to display the menu.

3. Tap Settings to display the Contacts Settings screen.

4. Tap Sort By to choose the sort order of the list of contacts in the Contacts app. You can sort the list by first name or last name.

5. Tap Name Format to choose how each contact is displayed. You can tap "First, Last" to display contacts with the first name first or tap "Last, First" to display the last name first.

6. Tap Share Multiple Contacts to choose how to transmit multiple contacts you share at once. The Share Multiple Contacts screen appears.

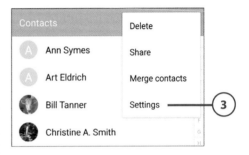

**7.** Select the As One File radio button to send a single file containing all the contacts, or select the Individually radio button to send a separate file for each contact. When you select one of these radio buttons, the Contacts Settings screen appears again; you don't need to tap the arrow button or the Back button to return to the Contacts Settings screen.

## Should You Share Multiple Contacts as One File or Individually?

Usually, it is best to share contact files individually. Sharing individual files typically takes longer than sharing a single file, because the receiving device accepts the files one at a time rather than all at once; but unless you transfer large numbers of contacts, the extra time is unlikely to inconvenience you unduly.

Sharing individual files helps you avoid a problem with transferring multiple contacts in a single file: If the receiving device doesn't support vCard files containing multiple contact records, the device receives only the first contact record. Most modern devices do support vCard files containing multiple contact records, but you might still run into devices that do not.

**8.** Tap the arrow button or the Back button to save the settings and return to the Contacts app.

← Share multiple contacts

◉ As one file

Share multiple contacts together in one file to reduce transmission time. If the receiving device does not support this, only one contact will be shared.

○ Individually — ⑦

Share multiple contacts individually. This may take longer because the receiving device must accept them one at a time.

⑧

← Contacts settings

Manage and back up contacts

# Create Contact Groups

You can create contact groups—such as Friends, Family, Inner Circle—and then divide your contacts among them. This can be useful if you don't want to search through all your contacts. For example, to find a family member, you can simply tap the Family group and see only family members.

1. On the Contacts screen, tap the Groups button to display the Groups screen.

2. Tap the Add button to display the New Group screen.

3. Tap the button at the top, select the accounts in which to create the group, and then tap Done to return to the New Group screen. The button's name varies depending on the accounts selected. For example, the button shows Device if Contacts will store the group only on your Galaxy Note 5; Google if only your Google account is selected; or Device Storage and All Accounts if the device and all your accounts are selected.

4. Tap Group Name and type a name for your new group.

5. Optionally, tap Group Ringtone to set a specific ringtone for the group. You can use the ringtone and vibration pattern to make calls from the group easy to distinguish.

6. Tap Add Member to add members to the group.

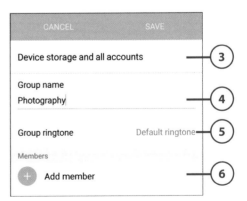

7. Tap the check box next to each contact's name to select the members of the group. A button appears for each contact at the top of the screen, including a – button that you can tap to quickly remove the contact from the group.

8. Tap Done. The New Group screen appears, now showing the members.

9. Tap Save to save the group.

**Tap Search and type search text to find contacts quickly.**

**Tap – to remove a contact from the group.**

| 3 | | DONE |
|---|---|---|

nn Symes  —    Christine A. Smith  —    Eddy Sempio  —

🔍 Search

A                                                                    #
                                                                     A
☐  Ⓐ  Alan's Taxis                                                   B
                                                                     C
                                                                     D
☑  Ⓐ  Ann Symes                                                      E
                                                                     F
                                                                     G
☐  Ⓐ  Art Eldrich                                                    H
                                                                     I
                                                                     J
                                                                     K
☐  Ⓐ  Arthur Orford                                                  L
        14155559086                                                  M
                                                                     N

**CANCEL**                                    **SAVE**

Device storage and all accounts

Group name
Photography

Group ringtone                              Default ringtone

Members

⊕  Add member

Ⓐ  Ann Symes                                         —

🖼  Christine A. Smith                                 —

# Change the Contacts in a Contacts Group

1. On the Contacts screen, tap the Groups button to display the Groups screen.

Contacts                              GROUPS    MORE

Ⓐ  Ann Symes

2. Tap the group to edit. A screen appears showing the group.

3. Tap the Edit button to open the group for editing.

4. Tap the Add Member button to add members to the group. On the resulting screen, check the box for each contact you want to add and then tap Done.

5. Tap the – button for each contact you want to remove.

6. Tap the Save button to save your changes to the group.

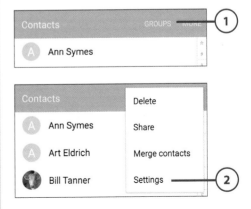

# Choose Which Contacts to Display

You can choose to hide certain contact groups from the main contacts display. For example, you can choose to show only contacts from Twitter. You can also choose which contact groups in each account to include.

1. On the Contacts screen, tap the More button to display the menu.

2. Tap Settings to display the Contacts Settings screen.

3. Tap Contacts to Display to show the Contacts to Display screen.

4. Tap All Contacts to display all contacts from all accounts.

5. Tap an account to show only contacts in that account.

6. Tap Customized List to choose a customized selection.

7. Tap the Settings icon (the cog) to customize which groups in each account are displayed.

8. Tap a downward caret to expand an account to see subgroups of contacts. Tap the resulting upward caret to collapse an account again, hiding its subgroups.

9. Tap a check box to select or deselect a subgroup of contacts.

10. Tap Done to save your settings.

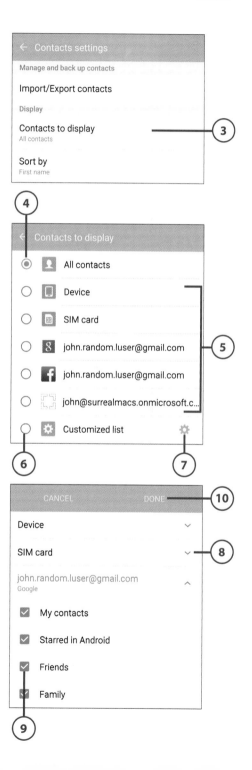

# Link and Unlink Contacts

As you add contacts to your Galaxy Note 5, the Contacts app automatically links them if the new contact name matches a name that's already stored. Sometimes you need to manually link contacts or unlink them if your Galaxy Note 5 has joined them in error.

## Link Contacts Manually

1. In the Contacts app, tap the contact you want to link a contact to. The contact record opens.

2. Tap the More button to display the menu.

3. Tap Link Contacts to display the Link Contact screen. The Suggested Contacts list shows contacts in which Contacts has found apparently suitable data, but you can choose a contact from the main list if necessary.

4. Check the box for each contact you want to link with.

5. Tap Link to link the contacts.

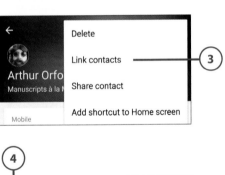

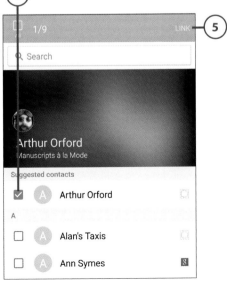

## Unlink Contacts

1. In the Contacts app, tap the contact you want to unlink. The contact record opens.

2. Tap the More button to display the menu.

3. Tap Manage Linked Contacts to display the Linked Contact screen.

4. Tap the red – icon to the right of each contact you want to unlink.

5. Tap the arrow button or the Back button to return to the contact record.

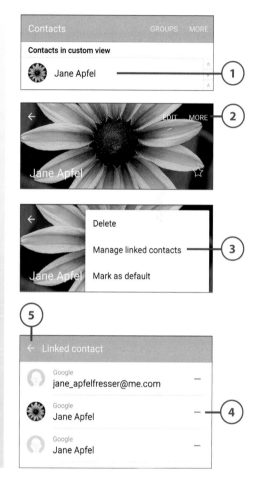

# Adding a Contact to Your Home Screen

If you communicate with any contact so much that you are constantly opening and closing the Contacts app, you can save time and effort by adding a shortcut to that contact on the Home screen.

1. In the Contacts app, tap the contact you want to add to the Home screen. The contact record opens.

2. Tap the More button to display the menu.

3. Tap Add Shortcut to Home Screen. Android adds a shortcut for that contact to the Home screen.

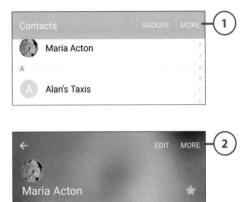

## >>>Go Further
# IMPORTING AND EXPORTING CONTACTS

You can import any contacts that are stored on your SIM or vCards that you have saved to your Galaxy Note 5's internal storage. You can also export your entire contact list to your Galaxy Note 5's SIM card or to a USB storage device. To access the import/export functions, open the Contacts app, tap the More button, and then tap Settings. On the Contact Settings screen, tap Import/Export Contacts to display the Import/Export Contacts screen.

Import/Export contacts

Import contacts

Import vCard files (VCF) from your device storage to Contacts on your device.

IMPORT ————— **Tap the Import button to start importing contacts.**

Export contacts

Export contacts from your device storage to selected storage locations as vCard files.

EXPORT

Tap the Import button. The Import Contacts From dialog opens, and you can tap SIM Card. (If the SIM card contains no contacts, the Import Contacts From dialog doesn't open, and the Galaxy Note 5 searches the Download folder for contact files to import.)

Import contacts from

Device storage

SIM card ————— **Tap SIM Card.**

The Save Contact To dialog then opens, and you can tap the destination for the contacts. The Galaxy Note 5 then imports the contacts.

Save contact to

Device

Google
john.random.luser@gmail.com ————— **Tap the destination for the contacts.**

Microsoft Exchange ActiveSync
john@surrealmacs.onmicrosoft.com

Turn your current call
into a conference call.

In this chapter, you find out how to make and take phone calls (including conference calls) using your Galaxy Note 5. Topics include the following:

→ Making phone calls
→ Receiving phone calls
→ Making conference calls
→ Configuring the Phone app

8

# Making and Receiving Calls

As a cellular phone, your Galaxy Note 5 includes powerful features that enable you to make phone calls swiftly and easily.

## Getting to Know the Phone App

With the Phone app, you can quickly make and receive calls across the cellular network. This section introduces you to some of the features you might frequently use.

# Open and Navigate the Phone App

The Phone app contains three tabs that enable you to make calls in various ways and to track the calls you receive.

1. On the Home screen, tap Phone.

2. Tap the dialpad icon to display the dialpad. The dialpad icon is always visible on the bottom right of the screen while you are in the Phone app.

3. Tap the keys to dial a number.

4. If the Phone app displays a suggested contact with a matching number, you can tap the contact if it is the one you want.

5. Tap the green phone icon to place the call.

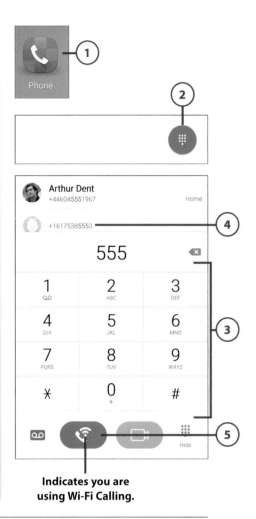

**Indicates you are using Wi-Fi Calling.**

---

## What Is Wi-Fi Calling?

The technical name for Wi-Fi Calling is Universal Media Access (UMA). This technology is provided by some carriers around the world and enables your Galaxy Note 5 to roam between the cellular network and Wi-Fi networks. Typically when you are connected to a Wi-Fi network, any calls you make are free and of higher audio quality because of the faster speeds. As you move out of Wi-Fi coverage, your Note 5 hands the call off to the cellular network—and vice versa—allowing your call to continue without interruption. The Phone app indicates when you are using Wi-Fi Calling by placing a Wi-Fi symbol next to the phone icon. If you want to read more about UMA or Wi-Fi Calling, read this online article: http://crackberry.com/saving-call-charges-recession-your-blackberry. The article is on a BlackBerry blog, but the descriptions of the technology still apply.

---

## Call Log

The Call Log tab shows all activity in the Phone app, including incoming calls, missed calls, rejected calls, and placed calls.

1.  Tap Log to see a list of the calls you have missed, placed, and received.

2.  Tap a log entry to see more information about the caller.

3.  Tap the phone icon to place a call to the caller.

4.  Tap the envelope icon to send an SMS (text message) to the caller.

5.  Tap Edit to delete one or more call log entries for this caller.

6.  Tap More to view the full contact record for this caller, or add the caller to your Auto Reject List.

**Rejected call**
**Incoming call**
**Outgoing call**

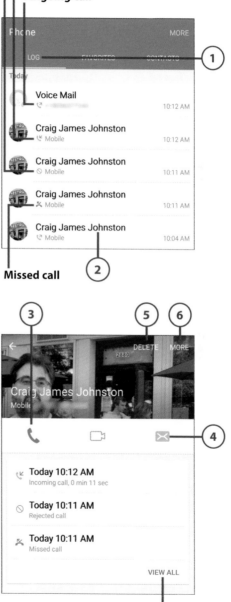

**Missed call**

**View all log entries.**

# Favorites

The Favorites tab shows contacts who you have marked as favorite and contacts who you call often.

1. Tap Favorites to see your favorite and frequently called contacts.

2. Tap the contact image of a favorite contact to place a call to them.

3. Tap the information icon to the right of a favorite contact's name to see all of the information about the contact.

4. Tap Add to add additional favorite contacts from your Contacts list.

5. Tap More to remove favorite contacts, or to reorder thair positions on the Favorites tab.

# Contacts

The Contacts tab shows all of the contacts that you have added to the Contacts app.

1. Tap Contacts to see all of your contacts.

2. Tap a contact to see all information about that contact.

3. Tap to search for a contact.

4. Tap Create to add a new contact.

5. Tap More to remove contacts or see your Speed Dial screen.

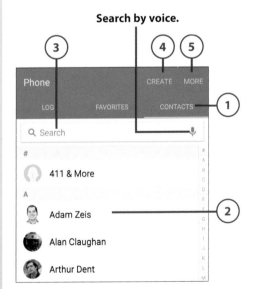

Search by voice.

# >>>Go Further

## SPEED DIAL

Speed dialing is a bit of a holdover from the 1980s and '90s when phones weren't as sophisticated as they are today. However, you might still find it useful to touch and hold one key to call a number. To add or edit your Speed Dial numbers, tap the Menu icon and tap Speed Dial. (Voicemail is already assigned to speed dial 1.) Tap the plus symbol for a numbered entry to add a contact for that Speed Dial number. To use Speed Dial, while the keypad is visible, touch and hold a number associated with a Speed Dial contact. That number will be dialed.

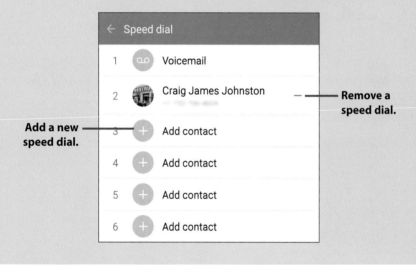

**Add a new speed dial.**

**Remove a speed dial.**

# Receiving a Call

When someone phones your Galaxy Note 5, you can accept the call, reject it, or reject it and send a text message.

# Accept a Call

1. When the phone rings, look at the contact name (if it is available) or the phone number (if it is not) and decide whether to take the call.

2. Swipe the green phone icon to the right to accept the call.

3. Tap to switch the call audio to the speaker.

4. Tap to switch the call audio to a Bluetooth device you have previously paired, such as a headset, your smartwatch, or your vehicle's built-in Bluetooth.

5. Tap to mute the call. Tap again to turn off muting.

6. Tap to show the keypad if you need to type extra numbers after the call is connected.

7. Tap to boost the call volume if the call volume is very quiet.

8. Tap to put the call on hold.

9. Swipe to the right to see more options, such as the ability to write a memo that is associated with the caller.

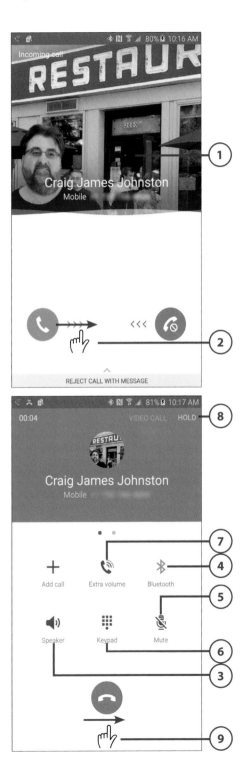

10. Tap to write a memo that is associated with the caller while you're on the call.

11. Tap to open the Calendar app, view the calendar, and create a new appointment if needed.

12. Tap to open the Internet browser and use it while on the call.

13. Tap to send an SMS (text message) to the caller.

14. Tap to send an email to the caller.

15. Tap to show the caller's information in the Contacts app.

16. Swipe to the left to return to the main call screen.

17. Tap to end the call.

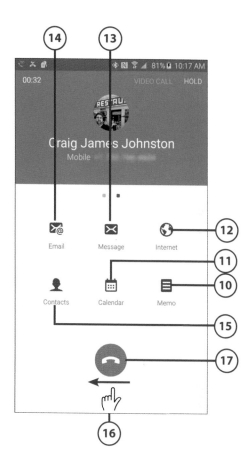

# Reject a Call

If you do not want to accept the call, you can reject it so that it goes to your voicemail.

1. When the phone rings, swipe the red phone icon to the left to reject the call.

   The call goes to voicemail, and your Galaxy Note 5 displays the screen you were using before the call came in.

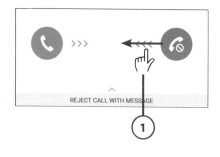

# Reject a Call and Send a Text Message

Instead of simply declining a call and sending it to your voicemail, you can send an SMS (text message) straight back to the caller. Your Galaxy Note 5 provides a selection of canned messages for general needs. You can also create your own messages or type custom messages for particular calls.

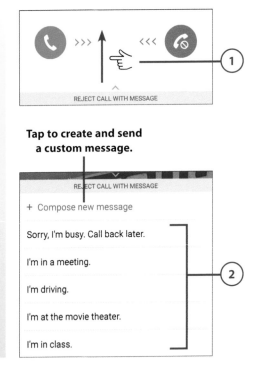

REJECT CALL WITH MESSAGE

**Tap to create and send a custom message.**

1. When the phone rings, swipe up to display the Reject Call with Message shade.

2. Tap to send one of the canned messages.

## It's Not All Good

**Bug with Custom Reject Message**

When you want to reject a call with a message, there is an option to compose a new message instead of using one of the on-screen choices. This option works unless your Note 5 is locked, and you use a lock screen PIN, password, pattern, or your fingerprint. The bug causes a new text message (SMS) compose screen to be created, correctly addressed to the caller, however you are unable to see the message compose screen to type your custom message. This means that the option of composing a custom message only works if you already have your Note 5 unlocked.

# Handle Missed Calls

If you miss a phone call, you can quickly locate it in the Phone app's logs so that you can return it, but you can also take actions on missed calls from the Lock screen or any other screen.

1. Tap to see the missed call from the Lock screen. If you use a Lock screen password or other method of locking your Note 5, you are required to use that method to unlock your Note 5 before you can continue.

2. Swipe from left to right across the missed call log entry to call the number back.

3. Swipe from right to left across the missed call log entry to send an SMS (text message) to the caller.

4. Tap the missed call log entry to see its details.

5. Tap to call the person back.

6. Tap to send an SMS (text message) to the caller.

7. Tap to delete one or more call log entries from this caller.

8. Tap to view the caller's full contact information (if you already have the person in your Contacts), or add the number to your Auto Reject list. When someone's number is on the Auto Reject list, your Note 5 automatically rejects calls from that number.

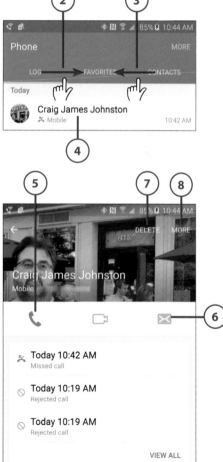

# Making Calls

Aside from making a call the traditional way—by using the dialpad to punch in the numbers—you voice-dial a call on your Galaxy Note 5, or you can make a conference call.

## Starting a Call from the Contacts App

Instead of launching the Phone app and then tapping the Contacts tab to go to the Contacts app, you can start a call directly from the Contacts app. Tap Contacts on the Home screen or the Apps screen to launch the Contacts app, tap the contact to display his or her details, and then tap the green phone icon to the right of the number you want to call.

## Dial Using Your Voice

With the S Voice feature, your Galaxy Note 5 enables you to dial calls using your voice.

1.  Say "Hi Galaxy" or whatever you set your S Voice Wake-up command to. A blue bar appears on the bottom of your screen indicating that S Voice is listening for a command. Please refer to the Prologue in the section "First-Time Setup" (step 36) to read more about the wake-up command.

2.  Say "Call," followed by the contact's name; if the contact has multiple phone numbers, say the type of number as well. For example, say "Call Dana Smith mobile" or "Call Craig at home."

3  Wait while S Voice dials the number. The Dialing screen appears.

# >>>Go Further

## USE "OK GOOGLE" TO MAKE A CALL

In addition to using S Voice, you can use Google to place your calls. Simply say "OK Google" and speak the call instructions. For example: "OK Google. Call Craig at home".

## Using Other Apps During a Call

During a call, you can use most other apps freely, but you cannot play music or video. You can take photos with the Camera app, but you cannot shoot videos. To switch to another app, either use the Recent Apps list or press the Home button and use the Apps screen as usual. While you are using another app, your Galaxy Note 5 displays a green bar at the top of the screen to remind you that you are in a call. Pull down the Notification panel to control the call or return to it or take actions such as switch to speakerphone, mute, and hang up.

**Green bar indicates call is in progress.**     **Tap to return to your call.**

## Make Conference Calls

You can quickly turn your current call into a conference call by adding other participants.

1. With a call in progress, tap Add Call on the call screen.

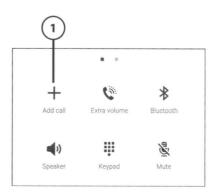

2. Dial the call in the most convenient way. For example, either type out the phone number or dial from the call log, Favorites, or Contacts.

3. Tap to swap between the original call and the one you just added, if you need to.

4. Tap Merge to merge the calls and complete the conference call setup.

5. Repeat steps 1–4 to add additional callers. The exact number of callers you can have on a conference call is governed by your wireless carrier.

6. Tap Manage if you need to hang up on only one of the conference call parties, or if you need to split one of the parties off the conference call while still keeping them connected and on hold.

7. Tap the red phone icon to the right of a conference party you want to hang up on and remove from the conference call.

8. Tap Split if you want to remove the party from the conference call, but need to keep them connected to your phone and on hold.

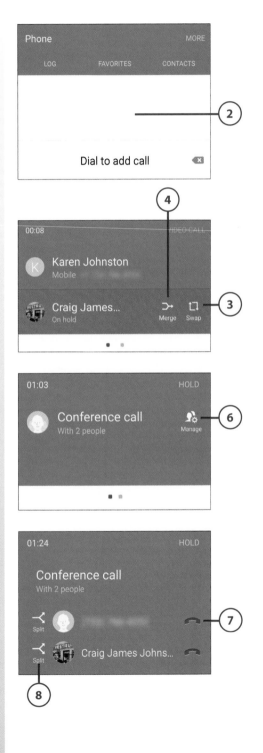

## *It's Not All Good*

**Manage Conference Calls May Not Work**

During the writing of this book, we noticed that the Conference call Manage icon was not on the screen during a conference call. This means that steps 6, 7, and 8 were not possible. It looks like a bug in the phone app, which Samsung will likely fix soon.

# Configuring the Phone App

To make the Phone app work your way, you can configure its settings.

1. Tap More.

2. Tap Settings.

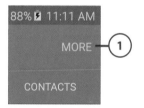

3. Tap to enable or disable the feature that allows you to swipe over a call log entry to either place a call to that number or send a text message to it.

4. Tap to enable or disable the feature that shows only contacts that include phone numbers in the phone app.

5. Tap to choose certain numbers for which calls will be automatically rejected. Tapping here also lets you edit your canned call rejection messages.

## What Does Call Rejection Do?

Your Galaxy Note 5's call rejection feature allows you to specify certain numbers to automatically reject, or to reject incoming calls that have no number or show as Unknown. Automatically rejecting specific numbers enables you to avoid calls from people you do not want to talk to.

6. Tap to choose whether you want to use Voice over LTE (VoLTE) when it is available.

← Call settings

Phone settings

**Swipe to call or send messages**
Make calls or send messages by swiping right or left across a contact's information in the Contacts tab, or a log item in the Log tab.   ON ③

**Only contacts with devices**
Show contacts with phone numbers and hide other contacts.   OFF ④

Call settings

**Call blocking** ⑤

**Voice over LTE settings**
Use VoLTE when available ⑥

Answering and ending calls

**Automatic answering**
Answer incoming calls automatically after 2 seconds while a headset or a Bluetooth device is connected.   OFF

**Call alerts**

**Ringtones and keypad tones**

Wi-Fi Calling

## What Is VoLTE?

LTE (or Long-Term Evolution) is the fourth generation of cellular data technology (not to be confused with the slightly faster version of 3G technology that has been incorrectly called 4G for years). VoLTE stands for Voice over LTE. Effectively, your voice call is sent as regular data over the LTE data channel as opposed to over the cellular voice channel. Voice quality is much better due to the higher rate at which the data is transmitted and received, and if the person you are calling also uses VoLTE, you can speak at the same time. Most wireless carriers treat VoLTE as regular voice minutes and don't let it count against your data plan. However, you should verify the situation with your local wireless carrier; otherwise, your data plan might take an unexpected hit.

7.  Tap to choose how you want to answer and end calls. You can choose to use your voice (saying "Answer" or "Reject"), press the Home button, or press the Power button.

8.  Tap to enable or disable a feature that automatically answers an incoming call if you have your Note 5 connected to a Bluetooth device or your vehicle's built-in Bluetooth.

9.  Tap to choose options for vibrations, cell status tones, and alerts during calls. You can choose whether your Galaxy Note 5 vibrates or plays a tone when someone answers your call and when they hang up. You can also choose to receive or suppress notifications during calls.

10. Tap to choose the ringtone that plays when you receive an incoming call. You can also choose whether you want your phone to vibrate when you receive an incoming call, and what vibration pattern to use.

11. Swipe up for more settings.

12. Tap to enable or disable Wi-Fi Calling, and choose how you want your Note 5 to utilize Wi-Fi Calling. You can choose to have your Note 5 prefer Wi-Fi but use cellular if Wi-Fi is unstable; prefer the cellular network, and only use Wi-Fi if cellular service is unavailable; or only use Wi-Fi for all calls.

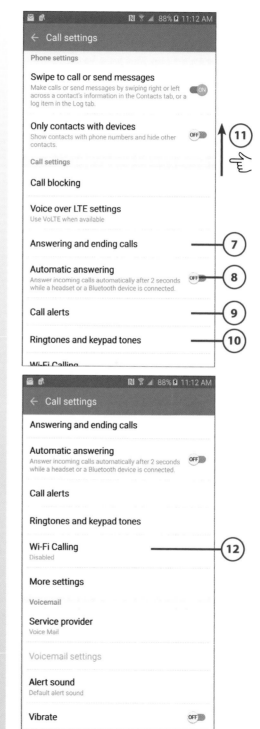

13. Tap to see additional settings, including how Caller ID is handled, call forwarding, call waiting, and Fixed Dialing Numbers (FDN). When you tap, the settings are loaded over the wireless network, so you might need to wait a few seconds before they appear.

14. Tap to choose which voicemail service to use (if you have more than one option). If you use Google Voice, it is common to use the Google Voice voicemail system as opposed to the one provided by your wireless carrier.

15. Tap to adjust voicemail settings (if options are available).

16. Tap to choose your ringtone for announcing voicemail.

17. Tap to choose to also vibrate when you are notified of a new voicemail.

18. Tap to save your changes and return to the main phone screen.

## What Is Video Calling?

Your mobile provider might offer video calling for your Note 5. If it does, you will see a video call icon to the right of the regular phone icon. If you place a video call by tapping the video call icon, if the person you are calling has a phone that supports video calling, you are able to make use of this feature. While on a video call, you can switch between the front-facing or rear-facing camera on your Note 5.

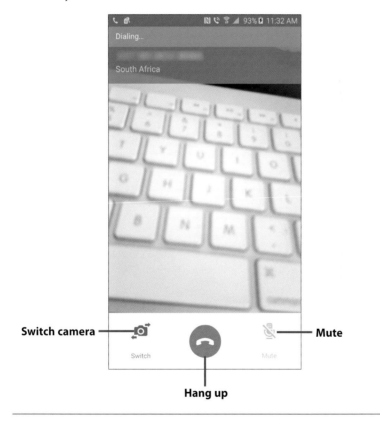

Switch camera

Mute

Hang up

Play your music through
the Galaxy Note 5's
speakers or through your
headphones.

In this chapter, you discover your Galaxy Note 5's audio and video capabilities, including how your Galaxy Note 5 plays video and music as well as how you can synchronize audio and video from your desktop or laptop computer or Google Music. This chapter also covers how to take pictures and videos. Topics include the following:

→ Using Google Music for music
→ Using the Gallery app for pictures and video
→ Shooting still photos and videos
→ Enjoying videos with the YouTube app

# Audio, Video, Photos, and Movies

Your Galaxy Note 5 is a powerful multimedia smartphone with the ability to play back many different audio and video formats. The large screen enables you to turn your Galaxy Note 5 sideways to enjoy a video in its original 16:9 ratio. You can also use your Galaxy Note 5 to take photos and videos, watch videos, and even upload videos to YouTube right from your phone. Android fully embraces the cloud, which enables you to store your music collection on Google's servers so you can access it anywhere.

## Enjoying Music with the Music Application

To get the most out of music on your Galaxy Note 5, you probably want to use the Play Music app, which enables you to listen to music stored on your phone as well as from your collection in the Google Music cloud.

# >>>*Go Further*

## INSTALL THE PLAY MUSIC APP IF NECESSARY

If your Galaxy Note 5 does not include the Play Music app, you need to install it. Tap Apps on the Home screen and look through the list of apps. The Play Music app may appear either directly on the Apps screen or in a Google folder that gathers apps such as Chrome, Gmail, and Google+ together with Play Newsstand, Play Movies & TV, and Hangouts.

If you don't find the Play Music app, tap the Apps icon on the Home screen and then tap the Play Store icon to open the Play Store app. Tap Apps, tap the search icon, and type **play music**. Tap the Google Play Music search result, tap Install, and then tap Accept & Download. Your Galaxy Note 5 downloads the Play Music app and installs it.

## Find Music

When you're certain the Play Music app is installed on your Galaxy Note 5, you can add some music. One way to add music is to purchase it from Google.

1. Tap the Play Music icon on the Apps screen or in the Google folder.

2. Tap the Menu button in the upper-left corner to display the menu panel.

3. Tap Shop to display the Play Store screen.

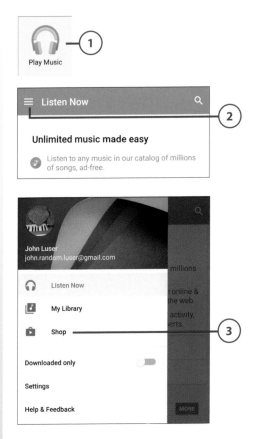

4. Tap New Releases to see new releases.

5. Swipe right or tap Genres to see a list of music genres.

6. Swipe left or tap Top Albums to see the Top Albums list. Swipe left again from the Top Albums list to see the New Releases list. Swipe left once more from the New Releases list to see the Top Songs list.

7. Tap the Search icon to search for music.

## Purchase Music

After you find a song or album you want to purchase, use the following steps to make the purchase.

### Free Music

Sometimes songs are offered for free. If a song is offered for free, you see the word "Free" instead of a price for the song. Even though the song is free, you still need to follow the steps outlined in this section; however, the price appears as 0.

1. Tap the price to the right of the song title or album.

2. Tap Buy. Google Play processes your payment, and Play Music downloads the song. You can then play it.

**The Play Store offers some songs for free.**

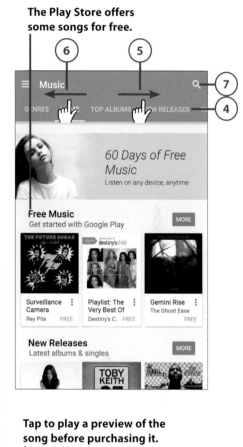

**Tap to play a preview of the song before purchasing it.**

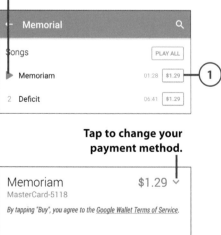

**Tap to change your payment method.**

## It's Not All Good

### Cloud and Data Usage

Although cloud storage (where your music is stored on Google computers as opposed to on your Galaxy Note 5) can be very beneficial, it does mean that any time you listen to your music collection it is streamed over the network.

If you are connected to Wi-Fi, this data streaming is free; however, if you are not connected to Wi-Fi, the data is streamed over the cellular network and counts against your data package. If you don't have a large or unlimited data package, you could incur large overage fees, so please be careful. Be extra careful about this when traveling abroad because international data-roaming charges are very expensive.

Another disadvantage of streaming from the cloud is that when you have no cellular or Wi-Fi coverage, or you have very slow or spotty coverage, you are unable to access and listen to your music collection, or the songs stutter because of the poor connection.

## Add Your Existing Music to Google Music

You can upload up to 50,000 songs from Apple iTunes, Microsoft Windows Media Player, or music stored in folders on your computer to your Google Music cloud account by using the Google Music Manager app on your desktop computer. If you haven't already installed Google Music Manager, open your web browser, go to https://play.google.com/music/listen, and download and install the app.

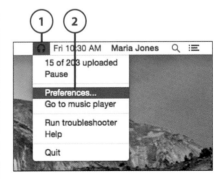

1. Click (right-click for Windows) the Google Music Manager icon. On the Mac, this icon appears in the menu bar at the top of the screen. On Windows, the icon appears in the taskbar at the bottom of the screen.

2. Choose Preferences on the Mac; choose Options on Windows.

**3.** Click Add Folder to add a folder of music to upload.

**4.** Click Remove Folder to remove the folder you have selected in the list box from your Google Play account.

**5.** Click Upload after you have made your selections.

**6.** Select the Automatically Upload Songs Added to My Selected Folders check box to allow Google Music Manager to automatically upload new songs added to the folders you have specified.

## Automatic Upload

If you choose to have your music uploaded automatically in step 6, Google Music Manager continually monitors the folders you specified to see if music has been added. If Google Music Manager finds new music, it automatically uploads it. After you install Google Music Manager, the app runs continuously, enabling it to detect music you add to iTunes, Windows Media Player, or your Music folders.

## Can I Download Music to My Computer?

You can download your entire music collection from Google Music to your computer, or just download music you have purchased on your Galaxy Note 5. While in Google Music Manager Preferences, click Download.

Click to download your free and purchased songs.

Click to download your entire library.

# Use the Music Application

Now that you have synced some music to Google Music, and maybe bought some music online, it's time to take a look at how to use the Play Music app on your Galaxy Note 5.

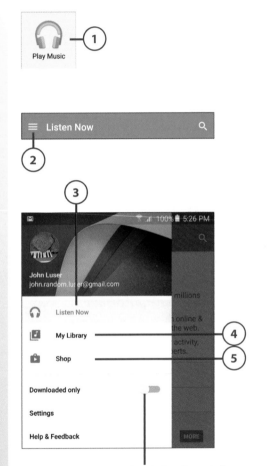

## Open the Music App and Navigate in It

1. Tap the Play Music icon on the Apps screen or in the Google folder.

2. Tap the button in the upper-left corner to display the menu panel. This panel enables you to switch among your different sources of music. You can also open the menu panel by swiping right from the left edge of the screen.

3. Tap Listen Now on the menu panel to display the Listen Now screen, which contains music you have added recently. Listen Now also recommends music to you based on the music you have and your recent listening habits.

4. Tap My Library to display your music library. Your library contains both the music on your Galaxy Note 5 and the music in your Google account.

5. Tap Shop to switch to the Play Store app and go to the Music section of Google Play, where you can browse and buy music as explained earlier in this chapter.

**Set the Downloaded Only switch to On when you want to see only the songs on your Galaxy Note 5.**

## Listen to Music in Your Library

1. Tap the button in the upper-left corner to display the menu panel.

2. Tap My Library to display your music library.

3. Tap to search for music using search terms.

4. Tap Instant Mixes to display the Instant Mixes screen, which contains both instant mixes you create yourself and ones that Google Play recommends to you. An *instant mix* is a selection of songs based on— and supposedly related to—a particular starting song. For example, you can create an instant mix based on "Walk on the Water" or "Bad Blood."

5. Tap Genres to display the list of genres. You can then tap the genre by which you want to browse your library.

6. Tap Artists to display the list of artists so you can browse by artists.

7. Tap Albums to display the list of albums so you can browse by albums.

8. Tap Songs to display the list of songs. You can then easily locate a song by name in the alphabetical list.

9. Tap the Menu button on an item to display a pop-up menu of commands you can perform for that item. In this example, you can start an instant mix for this artist, shop the artist's music at the Play Store, or shuffle the artist's songs.

10. Tap the Play button or Pause button to control playback on the current song or most recent song played.

11. Tap an artist to display information about the artist, plus the albums and songs your library contains by that artist.

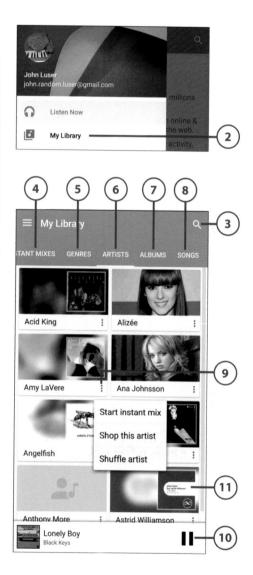

12. Swipe up to display further albums by the artist.

13. Tap the album you want to open. The album's songs appear.

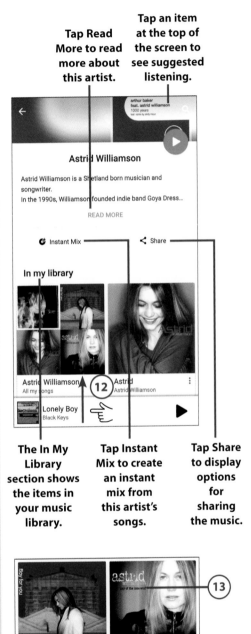

Tap Read More to read more about this artist.

Tap an item at the top of the screen to see suggested listening.

The In My Library section shows the items in your music library.

Tap Instant Mix to create an instant mix from this artist's songs.

Tap Share to display options for sharing the music.

14. Tap the song you want to start playing.

15. Tap Pause to pause playback. Tap the resulting Play button to start the music playing again.

16. Tap the album picture or any part of the Now Playing button except the Pause button or the Play button to display the Now Playing screen. This screen gives you full control of your music, as you see in the next section.

**The moving columns indicate the song that is playing.**

## Switching Between Your Songs Online and Your Songs on the Galaxy Note 5

The Play Music app enables you to play both the songs you have stored on your Galaxy Note 5 and the songs you have uploaded to Google Music. By default, Play Music presents both the songs on your Galaxy Note 5 and songs on Google Music as being available: When you go to play a song that is stored on Google Music, the Play Music app streams it automatically for you.

When you don't want to stream songs across the Internet—for example, when you are using a cellular connection—you can set Play Music to show you only the songs on your Galaxy Note 5. To do so, tap the button in the upper-left corner to display the menu panel, and then set the Downloaded Only switch to the On position (so it appears orange instead of gray).

# Control Playback

While playing music, you can control both how the music plays and the selection of music that plays.

1. Tap the Queue icon to display the queue, which shows the songs that are lined up to play. You can then tap a song to start it playing.

2. Tap the album art to return from the Now Playing screen to the previous screen. You can also tap anywhere on the button at the top apart from the Queue button and the Menu button.

3. Tap the Like (thumbs-up) icon to indicate you like the song. The Like icon turns solid to indicate you have applied the rating. Tap again to remove the rating. The Google Music app also adds the song to the "Thumbs Up" playlist.

4. Tap the Dislike (thumbs-down) icon to indicate you do not like the song. The Dislike icon turns solid to indicate you have applied the rating, and Play Music starts playing the next song.

5. Tap Previous once to go back to the start of the current song. Tap again to skip back to the previous song in the album, playlist, or shuffle.

6. Tap Next to skip ahead to the next song in the album, playlist, or shuffle.

7. Tap Pause to pause the song. The button turns into the Play button when a song is paused. Tap Play to resume playing a paused song.

8. Tap and drag the playhead to change the position in the song.

9. Tap Shuffle to enable or disable song shuffling. When Shuffle is enabled, songs in the current playlist, album, or song list play in a random order.

10. Tap Repeat to control repeating. Tap once to repeat all songs, tap again to repeat the current song only, and tap a third time to disable repeating.

11. Tap the Menu button to display the menu of actions you can take with the song.

12. Tap Start Instant Mix to create an instant mix based on the song.

13. Tap Add to Playlist to add the song to a playlist. In the Add to Playlist dialog that opens, you can either tap New Playlist to start creating a new playlist or tap the name of an existing playlist to use that playlist.

14. Tap Go to Artist to display the artist the song is by.

15. Tap Go to Album to display the album that contains the song.

16. Tap Clear Queue to clear the playback queue.

17. Tap Save Queue to save the playback queue. In the Add to Playlist dialog that opens, you can either tap New Playlist to create a new playlist containing the songs in the queue or tap the name of an existing playlist to add the songs to that playlist.

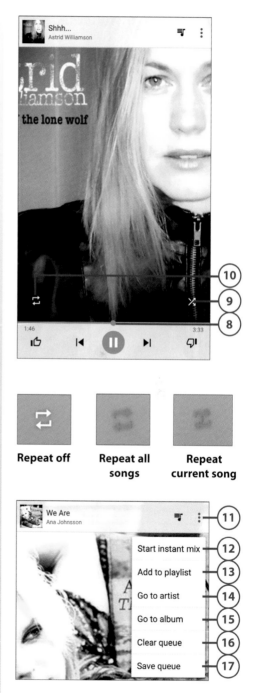

## What Is an Instant Mix?

If you are playing a song and choose to create an instant mix as mentioned in step 12, the Google Music app creates a new playlist and adds songs to it that are supposedly similar to the one you are currently playing. The name of the playlist is the name of the current song plus the word "Mix." For example, if you are playing the song "Piquant" and choose to create an instant mix, the playlist is called "Piquant Mix."

# Work and Listen to Music

You don't have to keep the Play Music app displayed while you are playing music. Instead, you can switch back to the Home screen and run any other app but still control the music easily.

**The headphones icon indicates that Play Music is open.**

1. Pull down the Notification bar.

2. Tap Pause to pause the song.

3. Tap Previous once to go back to the start of the song. Tap Previous again to go to the beginning of the previous song.

4. Tap Next to skip ahead to the next song in the list, album, or playlist.

5. Tap the song title or the album art to open the Play Music app for more control.

## What If I Get a Call?

If someone calls you while you are listening to music, your Galaxy Note 5 pauses the music and displays the regular incoming call screen. After you hang up, the music resumes playing.

# Work with Playlists

Playlists can be a great way of listening to music, enabling you to group related songs or simply those you want to hear in a particular sequence. On your Galaxy Note 5, you can create new playlists, add songs to existing playlists, rename playlists, and change the order of the songs they contain.

## Create a New Playlist on Your Galaxy Note 5

1.  Using the techniques described earlier in this chapter, navigate to a song you want to add to the new playlist.

2.  Tap the song's Menu button to display the menu of actions you can take with the song.

3.  Tap Add to Playlist. The Add to Playlist dialog opens.

4.  Tap New Playlist. The New Playlist dialog opens.

5.  Type the name for the new playlist.

6.  Optionally, type a description for the playlist to make it easier to identify.

7.  Set the Public switch to On if you want to make the playlist publicly accessible on Google Play.

8.  Tap the Create Playlist button. You can now add songs to the playlist as explained in the next section.

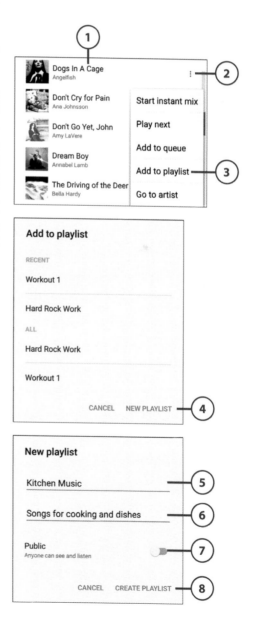

# Add a Song to an Existing Playlist

1. Using the techniques described earlier in this chapter, navigate to a song you want to add to the new playlist. You can also use the song on the Now Playing screen, as in this example.

2. Tap the song's Menu button to open the menu of actions you can take with the song.

3. Tap Add to Playlist. The Add to Playlist dialog opens.

4. Tap the playlist you want to add the song to.

①

| | | |
|---|---|---|
| Gotta Get Away<br>Black Keys | | ⋮ ② |
| Gourmandises<br>Alizée | Start instant mix | |
| A Great Divide<br>Amy LaVere | Play next | |
| Hands of the Hunter<br>Annabel Lamb | Add to queue | |
| | Add to playlist | ③ |

④

**Add to playlist**

RECENT

Kitchen Music

Workout 1

Hard Rock Work

ALL

Hard Rock Work

Kitchen Music

Workout 1

CANCEL    NEW PLAYLIST

# Delete a Playlist

When you no longer need a playlist, you can delete it in moments. Deleting the playlist doesn't delete its songs—only the list is deleted.

1. In the My Library view, swipe right on the categories if you cannot see the Playlists button.

①

2.  Tap the Playlists button to display the Playlists screen.

3.  Tap the Menu button for the playlist you want to delete.

4.  Tap Delete. A confirmation dialog opens.

5.  Tap the OK button.

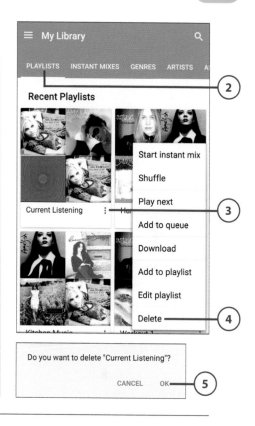

## Renaming a Playlist

To rename a playlist, go to the Playlists screen, tap the Menu button for the playlist, and then tap Edit Playlist on the menu. In the Edit Playlist dialog that opens, change the name and description as needed; you can also set the Public switch to On or Off, depending on whether you want to make the playlist public. Tap the Save button when you finish.

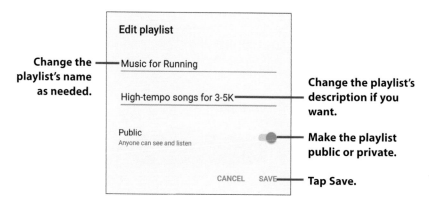

Change the playlist's name as needed.

Change the playlist's description if you want.

Make the playlist public or private.

Tap Save.

## Rearrange the Songs in a Playlist

You can keep a playlist fresh by adding songs to it, as explained earlier in this chapter, but you can also delete songs from the playlist and rearrange the songs it contains.

1. On the Playlists screen, tap the playlist to display its songs.

2. Tap and hold the song you want to move, drag it up or down until it is in the right place, and then release it. You can tap anywhere except for the Menu button on the right side of the song. If you prefer not to tap and hold, you can tap the handle on the left side of the song—the two horizontal lines, like an equal sign—and drag immediately.

3. To remove a song, swipe it to the left or to the right. You can also tap its Menu button and then tap Remove from Playlist.

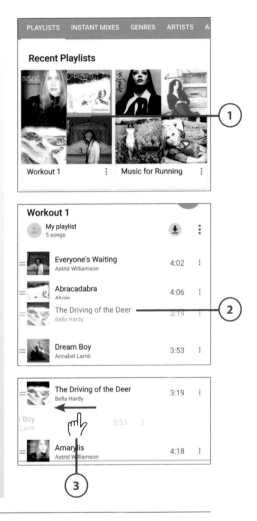

## Removed a Song by Mistake?

If you swipe a song off a playlist by mistake, you can put it back instantly. After you swipe, Play Music displays the message "Song removed" and an Undo button for a couple of seconds. Simply tap that Undo button to put the song back on the playlist.

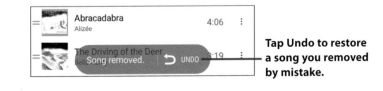

Tap Undo to restore a song you removed by mistake.

# Listen to Music with No Wireless Coverage

If you use Google Music and store your music online, your Galaxy Note 5 streams the music over the cellular or Wi-Fi network when you play the music. If you know you are going to be without a signal but still want to listen to your music, you need to store it on your Galaxy Note 5.

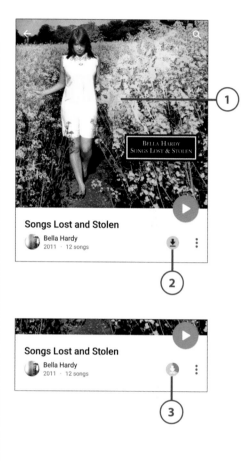

1. Using the techniques discussed earlier in this chapter, go to the music you want to store on your Galaxy Note 5.

2. Tap the gray download icon, which indicates that the music is not stored on your Galaxy Note 5.

3. The Play Music app downloads and stores the music. As it does so, the download icon displays a progress indicator, gradually turning the gray circle orange. When the music is available, a check-mark symbol appears on an orange circle.

## >>>Go Further

### SYNCHRONIZE MUSIC AND OTHER MEDIA USING A USB CABLE

If you don't use Google Music, or Google Music is not available in your country, you can synchronize music and other media using a USB cable or Wi-Fi. You can use Smart Switch, the program that Samsung provides for managing its newer phones and tablets, or another app such as doubleTwist (www.doubletwist.com). Alternatively, you can connect your Galaxy Note 5 via USB and access its file system using File Explorer or Windows Explorer on Windows (depending on which version of Windows you have) or Android File Transfer (www.android.com/filetransfer/) on the Mac.

# Use the Equalizer and Effects

You can use the Equalizer to change the sound of the music you play in the Play Music app. You can also use the Galaxy Note 5's sound quality and effects settings to change the sound output.

## The Equalizer and Sound Effects Are Systemwide Settings

You can access the Equalizer and the sound quality and effects settings from within the Play Music app, but both are systemwide settings. So when you set an equalization (say, Jazz) for Play Music, that equalization applies to other music apps as well. For example, if you open the Music app, which Samsung includes with most Galaxy Note 5 models, Music will be using the Jazz equalization as well.

The same goes for the sound effects, which work only when you have connected headphones or a compatible Bluetooth headset to your Galaxy Note 5. When you turn on a sound effect, such as SoundAlive+ or Tube Amp Pro, it affects all the audio that comes out through the audio jack or through your Bluetooth headset.

1. Connect your headphones or headset if you want to use sound effects. You might also want to start some music playing so that you can hear the results of the changes you make.

2. In the Play Music app, tap the button in the upper-left corner to open the menu panel.

3. Tap Settings to display the Music Settings screen.

4. Tap Equalizer to display the SoundAlive screen. At first, this screen shows two dials, the Bass/Treble dial at the top and the Instrument/Vocal dial at the bottom.

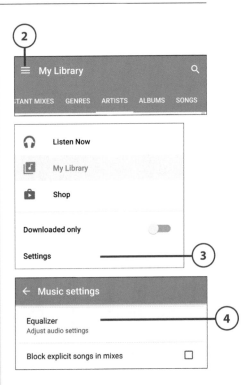

5.  If you want to apply a preset equalization, tap the Equalizer button. On the Equalizer screen that appears, tap the option button for the equalization (say, Rock), and then tap either the arrow button in the upper-left corner or the Back button below the screen to return to the SoundAlive screen.

6.  If you want to adjust the balance between bass and treble, tap the Bass/Treble dial and move the blue dot clockwise or counter-clockwise. As soon as you move the dial from the 12-o'clock position, the Equalizer button shows Custom, because you've applied a custom equalization.

7.  If you want to adjust the balance between instruments and vocals, tap the Instrument/Vocal dial and move the blue dot clockwise or counterclockwise, as needed. This feature works best for vocals that are in the normal singing range.

8.  If you want to use the full range of equalization controls, tap the Details button. The equalization sliders appear in place of the two dials, and four effect buttons—3D, Bass, Clarity, and Concert Hall—appear near the bottom of the screen.

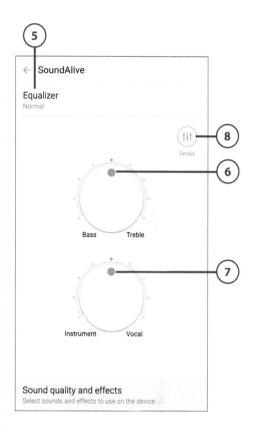

9. Tap and drag the equalization sliders up and down as needed to adjust the sound. The lowest frequencies are on the left and the highest frequencies on the right. Drag a slider up to get more of the frequency it controls, or drag it down to get less of that frequency. Any change you make to the equalization makes the Equalizer button show Custom.

10. If you want to apply one of the four sound effects, tap the 3D button, the Bass button, the Clarity button, or the Concert Hall button (which appears as Concert…).

11. Tap the Sound Quality and Effects button to display the Sound Quality and Effects screen.

12. Tap the Adapt Sound button if you want to create a custom audio profile. See the nearby note for more information.

13. Set the UHQ Upscaler switch to On if you want the Galaxy Note 5 to attempt to improve the quality of sound on music and videos you play. This feature attempts to calculate what data has been removed from the music file or video file by the compression technology and to restore that data. You might find that turning on UHQ Upscaler gives the sound more warmth or more punch.

14. Set the SoundAlive+ switch to On if you want the Galaxy Note 5 to use a surround-sound effect.

15. Set the Tube Amp Pro switch to On if you want the Galaxy Note 5 to simulate the slightly fuzzy sound of a tube amplifier.

16. Tap the arrow button or the Back button below the screen three times to return to the Play Music app.

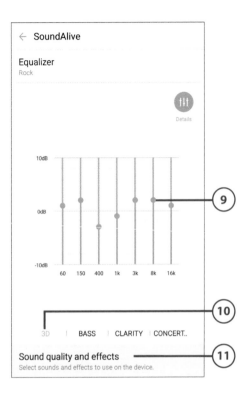

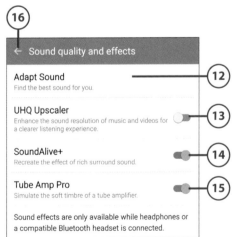

## What Does Adapt Sound Do?

The Adapt Sound enables you to create a customized audio profile tailored to the strengths and weaknesses of your hearing. Wearing headphones, you listen to a series of beeps at different frequencies and indicate which you can hear. Your Galaxy Note 5 builds an audio profile that you can then apply to change the device's audio output to compensate for areas in which you have suffered hearing loss.

# Playing and Sharing Videos

The Gallery app enables you to view pictures and video; you can also share pictures and video with people on Facebook, or via MMS, Bluetooth, YouTube, and email. This section explains how you can view and share videos. Later in this chapter, you learn how to take pictures and share them.

## Understanding the Two Ways to Access Videos

Your Galaxy Note 5 enables you to access videos in two main ways: through the Gallery app and through the Videos app. This section shows you how to use the Gallery app, which enables you to review your photos and videos at the same time and choose which to use or view. From the Gallery app, you can open the video for viewing in either the Photos app, as explained here, or in the Videos app.

1. Tap the Gallery icon on the Home screen or the Apps screen to launch the Gallery app.

2. Tap the navigation pop-up menu in the upper-left corner.

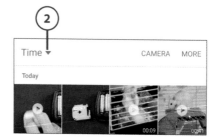

3. Tap Time to see the items listed by time; tap Albums to see the items listed by albums, such as Camera (photos taken with the Camera app) or DCIM (photos stored in the DCIM folder); tap Events to see items listed by events, such as a particular day; or tap Categories to see items listed by categories, such as Images, Videos, and Scenery. This example uses Categories, because this gives you direct access to the videos you've shot.

4. Tap an item to open it, revealing the pictures and videos it contains. This example shows the Videos category being opened.

5. Tap a video to open it for playback. Videos have a little Play icon on them, so they're easy to spot in folders that contain pictures as well.

6. Tap the Play icon to start the video playing.

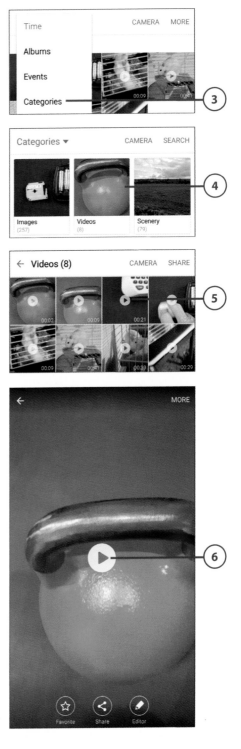

# Choosing the App to Use for Playing Videos

The first time you tap the Play icon for a video in the Gallery app, your Galaxy Note 5 displays the Complete Action Using dialog to let you choose between the available video players. Normally, these are the Photos app and the Video Player app, but you might have installed other video-capable apps on your Galaxy Note 5. If you have the choice of the Photos app or the Video Player app, tap Video Player; if you have more choices, tap your preferred app.

**Open with**

Photos          Video Player

— **Tap Video Player to use the Video Player app for playing the video.**

7. Tap the screen while the video is playing to reveal the video controls. If you do not use the controls, they disappear after a few seconds.

8. Tap Pause to pause the video. Tap the Play button (which replaces the Pause button) to resume playback.

9. Drag the playhead to scrub quickly forward and backward.

10. Tap Next to skip to the end of the video.

11. Tap Previous to return to the beginning of the video.

12. Tap the Volume icon to display a pop-up slider for adjusting the volume.

13. Tap More to display a menu with other actions, such as opening the video in an editor, deleting it, or adjusting the playback speed.

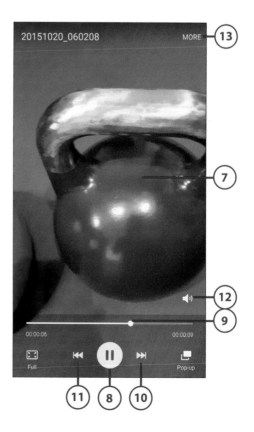

14. Tap Full to switch between viewing the video full screen and viewing it as best fits the Galaxy Note 5's screen.

## Changing the Orientation for a Video

When watching a video shot in landscape orientation, rotate your Galaxy Note 5 from portrait orientation to landscape orientation so you can enjoy the video full screen.

15. Tap Pop-Up to display the video in a pop-up window. You can then switch to another app and continue to watch the video as you work or play.

16. Tap the pop-up window to display the playback controls at the bottom and the × button in the upper-right corner.

17. Use the playback controls to control playback.

18. Tap the Full Screen button if you want to view the video full screen again.

19. Tap the × button to close the pop-up video window.

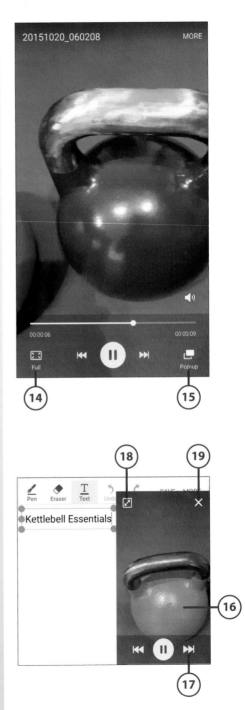

# Share Videos

From the Gallery app, you can share small videos with other people.

1. Tap and hold the video you want to share. After a moment, a green check mark appears on the video.

2. Tap Share to open the Share Via panel at the bottom of the screen.

3. Scroll left if necessary to display other methods of sharing.

4. Tap a method for sharing the video. Refer to the following sections for specific directions for sharing via YouTube or Facebook.

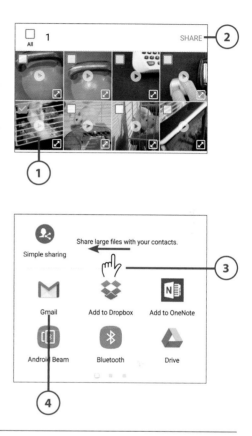

## Choose Effective Means for Sharing Videos of Different Sizes

Video files tend to be large, so it's important to choose suitable means of sharing them. For direct sharing, such as via email or messaging, it is best to share only small videos from your Galaxy Note 5, because large videos might not transfer successfully. For email, assume 10MB is the size limit; for messaging, videos should really be smaller than 1MB.

When you need to share larger video files, use an indirect means of sharing, such as Dropbox or Google Drive. In such sharing, you upload the file to the sharing site and then share a link with whomever you want to be able to download the file. Another option is to use the Simple Sharing feature at the top of the Share Via panel, which uses Samsung's servers. Or you can post the video on YouTube, as discussed next.

## Bluetooth Sharing Might Fail

Many phones do not accept incoming Bluetooth files, but devices such as computers do. Even on computers, the recipient must configure her Bluetooth configuration to accept incoming files.

# Share a Video on YouTube

YouTube gives you a quick, easy, and effective way to share your videos with the whole wired world.

If you have not previously set up your YouTube account on your Galaxy Note 5, you are prompted to do so before you can upload your video. You can read more about YouTube later in the chapter in the "Enjoying Videos with the YouTube App" section.

1. Tap the Music icon and choose any music you want to add to the video.

2. Tap the Effect icon and apply any effect your video requires. For example, you can apply the Silver Screen effect or the Sepia effect to give the video an older look.

3. Tap the left blue handle and drag it right to trim the beginning of the video as needed.

4. Tap the right blue handle and drag it left to trim the end of the video as needed.

5. Enter the title of your video.

6. Enter a description of your video.

7. Tap the Privacy pop-up menu and then tap Public, Unlisted, or Private, as needed.

8. Enter any tags for your video. Tags are keywords that help people find videos by searching.

9. Tap Upload.

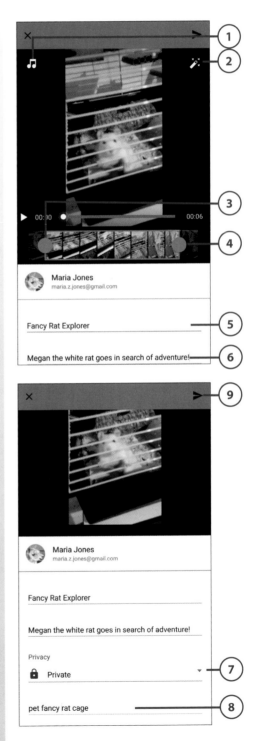

## Sharing a YouTube Video Only with Specific People

As well as the Public setting and the Private setting, the Privacy pop-up list provides an Unlisted setting. Choose Unlisted when you need to share the video with some people but not with everyone. The video then does not appear in the public view of your YouTube account, but you can send the URL for the video to anyone you want to view it.

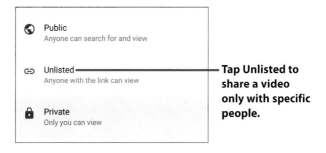

> **Tap Unlisted to share a video only with specific people.**

# >>>Go Further

## LIMITING YOUR YOUTUBE UPLOADS TO WI-FI NETWORKS

When you go to upload a video to YouTube, your Galaxy Note 5 might display the Upload dialog, prompting you to choose between uploading only when on Wi-Fi networks and uploading on any network. Normally, it is best to tap Only When on Wi-Fi and then tap OK, because uploading even relatively small video files over the cellular network can quickly become expensive.

**Upload**

Depending on your data plan, uploading videos when not connected to Wi-Fi may result in additional charges

⦿ Only when on Wi-Fi

○ On any network

*You can change this setting at anytime in the app settings*

> **Tap to restrict YouTube uploads to wireless connections.**

OK

> **Tap OK.**

If you need to change this setting later, open the YouTube app, tap the Menu button, and then tap Settings. Tap General to display the General screen, tap Uploads to display the Uploads dialog, and then tap Only When on Wi-Fi or On Any Network, as needed.

## Share Video on Facebook

After you have set up a Facebook account on your Galaxy Note 5, you can upload videos to your account.

1. Tap the To line and then tap the group with which you want to share the video, such as Friends or Public.

2. Enter a description of your video.

3. Tap the Location icon if you want to add the location to the video.

4. Tap Post to post the video.

## Delete Videos

1. In Time view or Albums view in the Gallery app, tap and hold the video you want to delete. After a moment, a green check mark appears on the video.

2. Tap the Delete icon to delete the video.

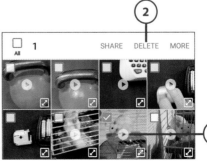

3. Tap Delete in the Delete confirmation dialog.

> 1 video will be deleted.
>
> CANCEL     DELETE —③

# Taking Photos and Videos with the Camera App

The Camera app enables you to take still photos and record videos. You can either shoot photos and videos with the default settings or choose among the many options the Galaxy Note 5 offers.

## Take Photos

1. Tap the Camera icon on the Home screen or the Apps screen to launch the Camera app. The Camera app opens and displays the input from the rear camera (the main camera) at first.

2. Tap the Switch Cameras icon to switch from the rear camera to the front camera so you can take photos of yourself. The front camera is lower resolution than the rear camera, but it works well for capturing candid self-portraits. When you switch to the front camera, the Camera app changes to the Selfie mode automatically on the assumption that you want to take a photo of yourself.

3. Tap the HDR readout to turn the HDR feature on or off. HDR stands for High Dynamic Range and tries to improve the color balance and lighting by taking multiple shots and combining them into a single shot.

4. Tap the Mode icon to switch the camera mode. You can read about camera modes later in this chapter.

5. Tap the Shutter icon to take a photo.

6. Tap the Video icon to start taking a video.

7. Tap the thumbnail to display the last photo or video you took.

## Taking a Burst of Photos

Instead of taking a single shot, the Camera app can take a burst of photos. This feature is great when you do not have time to compose your photo perfectly or your subject is moving. To take a burst of photos, tap and hold the shutter release.

# Zoom In and Out

Your Galaxy Note 5's Camera app includes a powerful digital zoom that enables you to close in on the objects you want to photograph.

1. Open the Camera app and point the lens so that your subject occupies the center of the screen.

2. Place two fingers (or a finger and a thumb) on the screen. A zoom indicator appears in the middle of the screen, with a readout showing the zoom factor. A factor of ×1.0 represents no zoom.

**The readout shows the zoom factor.**

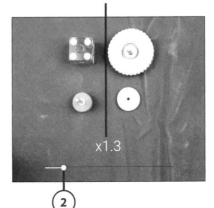

3. Move your fingers apart to zoom in. The readout shows the zoom factor you've reached.

4. Tap the Shutter icon to take the photo.

## Zooming Out

When you need to zoom back out, place two fingers (or a finger and a thumb) on the screen and pinch them together.

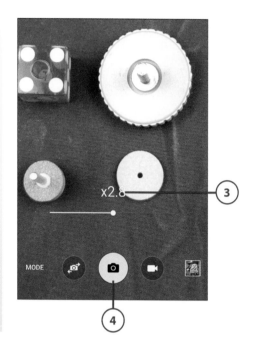

## It's Not All Good

### Digital Zoom Can Make Photos Grainy

In digital cameras, there are two main types of zoom: optical zoom and digital zoom. Optical zoom implements the zoom by moving the lens (or sometimes changing the lens used), which retains full quality even if you zoom in as far as the camera can. By contrast, digital zoom works by enlarging the pixels (the dots that make up the picture) of the part of the picture that you want to zoom in on.

Larger pixels can make the photos grainy, especially if you zoom in to extremes. So if you have the choice between moving your Galaxy Note 5 closer to your subject and using digital zoom, it's best to move closer because your photos will be higher quality. However, when moving closer isn't an option, digital zoom is still pretty good as long as you don't push it too far.

# >>>Go Further
## CHOOSE WHERE TO FOCUS

When you take a photo, the Camera app focuses on the center of the screen by default, because that's where the subject is most likely to be. Much of the time this works well, but at other times you might need to focus manually.

To focus manually, tap the point on the screen where you want the focus to be. The Camera app displays a white circle where you tap, and then it plays a chirping noise and displays a green rectangle momentarily to indicate it has refocused.

If the focus is correct, tap the Shutter button to take the photo. If the focus still isn't right, tap again to refocus.

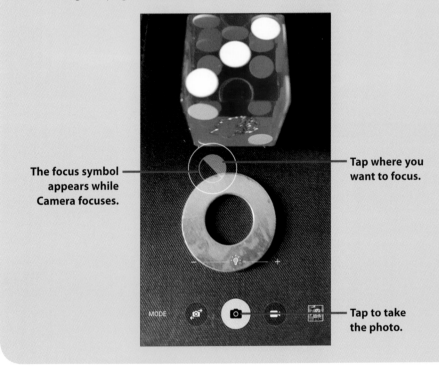

**The focus symbol appears while Camera focuses.**

**Tap where you want to focus.**

**Tap to take the photo.**

You can also lock the focus and exposure for a couple of seconds by tapping and holding the point on which you want to lock them. A dashed blue circle appears around where you tap and hold, and the Focus/Exposure readout appears. Tap the Shutter icon to take the photo as usual.

**Tap and hold to lock the focus and exposure.**

# Apply Effects to Photos

To make your photos more glamorous, more artistic, or simply more fun, you can apply effects to them. The Camera app includes effects such as Cartoon, Faded Color, Fisheye, Grayscale, Moody, Oil Pastel, Rugged, Sepia, Tint, Turquoise, Vignette, and Vintage.

1. Tap the Effect icon to display the Effect screen.

2. Tap the effect you want to apply. The effect appears full screen.

**Tap No Effect to remove the existing effect.**

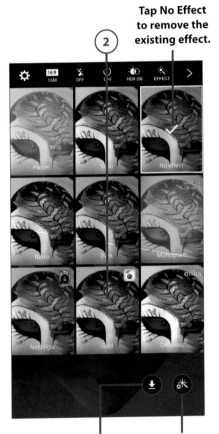

Tap to download other effects.

Tap to rearrange the effects on the screen.

3. If controls appear at the top of the screen, you can drag them to adjust the effect. You might need to tap a Settings button (the icon shows two horizontal sliders) in this area to display the controls.

4. Tap the Shutter icon to take the photo.

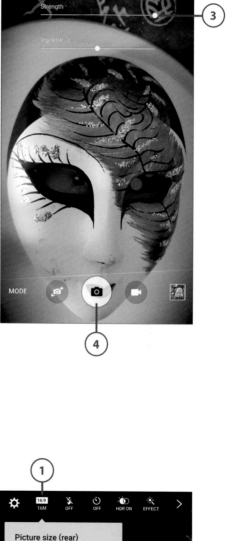

# Change Key Camera Settings

You can get good photos by using your Galaxy Note 5 as a point-and-shoot camera, as described in the "Take Photos" section. However, you can get better photos by changing settings to harness the full power of the Camera app.

1. Tap the Picture Size (Rear) icon to display the Picture Size (Rear) pop-up panel.

2. Tap the resolution you want to use.

## Choose Picture Size for the Front Camera

To choose picture size for the front camera, tap the Switch Cameras button to make the front camera active, and then tap the Picture Size (Front) icon, which takes the place of the Picture Size (Rear) icon. In the Picture Size (Front) pop-up panel, tap the resolution you want.

3. Tap the Flash icon to cycle the flash setting among Off, On, and Auto Flash.

## Making the Most of the Flash

Choose the Off setting for the flash when you need to take photos where the flash would be disruptive. Choose the On setting when you need to light the foreground of a shot, even though the rest of the scene is amply lit—for example, to light your subject's face in front of a bright background. Choose the Auto setting for general use.

**Tap to hide the Settings bar.**

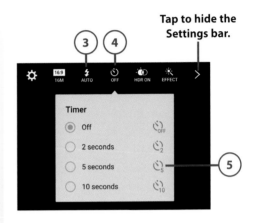

4. Tap the Timer icon to display the Timer pop-up panel.

5. Set the timer by tapping the 2 Seconds radio button, the 5 Seconds radio button, or the 10 Seconds radio button. Tap the Off radio button to turn the timer off.

## Choose Settings on the Camera Settings Screen

Beyond the key settings that appear in the Settings bar, the Camera app has other settings that you can configure on the Camera Settings screen.

1. Tap the Settings icon (the gear icon) in the upper-left corner of the Camera screen. The Camera Settings screen appears.

2. Tap Video Size (Rear) to display the Video Size (Rear) screen.

**3.** Tap the radio button for the video size you want: UHD, 3840×2160; QHD, 2560×1440; FHD (60fps), 1920×1080, for shooting 60 frames per second; FHD, 1920×1080, for shooting at the regular 30 frames per second; HD, 1280×720; or VGA, 640×480. Unless you need to shoot at super-high resolution or at 60 frames per second, FHD is a good choice, because it offers high quality and a widely used resolution. When you choose a setting, the Camera Settings screen appears again.

## Pitfalls of Shooting at High Resolution or Frame Rates

If you use the UHD (3840×2160) resolution, make sure you have plenty of free space, because this format takes up four times as much space as 1920×1080—around 1GB for three minutes of shooting.

If you use UHD, QHD, or FHD (60fps), be aware that you are not able to use video effects, video stabilization, or the Tracking AF feature. You also are not able to use HDR or to take photos while shooting video.

**4.** Set the Tracking AF switch to On when you want to use the Tracking Auto-Focus feature. This feature enables you to lock the focus onto an object in the view. The Camera app keeps the focus on this object even when you move the Galaxy Note 5 so that the object moves to a different part of the view.

**5.** Set the Video Stabilization switch to On to enable video stabilization.

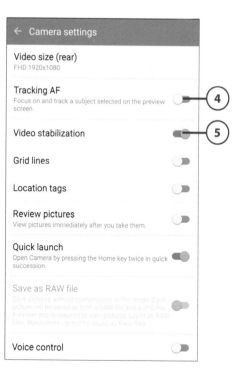

6. Set the Grid Lines switch to On if you want the Camera app to display grid lines on screen. You can use these lines to help you compose your shots and clips.

7. Set the Location Tags switch to On if you want the Camera app to record the location in photos and videos you shoot.

8. Set the Review Pictures switch to On if you want the Camera app to display each photo immediately after you take it. This setting can be useful for studio work, but it's a bane when shooting live subjects.

9. Set the Quick Launch switch to On if you want to be able to open the Camera app by double-pressing (double-clicking, if you like) the Home button. This shortcut can be handy.

10. Set the Save as RAW File switch to On if you want to be able to shoot uncompressed photos in the RAW format when using Pro mode. (You learn about modes later in this chapter.) RAW photos are great for serious work, but you need to get a viewer app if you want to be able to view them on the Galaxy Note 5.

11. Set the Voice Control switch to On if you want to be able to take a photo by giving commands such as "Smile!", "Cheese!", "Capture!", or "Shoot!" (no, really), or start shooting video by ordering "Record video!"

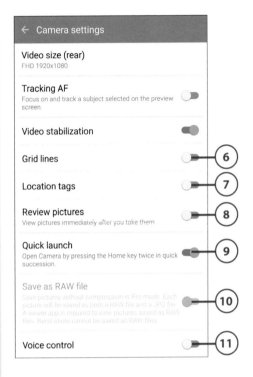

**12.** Tap the Volume Keys Function button to open the pop-up menu, and then tap the feature you want the physical volume buttons to perform: Take Pictures, Record Video, or Zoom.

**13.** If you mess up the settings, you can tap the Reset Settings button to reset them to their defaults.

**14.** Tap the arrow button or the Back button below the screen to return to the Camera app.

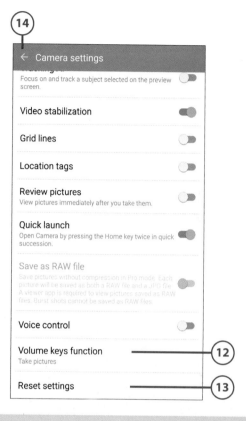

# >>>*Go Further*

## USING THE SHOOTING MODE SETTINGS

Your Galaxy Note 5's Camera app gives you a wide choice of shooting modes. By choosing the right mode for the type of photos you are taking, you improve your chances of getting high-quality pictures that look the way you want them to.

**Tap Mode to display the Modes screen.**

To choose the shooting mode, tap Mode on the main Camera screen. You can then tap the mode you want to apply.

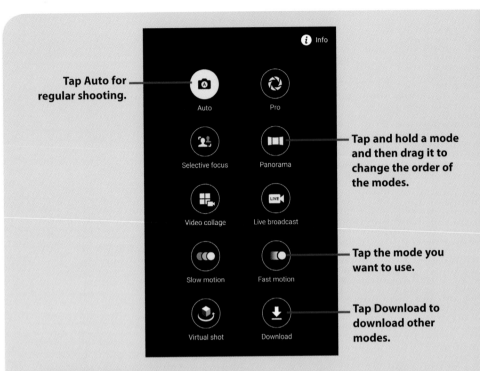

Tap Auto for regular shooting.

Info

Auto

Pro

Selective focus

Panorama — Tap and hold a mode and then drag it to change the order of the modes.

Video collage

Live broadcast

Slow motion

Fast motion — Tap the mode you want to use.

Virtual shot

Download — Tap Download to download other modes.

After you've found out which modes you find most useful, you might want to rearrange the modes. You can do this by tapping and holding the mode you want to move, and then dragging it to change its position.

Some of the shooting modes are straightforward. For example, tap Auto to have the Camera app handle as many decisions as possible, leaving you free to shoot; or tap Panorama when you need to stitch together a sequence of photos into a panorama photo.

Pro mode enables you to adjust a wide range of settings including the exposure value, the shutter speed, the focal length, and the white balance. If you've been looking at the Camera app and wondering where all the serious settings have gone, turn on Pro mode, and you'll find them.

Selective Focus mode helps you to make your subject stand out from the background. The subject must be positioned close to the lens (Samsung recommends within 18 inches) and at least three times as far from the background (say, 5 feet for that 18 inches). As you take the photo, you move the Galaxy Note 5 up to help the Camera app establish the relative distance of the objects.

Video Collage mode helps you to make short collages of videos without any serious editing. This mode is designed for creating videos suitable for sharing via social media.

Live Broadcast mode is for broadcasting live on YouTube. Your Galaxy Note 5 creates a link that you can share with your friends so that they can watch your broadcast in real time.

Slow Motion mode enables you to shoot video clips at a high frame rate so that they play back in slow motion. Similarly, Fast Motion mode enables you to shoot video clips for viewing in fast motion—for example, to create a dramatic or humorous effect.

Virtual Tour enables you to make a walkthrough of a location. This mode works surprisingly well but benefits from a device to steady the Galaxy Note 5, such as a monopod or a Steadicam rig.

## View the Photos You Take

After taking photos, you can quickly view the ones you have taken, mark them as favorites, share them with other people, or simply delete them.

1. In the Camera app, tap the thumbnail to view the last photo you took.

### Zooming In and Out on Your Photos

When viewing a photo, you can zoom in by placing two fingers on the screen and pinching outward or by double-tapping on the area you want to expand. Pinch inward or double-tap again to zoom back out.

2. Tap the photo to display the onscreen controls. They disappear after a few seconds of not being used.

3. Tap the Favorite icon to make the photo a favorite.

4. Tap the Share icon to display the Share Via panel, in which you can tap the means of sharing you want to use.

5. Tap the Edit icon to edit the photo. You can rotate it, crop it, apply a color filter, apply an effect, or take other actions.

6. Tap the Delete icon if you want to delete the photo. Tap Delete in the Delete confirmation dialog that opens.

7. Swipe left to display the previous photo. After that, you can swipe either left or right.

8. Tap the More button to access other commands, such as the Set as Contact Picture command and the Set as Wallpaper command.

9. Tap the Album button to display the album that contains the photo.

10. Tap the arrow button or the Back button below the screen to return to the Camera screen.

# Record Videos with the Camera App

Camera

Recording videos with the Camera app is even easier than taking still photos because there are fewer options to choose.

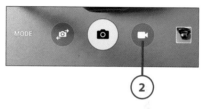

1. Tap Camera on the Home screen or the Apps screen to launch the Camera app.

2. Tap Video to switch to the video camera and start recording video.

3. If necessary, place two fingers (or a finger and a thumb) on the screen and pinch apart to zoom in. Pinch together to zoom back out.

4. Tap the Capture icon to take a still photo.

5. Tap the Pause icon to pause recording.

6. Tap the Stop icon to stop recording.

## Using Automatic and Manual Focusing

While the Camera app is recording video, it automatically adjusts the focus for the object in the center of the screen. If you need to focus on another part of the screen, tap it.

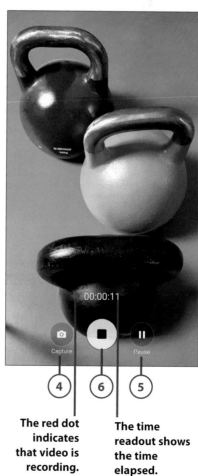

**The red dot indicates that video is recording.**

**The time readout shows the time elapsed.**

# Enjoying Videos with the YouTube App

Your Galaxy Note 5 comes with a YouTube app that enables you to find and watch videos, rate them, add them to your favorites, and share links with other people. The app even enables you to upload your own videos to YouTube.

## Meet the YouTube Main Screen

1. Tap the YouTube icon on the Apps screen to launch the YouTube app.

2. Tap the Search icon to search YouTube using keywords.

3. Tap Home to display the Home screen, which contains recommendations for you.

4. Tap Subscriptions to display the Subscriptions screen, which shows updates from the channels you have added.

5. Tap Account to display the Account screen, which includes your history (for returning to videos you watched earlier), the videos you have uploaded, notifications, and your Watch Later list, which contains any videos you have marked for watching later.

6. Tap Upload to display the Recent screen, which shows the videos you have shot and worked on recently. From here, you can navigate to other folders, such as your Videos folder. Once you locate the video you want to upload, you can start to upload it.

7. Tap an item to display its screen. You can then tap a video to display more information about it and play it. You can also tap Subscribe to subscribe to a channel.

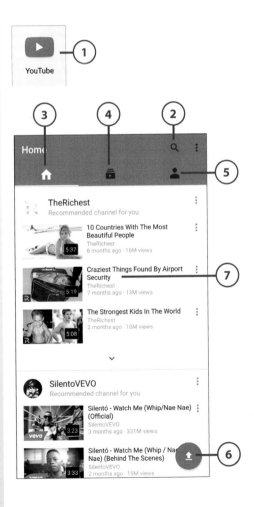

# Play a Video

While playing a YouTube video, you can rate the video, read comments about it, or share it with other people.

1. Tap the video to display the onscreen controls for a few seconds.

2. Tap Play to start the video or tap Pause to pause it.

3. Tap Full Screen to switch the video to full screen in Landscape mode.

4. Drag the playhead to scrub forward or backward through the video.

5. Tap + to display the Add Video To dialog, where you can add the video to your Watch Later list, your Favorites list, or a playlist.

6. Tap the Share icon to share the video's link (its URL) via apps such as Gmail, Facebook, or Twitter.

7. Tap the Info button to display the More Info panel, which shows related videos. Tap the × icon in the upper-right corner of the More Info panel to close it.

8. Tap the down-arrow icon to see information about the video, including who uploaded it, the video title, a description, and how many times it has been viewed.

9. Tap the channel icon to see the YouTube channel of the person who uploaded the video.

10. Tap the Like (thumbs-up) icon to like the video.

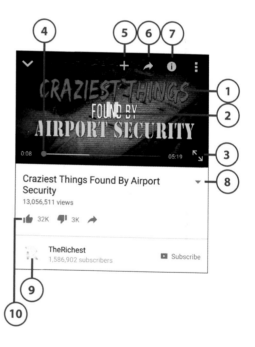

11. Tap the Dislike (thumbs-down) icon to dislike the video.

12. Tap Subscribe to subscribe to this channel.

13. Tap the Menu button to display the Captions icon, Quality icon, and Report icon.

14. Tap the Report icon to report the video as inappropriate—for example, for hateful or abusive content, or because it infringes upon your rights.

**Tap to choose the video quality.**

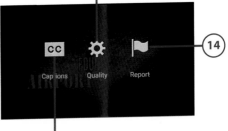

**Tap to watch with closed captioning.**

# Change YouTube Settings

To get more out of YouTube, you might want to change your settings. Your options include choosing whether to watch high-quality videos on cellular connections, clearing your YouTube search history, and enabling the preloading of items on your subscriptions list or your Watch Later list.

1. From within the YouTube app, tap the Menu button.

2. Tap Settings to display the Settings screen.

**3.** Tap General to display the General screen.

**4.** Set the Limit Mobile Data Usage switch to On to prevent the YouTube app from streaming high-definition (HD) video across cellular connections. This is normally a good idea. When your Galaxy Note 5 is connected to a Wi-Fi network, the YouTube app streams HD video.

**5.** Tap Uploads to choose when your Galaxy Note 5 uploads videos to YouTube. Your choices are Only When on Wi-Fi or On Any Network.

**6.** Tap Content Location to choose a specific country or region that you want to prioritize—for example, the country you live in.

**7.** Set the Restricted Mode switch to On if you want YouTube to hide videos that might contain inappropriate content.

**8.** Set the Enable Stats for Nerds switch to On if you want to see detailed statistics about YouTube viewing.

**9.** Tap the arrow button or the Back button below the screen to return to the main Settings screen.

**10.** Tap Connected TVs to display the Connected TVs screen.

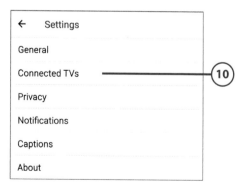

11. Tap Add a TV to pair your Galaxy Note 5 with a TV so you can broadcast to the TV.

12. Tap Edit TVs to edit your list of paired TVs. You can rename a TV for clarity or remove a TV you no longer want to use.

13. Tap Connected TVs or the Back button to return to the main Settings screen.

14. Tap Privacy to display the Privacy screen.

15. Tap Clear Watch History to clear the list of videos you have watched. Tap OK in the confirmation dialog that opens.

16. Tap Clear Search History to clear your YouTube search history. Tap OK in the confirmation dialog that opens.

17. Set the Pause Watch History switch to On if you want to temporarily stop YouTube logging the videos you watch.

18. Set the Pause Search History switch to On if you want to temporarily stop YouTube from storing the details of your searches.

19. Tap the arrow button or the Back button below the screen to return to the main Settings screen.

20. Tap Notifications to display the Notifications screen.

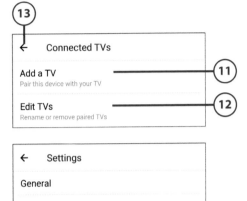

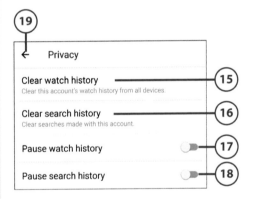

21. Set the Receive Notifications switch to On or Off to control whether you receive YouTube notifications on your Galaxy Note 5.

22. Set the Subscription Activity switch to On or Off to control whether YouTube notifies you of new videos and activity from your subscriptions.

23. Tap the Notify Me Via button to display the Notify Me Via dialog, and then tap the Mobile and Email radio button, the Mobile Only radio button, or the Email Only radio button, as needed.

24. Set the Recommended Videos switch to On or Off to control whether YouTube notifies you of videos it thinks you might like.

25. Set the Comments and Replies switch to On or Off to control whether YouTube notifies you about comments on your videos or sends you replies to messages.

26. Tap View Recent if you want to view your recent notifications.

27. Tap the arrow button or the Back button below the screen to return to the main Settings screen.

28. Tap Captions to display the Captions screen.

(27)

← Settings

Mobile notifications

Receive notifications — (21)
Notify on this device

Channel subscriptions

Subscription activity — (22)
Occasionally notify me of new videos and activity from my subscriptions

Notify me via — (23)
Mobile and email

Other notification types

Recommended videos — (24)
Notify me of videos that I might like

Comments and replies — (25)
Notify me when someone comments on my video or replies to me

Notification history

View recent — (26)

← Settings

General

Connected TVs

Privacy

Notifications

Captions — (28)

About

29. Tap Text Size to display the Text Size dialog, and then tap the radio button for the text size you want for captions: Very Small, Small, Normal, Large, or Very Large.

30. Tap Subtitles Styles to display the Subtitles Style dialog, and then tap the radio button for the caption style you want, such as White on Black or Yellow on Blue.

31. Tap the arrow button or the Back button below the screen to return to the main Settings screen.

32. Tap the arrow button or the Back button below the screen to return to the YouTube app.

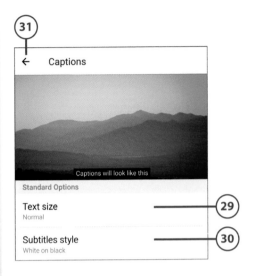

Take your library with you and read books anywhere.

In this chapter, you discover your Galaxy Note 5's capabilities for carrying and displaying books and magazines. Topics include the following:

→ Reading books with the Play Books app
→ Installing and using Amazon's Kindle app
→ Finding free e-books online
→ Reading newspapers and magazines with the Play Newsstand app

# Books, Newspapers, and Magazines

With its large, bright screen, your Galaxy Note 5 is great for reading books, newspapers, and magazines. You can load an entire library and newsstand onto your Galaxy Note 5, take the device with you anywhere, and read to your heart's content.

## Reading Books with Play Books and Kindle

Books are perfect media for your Galaxy Note 5 because their file sizes are mostly small but they deliver long-lasting entertainment. Your Galaxy Note 5 might come with one or more apps for reading books; if it doesn't, you can easily install such apps from the Play Store.

## Installing the Play Books App

Your Galaxy Note 5 might include Google's Play Books app, so tap the Apps button on the Home screen and see if Play Books appears on the Apps screen. The Play Books icon might appear directly on the Apps screen or in the Google folder, which may be either on the Apps screen or on the Home screen.

If the Play Books app is not already installed on your Galaxy Note 5, install it from the Play Store. Tap Play Store on the Home screen or the Apps screen, tap Apps on the Google Play screen, tap the Search icon, and type google play books. Tap the Google Play Books result and then tap Install. Review the permissions and tap Accept if you want to proceed.

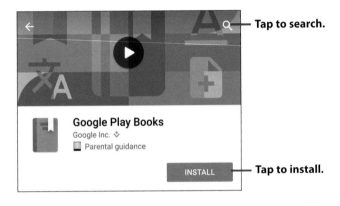

Tap to search.

Tap to install.

## Open the Play Books App and Meet Your Library

Google's Play Books app provides straightforward reading capabilities and ties in to the Books area of Google's Play Store, from which you can buy many books and download others for free.

1. On the Apps screen, tap Play Books. If you don't find the Play Books icon on the Apps screen, go to the Google folder, which is either on the Apps screen or the Home screen. Tap the Google folder and then tap Play Books. The Read Now screen usually appears at first.

## Should You Turn On Sync for Play Books?

When you launch Play Books, the app might display the Sync Is Currently Turned Off for This App dialog. If this dialog opens, tap the Turn Sync On button to enable syncing your books. With sync on, Play Books automatically updates your reading positions, so no matter which device you use to open a book, the app automatically displays your current page. Sync also synchronizes, bookmarks, notes, and other features.

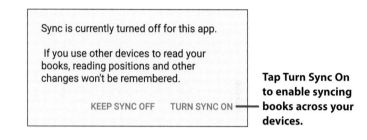

Sync is currently turned off for this app.

If you use other devices to read your books, reading positions and other changes won't be remembered.

KEEP SYNC OFF    TURN SYNC ON

**Tap Turn Sync On to enable syncing books across your devices.**

2. Tap the navigation panel button in the upper-left corner to display the navigation panel.

3. Tap My Library to display the books in your library.

### Where to Get Books

Depending on where you bought your Galaxy Note 5, your library might include several public-domain books as samples—plus any books you have already added to your library on your Galaxy Note 5 or another Android device. If your library is empty, you can get books from the Play Store.

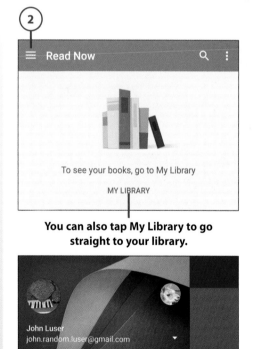

**You can also tap My Library to go straight to your library.**

4. Tap the tab for the list of books you want to view. Your choices are All Books (which this example shows), Uploads, Purchases, and Samples. Uploads are books you have uploaded to your Google account. You find out how to upload books later in this chapter.

5. Tap the Search icon to search your library for books by keyword. Searching is useful when you have built up a large library. When your library contains only a few books, it is usually easier to browse through them.

6. To control how Play Books sorts your library, tap the Sort By button. The Sort By dialog opens.

## Downloading a Book to Your Galaxy Note 5

A white pushpin on a blue circle indicates the book is stored on your Galaxy Note 5, so you can read it offline. To download a book to your Galaxy Note 5, tap the book's Menu button (the button showing three vertical dots) and then tap Keep on Device on the pop-up menu.

**Tap Download.**

**Tap the book's menu button.**

**A blue circle with a check mark indicates the book is stored on your Galaxy Note 5.**

## Refreshing Your Library

If you cannot see a book you know you have purchased, uploaded, or otherwise acquired, you might need to refresh your library by tapping the Menu button and then tapping Refresh on the menu. Refreshing makes the Play Books app sync your books from the Google Play service, so it should fill in any gaps in your library.

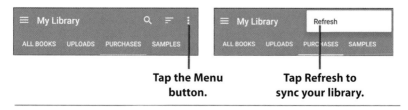

**Tap the Menu button.**

**Tap Refresh to sync your library.**

7. Tap the Recent radio button, the Title radio button, or the Author radio button, as needed. Play Books displays your books sorted into the order you choose.

8. Tap a book to open it. If the book is not stored on your Galaxy Note 5, Play Books downloads the book and then opens it.

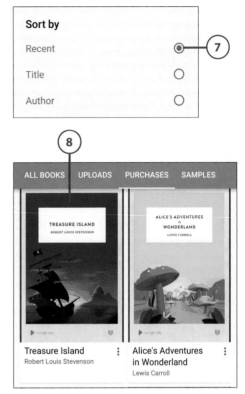

## Get Books from the Play Store

The Books area of the Play Store offers a fair number of e-books for free and a much larger number of e-books for sale. You can easily access the Books area of the Play Store from the Play Books app.

1. Tap the button in the upper-left corner of the Play Books app to display the navigation panel.

2. Tap Shop to display the Books area of the Play Store. The Play Books Home screen appears first.

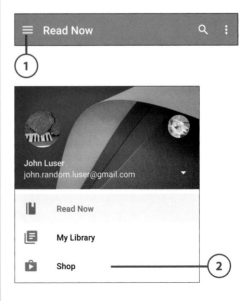

3. Tap the Search icon to search for books.

4. Tap the Top Selling tab or swipe left once to see the list of top-selling books.

5. Tap the Deals tab or swipe left twice to see special offers.

6. Tap the New Releases in Fiction tab or swipe left three times to see fiction books that have been newly added to the Play Store. Swipe once more (four times total) to display the New Releases in Nonfiction list; swipe one more time (five times total) to display the New Free list.

## Navigate Quickly Among Tabs by Swiping

The Books area of the Play Store contains various tabs, including Categories, Home, Top Selling, New Releases in Fiction, New Releases in Nonfiction, and Top Free. You can navigate among these tabs by tapping their names on the tab bar or scrolling the tab bar as needed, but it is usually quicker to swipe left or right one or more times to change tabs.

7. Tap a featured book or a recommended book to see its details.

8. Tap the More button for a featured category to see the books it contains.

9. Tap Categories to display the list of categories. You can also swipe right once from the Home screen to display the list of categories.

10. Tap the category you want to display. The Top Selling list for the category appears first.

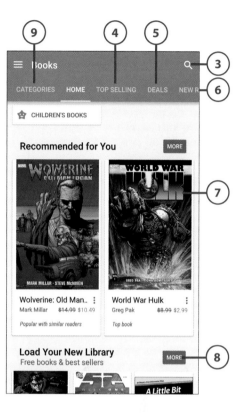

11. Swipe up to see more of the list.

12. Tap the New Releases tab or swipe left to see the New Releases list for the category.

13. Tap a book to display its details.

14. Tap the blue bookmark symbol bearing a + sign to add the book to your wish list.

15. Tap Read More to expand the description.

16. Swipe up to read the reviews or to rate the book yourself (which you can do even if you haven't yet read it), to read the About the Author blurb, and to see lists of other books by the same author and similar books.

17. Tap Free Sample to download a free sample of the book. Reading the sample can be a great way to decide whether to spend your money on the book. Android downloads the book and displays its first page in the Google Books app.

## Buying Books from the Play Store

To buy a book from the Play Store, you must either add a credit card or debit card to your Google account or redeem a voucher. See Chapter 11, "Working with Android Apps," for information on setting up Google Wallet and adding a means of payment to it.

18. Tap the price button to buy the book, and then follow through the payment process on the next screen. If the book is free, tap the Add to Library button. Android downloads the book and displays its first page in the Play Books app.

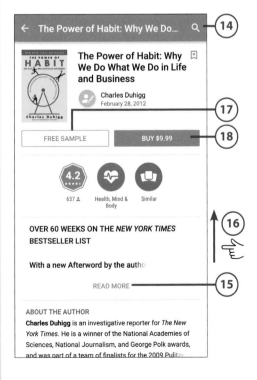

## Share a Book with Other People

When you find a book you simply must tell someone about, you can do so easily from the Play Store app. Tap the Share button at the bottom of the screen to display the Share screen, tap the means of sharing you want to use, and then complete the sharing in the app that Android opens.

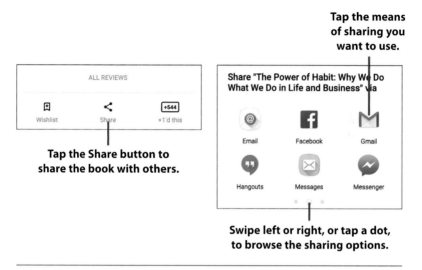

Tap the means of sharing you want to use.

Tap the Share button to share the book with others.

Swipe left or right, or tap a dot, to browse the sharing options.

## Finding Free E-Books Online

Apart from buying e-books online at the Play Store or other stores such as Amazon (www.amazon.com) and Barnes & Noble (www.barnesandnoble.com), you can find many free books. Most online stores offer some free e-books, especially out-of-copyright classics, so it is worth browsing the Free lists. Other good sources of free e-books include ManyBooks.net (www.manybooks.net) and Project Gutenberg (www.gutenberg.org).

# Read Books with the Play Books App

1. Tap the button in the upper-left corner to display the navigation panel, and then tap Read Now to display your Read Now screen. This screen shows the books you have been reading recently plus books you have recently bought (or downloaded for free) or uploaded to your Google account. Further down the screen is a Recommended for You section that suggests books you might be interested in based on the books you have.

2. Tap the book you want to open. The cover or default page appears if this is the first time you have opened the book. Otherwise, the page at which you last left the book appears.

3. Tap the middle of the screen to shrink the page a little and display the navigation controls at the top and bottom of the screen. The controls remain onscreen until you tap the screen again.

4. Tap the Search icon to search within the book for specific text.

5. Tap the Contents icon to display the Contents screen. From here, you can tap Chapters to display a list of the book's chapters and major headings, and then tap the place you want to display; tap Bookmarks to display a list of the bookmarks you have created in the book, and then tap the bookmark you want to go to; or tap Notes and then tap the note you want to view.

6. Drag the slider to move quickly through the book.

7. Swipe left to move further through the book, or swipe right to move back through it.

8. Tap the middle of the screen to restore the current page to full screen, hiding the controls.

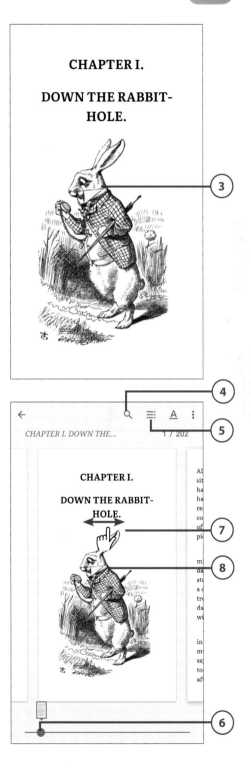

9. Tap the right side of the screen or drag left to turn the page forward. Dragging lets you turn the page partway to peek ahead.

10. Tap the left side of the screen or drag right to turn the page back.

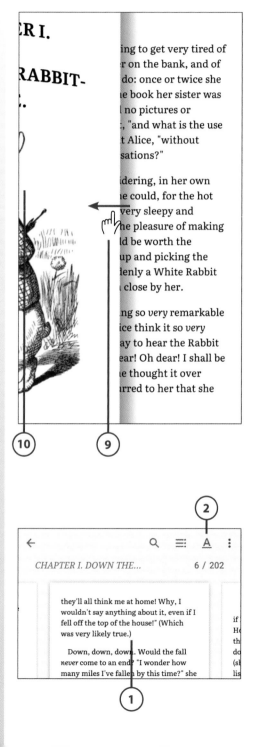

# Configure Display Options for the Play Books App

You can configure the Play Books app to display the text the way you prefer to see it. You can change the overall theme of the text display to get a background color that suits you. You can also change the font, alignment, font size, and line spacing.

1. With the Play Books app open and active, tap the middle of the screen. The controls appear.

2. Tap Display Options. The controls disappear, the page returns to full size, and the Display Options panel opens.

3. Tap the Day button, the Night button, or the Sepia button to set the overall theme. The Day theme uses black text on a white background, the Night theme uses white text on a black background, and the Sepia theme uses black text on a sepia background.

4. Drag the Brightness slider to adjust the brightness manually.

5. Tap the Auto button to enable or disable automatic brightness.

6. Tap the Typeface pop-up menu to change the typeface used.

7. Tap the Text Alignment pop-up menu to change the text alignment. The choices are Default, Left, and Justify.

8. Tap the small T button to decrease the font size.

9. Tap the large T button to increase the font size.

10. Tap the left Line Height button to decrease the spacing between lines.

11. Tap the right Line Height button to increase the spacing between lines.

12. Tap the book page to close the Display Options panel.

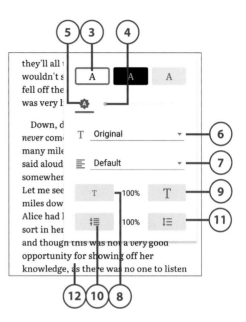

# Choose Options for the Play Books App

You can configure the Play Books app to make it work your way. Options include switching between flowing text and the original pages of the book, adding bookmarks, and having your Galaxy Note 5 read aloud to you.

1. With the Play Books app open and active, tap the screen to display the controls.

2. Tap the Menu button to display the menu.

3. Tap Original Pages to display the book's pages as they are laid out in the physical book. This option is available only for some books. Tap the Menu button again and then tap Flowing Text when you want to change the display back to flowing text.

4. Tap About This Book to display the book's page in the Play Store. If the book is a sample, you can tap Buy on the menu to start the process of buying the book.

5. Tap Share to share the book's URL on the Play Store via Facebook, Gmail, Twitter, or another means of sharing.

6. Tap Add Bookmark to add a bookmark to the current page. To remove the bookmark, go to the page, tap the Menu button, and then tap Remove Bookmark.

7. Tap Read Aloud to start Android reading the text out loud. To stop it, tap the Menu button and then tap Stop Reading Aloud.

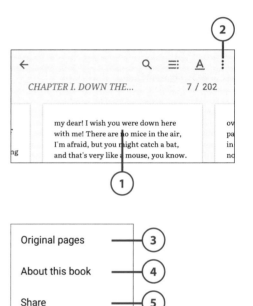

**8.** Tap Help & Feedback to display the Help screen, from which you can access various help resources, such as Help Center, Contact Us, and Report a Problem.

**9.** Tap Settings to display the Settings screen.

**10.** Tap Auto-Rotate Screen to display the Auto-Rotate Screen dialog.

**11.** Tap the means of rotation you want to use. Your options are Use System Setting, Lock in Portrait, and Lock in Landscape. For example, if you prefer to read books in landscape orientation, you can tap Lock in Landscape to prevent the screen from rotating automatically as you move the Galaxy Note 5 back to a portrait orientation.

**12.** Check the Download over Wi-Fi Only box if you want to prevent Play Books from downloading books over a cellular network. This is a good move if your cellular plan gives you only a miserly data allowance.

**13.** Check the Use Volume Key to Turn Pages box if you want to use the physical volume key to turn the pages in the Play Books app. This setting can be helpful if you normally hold your Galaxy Note 5 with your fingers over the volume key.

**14.** Check the Use 3D Effect for Page Turning box if you want Play Books to use the 3D animation for turning pages.

**15.** Check the Enable PDF Uploading box if you want to be able to upload PDFs to Play Books from sources such as email and your Downloads folder.

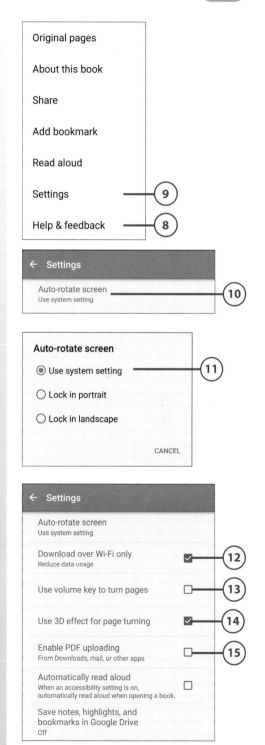

16. Check the Automatically Read Aloud box if you want Android to start reading aloud automatically when you open a book in Play Books.

17. Tap Save Notes, Highlights, and Bookmarks in Google Drive. The Save Notes, Highlights, and Bookmarks in Google Drive dialog opens.

18. Type the name for the folder in which to save the notes, highlights, and bookmarks. You can also accept the default name— Play Books Notes.

19. Check the Save My Notes, Highlights, and Bookmarks box.

20. Tap OK to close the dialog.

21. If you want to prevent books marked as sexually explicit from appearing in Play Books, tap Parental Controls and check the Books box. See the section "Manage Google Play Settings" in Chapter 11 for coverage of the Parental Control features.

22. If you want to be able to use the dictionary feature of Play Books offline, tap Offline Dictionary. In the Offline Dictionary dialog that opens, check the box for the language you want to use (such as English), and then tap OK to download and install the language.

23. Tap the arrow button or the Back button to leave the Settings screen and return to the screen you were previously using in the Play Books app.

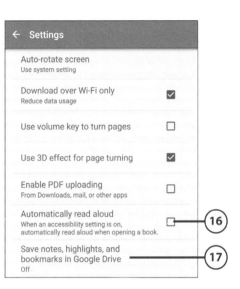

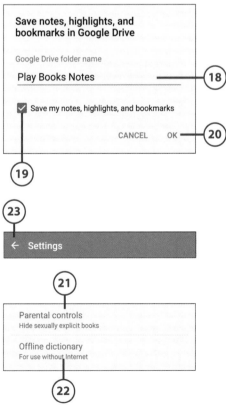

# Remove or Delete a Book from Your Play Books Library

When you no longer want a particular book on your Galaxy Note 5, you can remove the download. The book remains in your library, so you can download it again if necessary, or read it on your other devices.

If you no longer want a particular book in your library, you can delete it. Deleting the book removes it from your Google Play library entirely, not just from your Galaxy Note 5 (or whichever other device you're using), so Play Books makes you confirm the action.

1.  In the My Library view in Play Books, tap the Menu button on the book's listing.

2.  Tap Delete from Library. The Delete from Library dialog opens.

3.  Tap Delete.

**Tap Remove Download to remove the downloaded book from your Galaxy Note 5.**

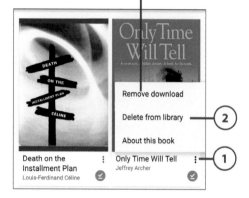

>>>*Go Further*

## UPLOAD YOUR DOCUMENTS TO GOOGLE PLAY BOOKS

The Play Books app is great for reading books you buy or get for free from the Play Store, but you can also use it to read your own PDF files and e-books in formats such as the widely used ePub format. To do so, you use your computer to upload the files to your Google account, from which the Play Books app can then access them.

To upload the files, open your computer's web browser and go to play.google. com. Click the Sign In button, and then sign in with your Google account. Click Books in the navigation panel on the left, and then click My Books to display the screen containing your books. Now click the Upload Files button in the upper-right corner of the window, and then follow the instructions onscreen to select the file or files.

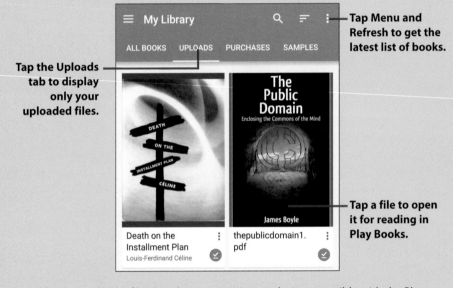

Tap Menu and Refresh to get the latest list of books.

Tap the Uploads tab to display only your uploaded files.

Tap a file to open it for reading in Play Books.

After you upload a file, Google processes it to make it compatible with the Play Books app. The books appear in your library, but you might find it easier to access them on the Uploads screen; to display this screen, either tap the Uploads tab in the tab bar or swipe left or right until the Uploads screen appears. If the books do not appear, tap the Menu button and then tap Refresh to force Play Books to refresh the list. You can then tap a book to download it and read it.

## Install the Kindle App

Google's Play Store has a good selection of books, but if you want books in Amazon's vast bookstore, you need to use the Kindle app. If you already own any Kindle books, installing the Kindle app gives you most of the benefits of owning a Kindle reader without having to buy or haul around an extra device.

## Installing the Kindle App

If the Kindle app is not already installed on your Galaxy Note 5, install it from the Play Store. Tap Play Store on the Apps screen, tap Apps on the Google Play screen, tap the Search icon, and type kindle. Tap the Amazon Kindle result and then tap Install. Review the permissions and tap Accept if you want to proceed.

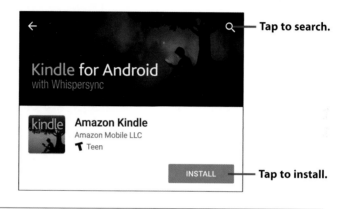

Tap to search.

Tap to install.

## Sign In and Navigate the Kindle App

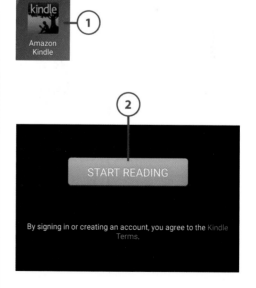

1. On the Apps screen, tap the Amazon Kindle icon. The first time you run the Kindle app, it displays the Start Reading screen.

2. Tap the Start Reading button to display the Sign In screen. This screen also appears only the first time you use the app.

3. Type your email address or mobile phone number.

## Creating an Amazon Account

To buy books or download free books from Amazon, you must have an Amazon account. If you do not have one, tap the Create an Account button on the Sign In screen and then follow through the screens to create an account.

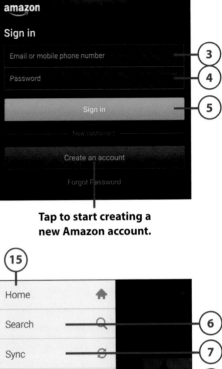

Tap to start creating a new Amazon account.

4. Type your Amazon password.

5. Tap Sign In. The Kindle app signs you in to your account and then displays its Home screen with the menu panel open.

6. Tap Search to search your Kindle library for the terms you type.

7. Tap Sync to refresh the display of books. You would do this if you have just bought a book using your computer or a different device and the book hasn't yet appeared on the Kindle app on your Galaxy Note 5.

8. Tap Store to go to the Kindle Store, where you can browse and buy books.

9. Tap All Items to display the All Items screen. This screen shows all the items in your Kindle library, whether they are on your Galaxy Note 5 or not.

10. Tap On Device to see the list of books and other items stored on your Galaxy Note 5.

11. Tap Collections to display the Collections screen, which contains the collections you have created to organize your library.

12. Tap Books to see the list of books, rather than documents, newspapers, and magazines.

13. Tap Docs to display the documents stored in your Kindle account. These are documents you have sent via email to your Send to Kindle email address, a Kindle-only address that Amazon provides with Kindle accounts.

14. Tap Newsstand to display your Newsstand items.

15. Tap Home to close the menu panel. The Home screen appears, showing the books in your Kindle library on a carousel.

16. Scroll left or right to find the book you want.

17. Tap the Store icon to go to the Kindle Store to browse or buy books.

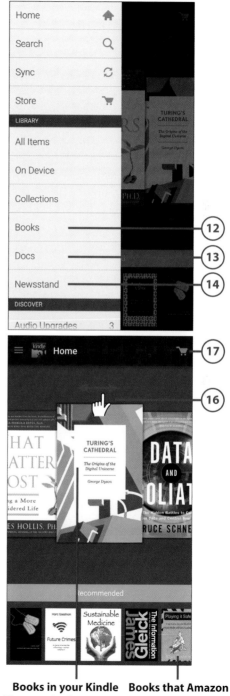

**Books in your Kindle library, whether on your Galaxy Note 5 or not.**    **Books that Amazon recommends for you.**

# Read a Book with the Kindle App

1. In the Kindle app, tap the book you want to open. This example uses the On Device screen, but you can also start from another screen, such as the Home screen or the All Items screen.

---

### Reaching the On Device Screen from a Book

If you currently have a book open in the Kindle app, tap the Back button to go back to the main screen, tap the Menu button, and then tap On Device.

---

2. Tap the middle of the screen to display the controls. Tap again to hide these items.

3. Drag the slider to change the location in the book.

4. Tap the right side of the screen to display the next page. You can also display the next page by dragging or swiping left.

5. Tap the left side of the screen, or drag or swipe right, to move back a page.

6. Tap the Menu button to display the menu.

**Tap to display the books as a list instead of as a grid of covers or to change the sort order.**

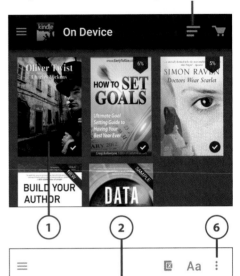

lent a hand in bringing him here. He's a thief, a liar, a devil, all that's bad, from this night forth. Isn't that enough for the old wretch, without blows?'

'Come, come, Sikes,' said the Jew appealing to him in a remonstratory tone, and motioning towards the boys, who were eagerly attentive to all that passed; 'we must have civil words; civil words, Bill.'

'Civil words!' cried the girl, whose passion was frightful to see. 'Civil words, you villain! Yes, you deserve 'em from me.
I thieved for you when I was a child not half as old as this!' pointing to Oliver. 'I have been in the same trade, and in the same service, for twelve years since. Don't you know it? Speak out! Don't you know it?'

'Well, well,' replied the Jew, with an attempt at pacification; 'and, if you have, it's your living!'

'Aye, it is!' returned the girl; not speaking, but pouring out the words in one continuous and vehement scream. 'It is my living; and the cold, wet, dirty streets are my home; and you're the wretch that drove me to them long ago, and that'll keep me there, day and night, day and night, till I die!'

Page 74 of 264                                    28%

7. Tap Shop in Kindle Store to go shopping for Kindle books.

8. Tap My Notes & Marks to view the list of notes and bookmarks you have added to the current book. From there, you can tap one of your bookmarks or notes to go to its page.

9. Tap Add a Bookmark to bookmark the current page, or tap Remove Bookmark to remove a bookmark from the current page. Adding a bookmark gives you an easy way to return to a particular page by using the View My Notes & Marks command on the menu.

10. Tap Share Progress to display the Share Progress dialog, in which you can pick a way to share your reading progress. For example, you can post a link to Facebook or send an email message saying you're 50% through the book.

11. Tap Word Wise to display the Language Learning screen, on which you can enable or disable the Word Wise feature, which displays hints above words that are considered challenging. If you enable Word Wise, you can also choose to show multiple-choice hints—when Kindle isn't sure of the exact meaning of a word in context, it displays a list of possible meanings so that you can select the right one.

12. Tap the menu-panel button to display the menu panel.

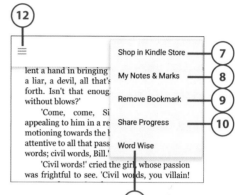

13. Tap About This Book to display the About This Book pane, which contains brief information about the book and its author.

14. Tap the Go To button to go to a page by number or to go a location. The locations are numbered divisions of the text. You can see the number of the current location by tapping the middle of the screen and looking at the Location slider. However, unless you know the number of the location to which you want to go, this command is of little use.

15. Tap Search to search in the book. For example, you can search for a distinctive word on a page.

16. Tap Sync to go to the furthest page you've read in this book on any of your Kindle devices. Normally, you do this after reading the book on another device.

17. Tap Upgrade with Audio to see options for adding professional narration to the Kindle book.

18. Tap Popular Highlights to see a list of passages that many people have highlighted in the book.

19. Tap Before You Go to display a screen for rating the book and for exploring other books recommended to you based on this book.

20. Tap Cover or a section in the Table of Contents list to go straight to that section. Scroll down as needed to find the section you want.

| Library | ⌂ |
| About This Book | ——— 13 |
| Go to | ——— 14 |
| Search | ⌕ ——— 15 |
| Sync | ↻ ——— 16 |
| Upgrade with Audio | ⌁ ——— 17 |
| Popular Highlights | ——— 18 |
| Before you go | ——— 19 |

**TABLE OF CONTENTS**

| Cover | ——— 20 |
| CHAPTER I | 1 |
| CHAPTER II | 3 |

# >>>Go Further

## ADDING MARKS TO A BOOK

You can easily add a bookmark to the current page by tapping the Menu button and then tapping Add a Bookmark, but the Kindle app also enables you to add highlights, add notes, and copy text to the clipboard so that you can paste it elsewhere.

**Tap to add a note.** **Tap to copy the text.**

**Tap to highlight the text.**

other pursuits of a similar kind: all undertaken with his characteristic impetuosity. In each and all he has since become famous th most profo 1ood, as a

Before his removal, he had managed to contract a strong friendship for Mr. Grimwig, which that eccentric gentleman cordially reciprocated. He is accordingly visited by Mr. Grimwig a great many times in the course of

**Tap to access the search commands.**

**Tap and hold on the page to display the controls.** **Drag the blue handles to select the text you want to mark.**

Tap and hold the relevant part of the text until the Kindle app selects it. Drag the blue selection handles to encompass the text you want to mark, and then tap the appropriate button on the pop-up toolbar.

## Choose View Options for the Kindle App

To make your books easy to read, you can choose view options for them.

1.  With a book open in the Kindle app, tap the screen to display the controls.

2.  Tap the Aa icon to display the View Options panel.

3.  Drag the Brightness slider to adjust the screen brightness.

4.  Check the Use System Brightness box to make the Kindle app use the same brightness as the Galaxy Note 5 as a whole.

5.  Tap the – icon to decrease the font size.

6.  Tap the + icon to increase the font size.

7.  Tap the Font pop-up menu to change the font.

8.  Tap the Color pop-up menu to choose the color scheme. Your choices are White, Black, Sepia, and Green.

9.  Tap the Margins pop-up menu to adjust the margin width.

10. Tap the Line Spacing pop-up menu to change the line spacing. Your choices are Narrow, Normal, and Wide.

11. Tap the document to close the View Options panel.

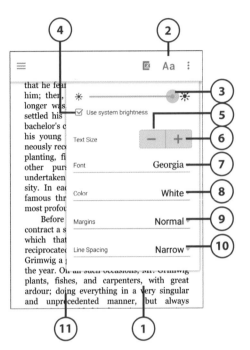

## >>>*Go Further*
### EXPLORE OTHER BOOK READERS

Between them, the Play Books app and the Kindle app give you access to a phenomenal range of books. However, there are many other book readers you might want to explore to give yourself access to other bookstores and other books. In particular, the Aldiko app, the Kobo app, and the Nook app are worth trying. Each of these apps are free in the Play Store. The Nook app ties into Barnes & Noble's online bookstore.

# Reading Newspapers and Magazines with Play Newsstand

To read newspapers and magazines, you can use Google's Play Newsstand app. Your Galaxy Note 5 might include Play Newsstand; if it doesn't, launch the Play Store app, search for play newsstand, and install the Google Play Newsstand app.

### Exploring Other News and Magazine Apps

If the Play Newsstand app does not deliver the content you need, or does not otherwise suit you, explore other news and magazine apps such as PressReader and Zinio. Both these apps are free in the Apps section of the Play Store.

## Open the Play Newsstand App and Choose Your Topics

The first time you open Play Newsstand, the app prompts you to select the topics you like, so that it can show you relevant stories.

1. On the Apps screen or in the Google folder, tap Play Newsstand. The first time you open it, the app displays the Welcome to Newsstand dialog, prompting you to tell the app what you like to read.

2. Tap Customize to display the What Topics Do You Like to Read About? screen.

3. Tap an unchecked topic that you want to add. A check mark appears on the topic.

4. Tap any checked topic that you want to remove. The topic's check mark disappears.

5. Tap Next. The What News Sources Do You Like to Read? screen appears.

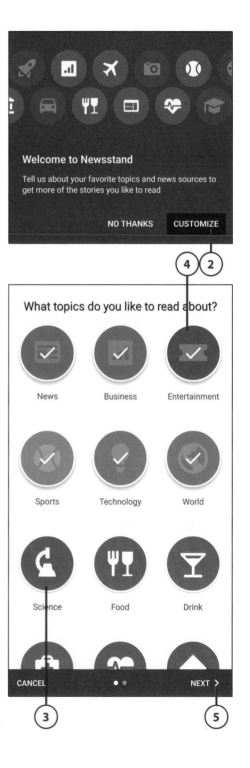

6.  Tap any unchecked news source that you want to add.

7.  Tap any checked news source that you want to remove.

8.  Tap Done when you finish making your choices. The news screens appear.

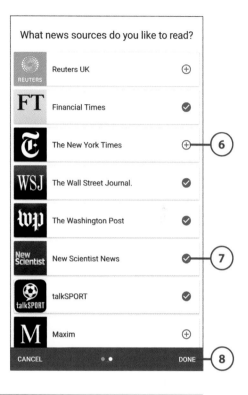

## Adding Paid Content to Play Newsstand

After performing the initial setup on Play Newsstand, you can add other content, including paid content, at any point. To do so, tap the button in the upper-left corner of the screen to display the menu panel, and then tap Explore. On the Explore screen, tap the topic you want to browse, such as News & Politics or Science & Technology. The available content for the topic appears, and you can choose which items to add.

Any item for which you have to pay displays a price button. When you tap such an item, Android switches you to the Play Store app and displays the page for that item. You can then pay for the item using the means of payment you have set up for the Play Store.

# Read News with the Read Now Feature

1. Tap the category of news you want to view, such as Highlights, News, Business, or Sports. You can also swipe left or right to move from one category to another.

2. Tap the story you want to display.

3. Tap the screen to display the controls at the top. Tap the text rather than a picture, because tapping a picture displays that picture and its caption.

4. Tap the Share icon to share the story using the means you select in the Choose an Action screen that opens. For example, you can share the story on Facebook, add it to Dropbox, or share it via email.

5. Tap Bookmark to create a bookmark for the story so that you can access it again easily.

6. Tap the arrow or the Back button to return to the previous screen so that you can browse and read other stories.

# Build Your Newsstand Library

The Play Newsstand app enables you to build a library containing the publications you prefer to read.

1. Tap the navigation button to display the navigation panel.

2. Tap My Library to display the My Library screen.

3. Tap News, Magazines, or Topics to display the content type you want to customize.

4. Tap the menu button on one of the items.

5. Tap Download to download the item.

6. Tap Move to Top to move the item to the top of the list.

7. Tap Share to share the item via any of the means available, such as Twitter or Email.

8. Tap Remove Source to remove this news source from your library.

9. Tap Add to Home Screen to add this news source to your Home screen.

10. Tap More to start adding another news source.

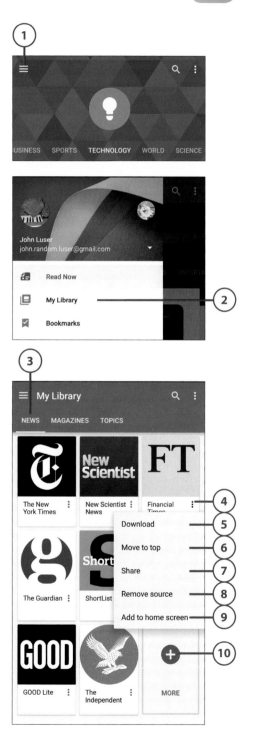

# Choose Options for the Play Newsstand App

The Play Newsstand app has several settings you can choose to control when it downloads magazines and when it notifies you about new issues. You can also change the account you use to pay for Play Newsstand.

1. Tap the navigation button to display the navigation panel.

2. Tap Settings to display the Settings screen.

3. Tap Article Text Size to display the Article Text Size dialog, where you can tap the Small radio button, the Normal radio button, or the Large radio button, as needed.

4. Check the Show Notifications box if you want to receive notifications when a new issue is available of a magazine that you have added to your library.

5. Check the Download via Wi-Fi Only box if you want to restrict Play Newsstand to downloading content to when your Galaxy Note 5 has a Wi-Fi connection. Because newspaper and magazine files can be relatively large, checking this box is a good idea if your cellular data plan is limited.

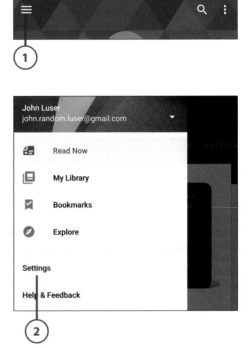

6. Check the Download While Charging Only box if you want Play Newsstand to download content only when your Galaxy Note 5 is charging. You might want to do this if your Galaxy Note 5 tends to run out of battery power.

7. Check the Auto-Download Magazines box if you want Play Newsstand to automatically download issues of magazines when they become available.

8. If you check the Auto-Download Magazines box, tap Options for Auto-Downloaded Issues to display the Auto-Download Magazines dialog, in which you can choose which issues to download and which to store. For example, you can choose to store only the latest issue to avoid running out of space on your Galaxy Note 5.

9. You can tap Clear All Downloads if you need to remove all downloaded content—for example, if you suddenly run out of space. This is a drastic action, so you have to tap OK in the Clear All downloads dialog to confirm it.

10. Tap the arrow or the Back button when you finish choosing settings.

Browse for apps.

Search for apps.

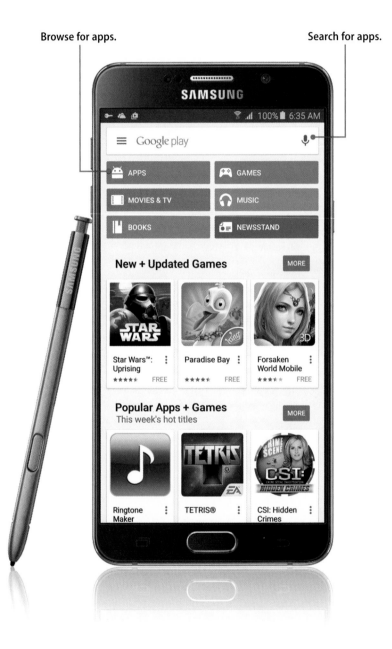

In this chapter, you find out how to purchase and use Android apps on your Galaxy Note 5. Topics include the following:

→ Finding apps with Google Play
→ Purchasing apps
→ Keeping apps up to date

# Working with Android Apps

Your Galaxy Note 5 comes with enough apps to make it a worthy smartphone. However, wouldn't it be great to play games, work on business or school documents, or keep a grocery list? Well, finding these types of apps is what the Google Play Store is for. Read on to learn about finding, purchasing, and maintaining apps.

## Configuring Google Wallet

Before you start buying apps in the Play Store app, you should sign up for a Google Wallet account. If you plan to only download free apps, you do not need a Google Wallet account.

1.  From a desktop computer or your Galaxy Note 5, open the web browser and go to https://wallet.google.com.

2.  Sign in using the Google account that you will be using to synchronize email to your Galaxy Note 5. See the Prologue or Chapter 4, "Email and Text Messages," for information about adding a Google account to your Galaxy Note 5.

3.  Choose your location. If your country is not listed, you have to use free apps until it's added to the list.

4.  Enter your name.

5.  Enter your ZIP Code.

6.  Enter your credit card number. This can also be a debit card that includes a Visa or MasterCard logo, also known as a check card, so that the funds actually are withdrawn from your checking account.

7.  Enter the month and year of the card's expiration date.

8.  Enter the card's CVC number, which is also known as the security code. This is a three- or four-digit number that's printed on the back of your card.

9.  Check this box if your billing address is the same as your name and home location. Otherwise, uncheck this box and enter your billing address and phone number when prompted.

10. Click Accept and Create when you finish filling in the form.

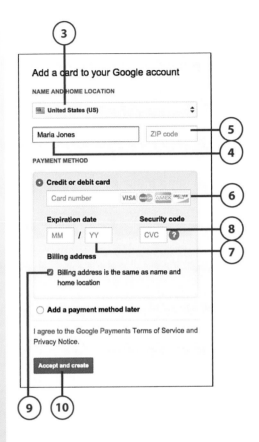

# Navigating Google Play

Android is the operating system that runs your Galaxy Note 5, so any apps that are made for your Galaxy Note 5 need to run on Android. The Google Play Store is a place where you can search for and buy Android apps.

1. On the Apps screen, tap the Play Store app icon to launch the Play Store app. You can also tap the Play Store icon on the Home screen if it appears there.

2. Tap Apps to browse all Android apps.

3. Tap Games to browse all Android games.

4. Tap the Search box to search Google Play.

5. Tap the Menu button to display the menu panel.

6. Tap Store Home to display the Home page of the Play Store.

7. Tap My Apps to display the list of apps you have already purchased or acquired for free.

8. Tap My Wishlist to display your wishlist. This is a list to which you can add items you want to buy or you want others to buy for you.

9. Tap People to see the People feed, which shows what apps people you know are downloading.

10. Tap My Account to display the My Account screen, on which you can manage your payment methods, your rewards, and your order history.

11. Tap Redeem to redeem a gift card or promotional code.

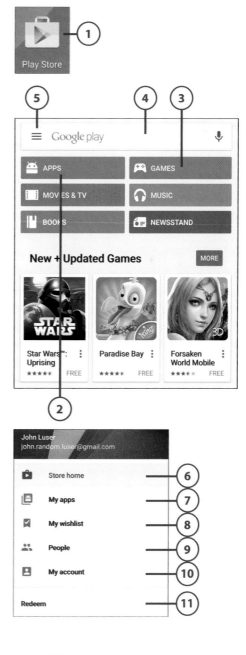

# Download Free Apps

You don't have to spend money to get quality apps. Some of the best apps are actually free. Other free apps are feature-light versions that give you a chance to test-drive the app without paying and decide whether you want to upgrade to the full version.

1. Tap the app you want to download. The screen for the app appears.

2. If the app has a video, tap the Play button to play the video. A video walkthrough can be a great way of getting a clear idea of whether the app does what you want.

3. Swipe up to read the app features, reviews by other people who installed it, and information on the person or company who wrote the app.

4. Scroll left and right to see the app screenshots.

5. Tap Install to download and install the app.

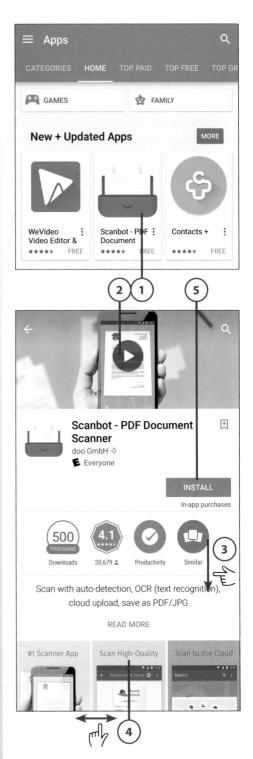

# What Are In-App Purchases?

The In-App Purchases notation below the Install button for an app on Google Play means that the app offers features for which you have to pay. You purchase the features from within the app rather than by making a separate purchase on Google Play.

Developers use in-app purchases widely because it enables them to offer their apps for free—which helps encourage people to try the apps—or for a low price. Game companies also sometimes require you to use in-app purchases for additional levels and features.

Generally speaking, in-app purchases are beneficial to both developers and their customers, but as a customer, you should keep your eyes open for the cost of in-app purchases, especially if others (such as your family) can use in-app purchases on apps linked to your credit card or debit card.

6. Tap Accept to accept the app permissions and proceed with the download.

## Beware of Permissions

Each time you download a free app or purchase an app from Google Play, you are prompted to accept the app permissions. App permissions are permissions the app wants to have to use features and functions on your Galaxy Note 5, such as access to the wireless network or access to your phone log.

Pay close attention to the kinds of permissions each app is requesting and make sure they are appropriate for the type of functionality the app provides. For example, an app that tests network speed will likely ask for permission to access your wireless network, but if it also asks to access your list of contacts, it might mean that the app is malware and just wants to steal your contacts.

**Tap an upward caret to collapse a section.**

**Tap a downward caret to expand a section.**

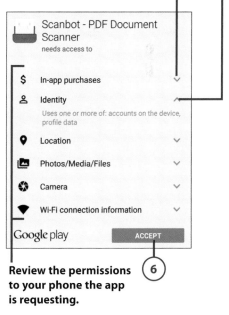

**Review the permissions to your phone the app is requesting.** (6)

**7.** After your Galaxy Note 5 downloads and installs the app, the
Open button appears in the Play
Store app. Tap Open to open the
app.

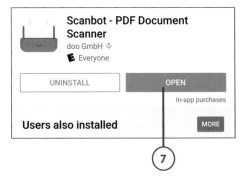

## >>>Go Further

# OPEN A NEWLY INSTALLED APP FROM THE NOTIFICATIONS PANEL

If you keep the Play Store app open while downloading an app, the Open button
on the app's screen provides a handy way to open the app and put it through
its paces. However, if the app is large or your Internet connection is slow, you
probably won't want to hang about in the Play Store app until the download
completes.

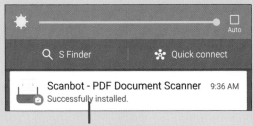

**Tap the Successfully Installed notification
to open a freshly installed app.**

When the installation finishes, a notification briefly appears telling you that the
app has been installed successfully. You can then launch the app by opening the
notifications panel and tapping the Successfully Installed notification for the app.

# Buy Apps

If an app is not free, the price appears next to the app icon. If you want to buy the app, remember that you need to already have a Google Wallet account. See the "Configuring Google Wallet" section, earlier in the chapter, for more information.

1. In the Play Store app, tap the app you want to buy. The app's screen appears.

## What If the Currency Is Different?

When you browse apps in Google Play, you might see apps that have prices in foreign currencies, such as in euros. When you purchase an app, the currency is simply converted into your local currency using the exchange rate at the time of purchase.

2. Swipe up to read the app's features, reviews by other people who have used it, and information on the person or company who created the app.

3. Scroll left and right to see the app screenshots.

4. Tap the price button to start the process of downloading and installing the app.

5. Review the app permissions and make sure you can accept them. Tap Accept to proceed with the purchase. Your purchase method appears.

6. If this is the means of payment you want to use, tap Continue. If not, tap the downward-arrow button to expand the dialog to show other payment options.

7. After selecting your means of payment, tap Continue to purchase the app, and then tap Buy. You will receive an email from Google Play after you purchase an app. The email serves as your invoice.

**Review the permissions the app requires, if any.**

**Tap to buy the app with this means of payment.**

**Tap Payment Methods to choose another means of payment.**

**Tap Redeem to redeem a gift certificate or prepaid card.**

## Getting a Refund on an App

If you realize you've bought the wrong app, or otherwise regret a purchase, you can return it within two hours and get a full refund. To do this, open the Play Store app, go to the My Apps screen, tap the app to display its screen, and then tap Refund.

**Tap Refund to get a refund on an app you've just bought.** ───

If the Refund button doesn't appear, you're too late for an automatic refund, but you might be able to get a refund manually. Open your web browser, go to the Play Store website (play.google.com), and then sign in. Click or tap the Gear icon and then click My Account to display the My Account screen. In the Order History list, click or tap the Menu button (the three vertical dots) in the row for the purchased item and select Report a Problem. In the Report a Problem dialog box, open the pop-up menu and select the most appropriate reason, such as I No Longer Want This Purchase. Type an explanation in the text box and click or tap the Submit button.

# Manage Apps

You can use the My Apps section of Google Play to update apps, delete them, or install apps that you have previously purchased.

1.  In the Play Store app, tap the button in the upper-left corner to display the menu panel.

2. Tap My Apps to display the My Apps screen.

3. Tap All to see all apps that you have purchased on this Google account.

4. Look for the Installed indicator to see whether the app is currently installed.

5. Tap the Update indicator to update an installed app with the latest version.

6. Tap an unmarked app to install it. The lack of marking indicates a free app. This might be either an app you installed but then removed or an app you "purchased" (downloaded for free) on another device.

7. Tap the × button to remove an app from the list of apps.

8. Tap an app marked as Purchased to reinstall an app that you previously purchased and installed, but that is no longer installed, or an app that you purchased on another device. Because you have already purchased the app, you do not need to pay for it again.

## Allowing an App to Be Automatically Updated

When the developer of an app you have installed updates it to fix bugs or add new functionality, you are normally notified in the Notification bar and Notification panel so that you can manually update the app.

Google Play enables you to choose to have the app automatically updated without your intervention. To do this, open the My Apps screen, tap the Installed tab, and then tap the app you want to update automatically. On the app's screen, tap the Menu button and then check the Auto-Update box. Be aware that if these updates occur while you are on a cellular data connection, your data usage for the month will be affected.

**Check this box to enable automatic updating.**

**Tap the Menu button.**

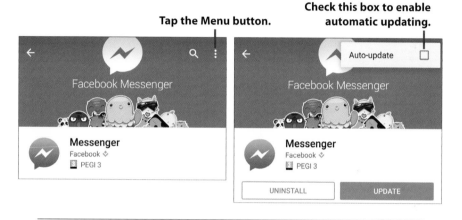

## Uninstalling an App

To uninstall an app, tap the app's button on the My Apps screen, and then tap Uninstall on the app's screen. Uninstalling the app removes both the app itself and its data from your Galaxy Note 5. Although the app no longer resides on your Note 5, you can reinstall it as described in step 7 because the app remains tied to your Google account.

**Tap this button to uninstall the app.**

# Manage Google Play Settings

1. In the Play Store app, tap the button in the upper-right corner to display the menu panel.

2. Tap Settings to display the Settings screen.

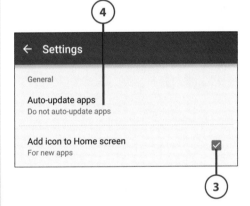

3. Check the Add Icon to Home Screen box if you want each app you install to add its app icon to the Home screen. If you want to keep the Home screen uncluttered, uncheck this box.

4. Tap Auto-Update Apps to display the Auto-Update Apps dialog.

5. Tap the appropriate radio button: Do Not Auto-Update Apps, Auto-Update Apps at Any Time, and Auto-Update Apps over Wi-Fi Only. Because apps can be large, choosing Auto-Update Apps over Wi-Fi Only is usually the best choice unless you want to disable automatic updating.

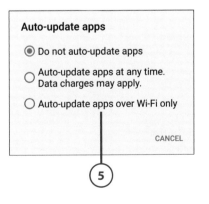

6. Tap Clear Local Search History if you want to clear the Google Play search history. There's no double-check or confirmation beyond a quick blink of the button.

7. Check the App Updates Available box if you want Android to notify you when updates are available for the apps installed on your Galaxy Note 5.

8. Check the Apps Were Auto-Updated box if you want Android to notify you after it has automatically updated apps.

9. Tap Require Authentication for Purchases to display the Require Authentication dialog.

10. Tap the radio button for the authentication you want: For All Purchases Through Google Play on This Device (the most secure option), Every 30 Minutes (which gives moderate security), or Never (which gives none).

11. If you need to enable parental controls for apps and content in Google Play, tap Parental Controls. The Parental Controls screen appears.

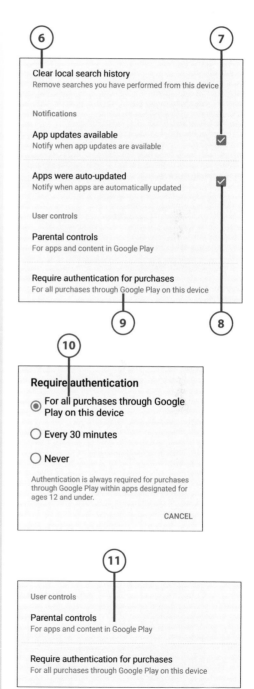

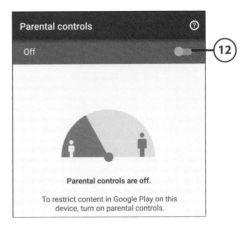

12. Set the Parental Controls switch to On. The Create Content PIN dialog opens.

13. Tap the keypad to set a four-digit PIN that must be typed in before changing the Google Play User Control.

14. Tap OK. The Create Content PIN dialog closes, and the Confirm PIN dialog opens.

15. Type your PIN again, and then tap OK once more (not shown). The Parental Controls screen appears again, now with the controls enabled.

16. Tap Apps & Games. The Allow Up To dialog opens, showing ratings for apps and games.

**Parental controls**                                        ⑫

Off

*Parental controls are off.*

To restrict content in Google Play on this
device, turn on parental controls.

---

**Create content PIN**

You'll use this PIN to change settings for
parental controls.

····|

                                    CANCEL        OK

                        ⑬                         ⑭

---

**Parental controls**                                        ⑦

On

Set content restrictions for this device
Each type of content has different options.

🖳  **Apps & Games** ————————————— ⑯
     Allow all, including unrated

🎞  **Movies**
     Allow all, including unrated

🖵  **TV**
     Allow all, including unrated

📖  **Books**                                           ☐
     Restrict sexually explicit books

🎧  **Music**                                           ☐
     Restrict music marked explicit by content
     providers

17. Tap the maximum level you will permit, such as Teen. The Allow Up To dialog closes.

18. Tap Movies and then tap the appropriate level in the Allow Up To dialog.

19. Tap TV and then tap the appropriate level in the Allow Up To dialog.

20. Check the Books box if you want to restrict sexually explicit books.

21. Check the Music box if you want to restrict music that content providers have marked Explicit. The Explicit rating usually refers to the lyrics, but you might find the occasional instrumental track that's marked Explicit.

22. Tap the Back button below the screen. Android returns you to the Play Store app (not to the Settings screen).

**Allow up to:**

| | |
|---|---|
| Everyone | **E** |
| Everyone 10+ | **E** |
| Teen | **T** |
| Mature 17+ | **M** |
| Adults only 18+ | **A** |
| Allow all, including unrated | |

(17)

| | | |
|---|---|---|
| Apps & Games | Highest rating: Teen | |
| Movies | Allow all, including unrated | (18) |
| TV | Allow all, including unrated | (19) |
| Books | Restrict sexually explicit books | (20) |
| Music | Restrict music marked explicit by content providers | (21) |

## Why Lock the User Settings?

Imagine if you buy a Galaxy Note 5 for your child but want to make sure that he doesn't get to any undesirable content. First, you set the content filtering to restrict the content visible in Google Play. Next, you set the PIN so he can't change that setting. A similar idea goes for limiting purchases.

**Enter content PIN**

Enter PIN to modify parental controls:

**Enter the PIN so you can change the settings.** — •••7

CANCEL    OK

## Accidentally Uninstall an App?

What if you accidentally uninstall an app or you uninstalled an app in the past but now decide you'd like to use it again? To get the app back, go to the My Apps screen in Google Play. Scroll to that app and tap it to display the app's screen. Tap Install to reinstall the app.

# Keeping Apps Up to Date

Developers who write Android apps often update their apps to fix bugs or to add new features. With a few quick taps, you can easily update the apps you have installed.

1. On the Apps screen, tap the Play Store icon to launch the Play Store app.

2. Tap the button in the upper-right corner to display the menu panel.

3. Tap My Apps to display the My Apps screen.

4. Tap Installed to display the Installed screen.

5. Tap Update to update an app.

## Starting an Update from the Notification Panel

When your Galaxy Note 5 detects an update available for one of the apps you have installed, it displays the update notification in the Notification bar. You can open the My Apps screen in Google Play quickly by pulling down the Notifications panel and tapping the notification.

**Tap Update All to apply all available updates at one time.**

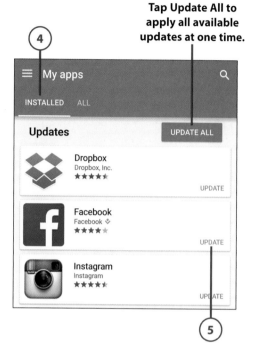

Swipe up
to read.

In this chapter, you discover how to set up your Android Wear smartwatch and use it with your Samsung Galaxy Note 5.

→ Setting up your Android Wear watch
→ Choosing settings and installing apps
→ Navigating the Android Wear watch's interface
→ Using the Android Wear watch's apps

# Using Your Samsung Galaxy Note 5 with an Android Wear Smartwatch

To get the most out of your Galaxy Note 5, you can link it to a Android Wear smartwatch. Android Wear watches are sold by vendors such as Samsung, LG, and Motorola and act as a companion for any Android smartphone, including your Note 5. The Android Wear watch enables you to display essential information, make phone calls, and allow simple interactions with apps without taking your Galaxy Note 5 out of your pocket.

## Setting Up Your Android Wear Watch

To set up the Android Wear watch, you need to use your Galaxy Note 5.

1. Unpack the Android Wear watch and identify its components: the Android Wear watch itself, a charging dock/clip, and the charger.

2. Fully charge your Android Wear watch.

3. Turn the Android Wear watch on by pressing and holding its button for a moment. The button is on the right side of the Android Wear watch.

4. Tap to choose your preferred language on the watch screen.

5. When you see a screen on your watch telling you to install the Android Wear app on your phone, switch to your Note 5 for steps 6–14.

6. Search the Google Play Store for the Android Wear app. When you find it, tap Install.

7. Tap Accept to accept the permissions that the Android Wear app needs to run correctly. After the app installs, run it to start setting up your watch.

8. Tap the right arrow to start setting up your watch.

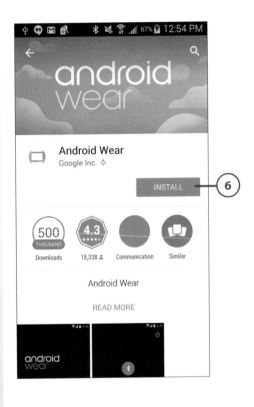

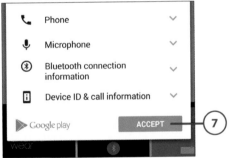

9. Tap Accept to accept that the Android Wear app will synchronize data between your watch and your Note 5.

10. Tap the name of the watch you want to use. In this example, it is a Samsung Gear Live, listed as "Gear Live 10C9."

11. When prompted, accept the Bluetooth Pairing PIN on both your Note 5 and your watch. The PIN should be the same on both devices.

12. When your watch and Note 5 are paired over Bluetooth, you see a screen preparing you to configure Android to allow the Android Wear app to have access to notifications. Tap Notification Settings.

13. Check the box to allow the Android Wear app to receive access to Android notifications.

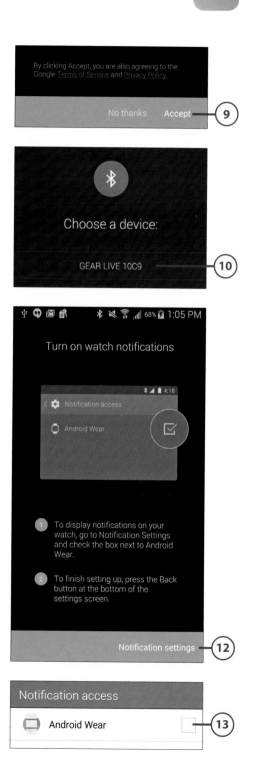

14. Tap OK to verify that you want the Android Wear app to have access to all Android notifications.

> **Allow Android Wear**
>
> Android Wear will be able to read all the notifications you receive, which may include personal information such as contact names and messages sent to you. It will also be able to dismiss these notifications or select actions related to them.
>
> Cancel          OK ——(14)

## Android Wear Smartwatches Explained

Android Wear is a framework that Google created to support smartwatches connecting to Android devices. This enabled different vendors to create and sell smartwatches that have their own unique look and build quality but can all be compatible with any Android device as long as the owner installs the Android Wear app. Smartwatches that use the Android Wear framework can have square or round faces. Examples of Android Wear watches that have a round face are the Motorola Moto 360 and the LG G Watch R. Examples of Android Wear watches that have a square face are the Asus ZenWatch, Sony SmartWatch 3, Samsung Gear Live, and the LG G Watch. No matter whom you buy your Android Wear–based smartwatch from, and regardless of whether it has a square or round face, the instructions and guidance in this chapter are relevant.

# Choosing Settings for Your Android Wear Watch

After pairing your Android Wear watch with your Galaxy Note 5, you'll probably want to spend some time customizing the Android Wear watch. You can use the Android Wear app on your Galaxy Note 5 to configure overall settings for the Android Wear watch, as explained in this section. To configure other settings, you use the Settings app on the Android Wear watch itself, as discussed in the following section.

# Navigate the Android Wear App

The Android Wear app gives you access to features and settings for configuring and managing your Android Wear watch.

1. Tap to launch the Android Wear app.

2. Tap a watch face to change it on your watch.

3. Tap to see all watch faces you have installed and find more.

4. Swipe up to see all voice actions and what apps are launched when the voice action triggers.

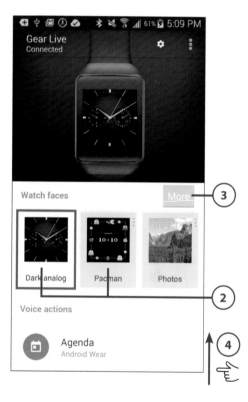

# Set Voice Actions

Voice actions are voice commands you speak to your watch. Based on what you say, your watch either launches an app or takes an action, or it tells your Note 5 to launch an app. Some voice actions can be customized to make use of third-party watch apps that you install. Voice actions that are gray are voice actions that cannot use third-party watch apps, or you have not installed a third-party watch app to make use of them.

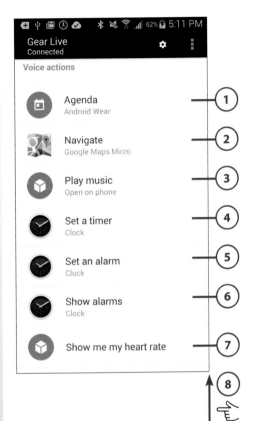

1. Your watch shows your agenda.

2. Your watch launches the Google Maps Micro watch app and enables you to get turn-by-turn directions. The Google Maps Micro watch app also launches the Google Maps app on your Note 5, which actually provides the navigation to your watch.

3. Opens the Google Play Music app on your Note 5 and plays music.

4. Sets a timer on your watch.

5. Sets an alarm on your watch.

6. Shows the alarms set on your watch.

7. Shows your heart rate. Tap to choose which watch app launches to show your heart rate.

8. Swipe up for more voice actions.

9. Shows how many steps you have walked with your watch on.

10. Starts a stopwatch on your watch. Tap to select which watch app launches to start the stopwatch.

## Why Is the Icon Gray?

In the following steps, each of the voice actions shown in the figure have a gray Google Play icon next to them. That icon indicates that there is currently no app installed to handle the function provided by the voice action. After you install an appropriate app on your Note 5, these actions will be available.

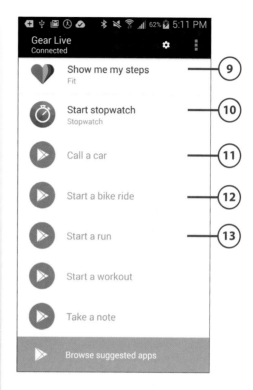

11. Call a car to pick you up. Install an app such as Lyft to make this voice action available. If you have two apps installed that both handle this function, tap Call a Car to choose the app you prefer to use.

12. Allows you to launch an app to start a bike ride. Install an app such as RunKeeper to make this voice action available. If you have two apps installed that both handle this function, tap Start a Bike Ride to choose the app you prefer to use.

13. Allows you to launch an app to start a run. Install an app such as RunKeeper to make this voice action available. If you have two apps installed that both handle this function, tap Start a Run to choose the app you prefer to use.

14. Allows you to launch an app to start a workout. Install an app such as RunKeeper to make this voice action available. If you have two apps installed that both handle this function, tap Start a Workout to choose the app you prefer to use.

15. Allows you to launch an app to take a note. If you do not install an app to handle this voice action, when you use this feature, the note you dictate is emailed to your Gmail address. Installing an app such as Chaos Control allows this voice action to launch your favorite note-taking app.

16. Tap to browse the Google Play Store for watch apps to handle voice actions and standalone watch apps that provide additional functionality.

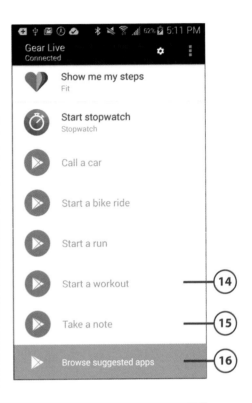

## How To Handle Riding, Running, and Workouts?

Start a Bike Ride, Start a Run, and Start a Workout are functions that will not work until you install an app on your Note 5 to handle them. It is your choice which apps you want to install to handle these functions. The one used for writing this chapter was RunKeeper. It just so happens that RunKeeper handles all three functions, however, that does not mean that you need to use just one app for all three functions. You can install three different apps to handle one of the three functions seperately. Your favorite apps that you already use for tracking bike rides, for example, might already support Android Wear. If that is the case, you will select that app to support the bike ride function. If you have two apps installed that handle one or more of the functions, tap the function to choose which app you want to use. For example, to change what app handles Start a Bike Ride, tap Start a Bike Ride and choose the app.

# Choose a Watch Face

Your watch comes with some pre-installed watch faces, and you can use the Android Wear app to choose which one you want to use. You can also browse the Google Play Store for more. Some are free; some you must purchase.

1. From the main Android Wear app screen, tap one of the three most recent watch faces to set your watch to use it.

2. Tap More to see all watch faces you have installed.

3. Select a watch face to use.

4. Scroll down to the bottom of the screen and tap Get More Watch Faces to find more watch faces in the Google Play Store.

5. Tap to install a watch face.

6. Once your new watch face has been installed, it automatically downloads to your watch and is visible in the Android Wear app. Tap the watch face to make your watch start using it.

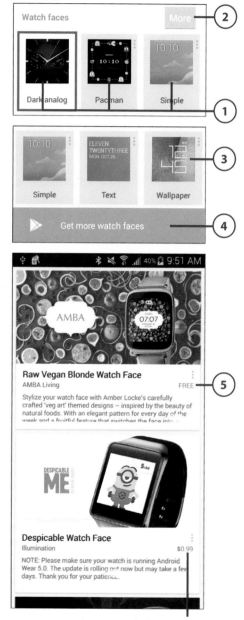

Some watch faces cost money.

7. Some watch faces have configuration options. If the watch face has settings that you can change that affect the way it works, the Settings icon displays over the watch face. Tap it to adjust the watch face's settings.

8. Tap to return to the main Android Wear app screen.

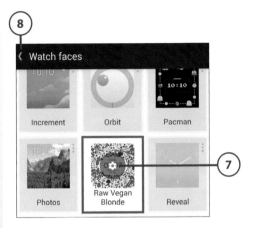

## Adjust the Android Wear App's Settings

The Android Wear app does allow for some configuration, and it also provides ways for you to view your watch's battery life and available memory.

1. From the main Android Wear app screen, tap the gear icon to see the settings.

**2.** Tap to choose which calendars you want to show event cards for on your watch.

**3.** Tap to choose apps that you no longer want to receive notifications for on your watch. By default, every notification from every app is sent to your watch. Use this setting to select which ones you really care about.

**4.** Tap the on/off button to mute any alerts, notifications, or any other interruptions on your Note 5 while it is connected to the watch. Having this enabled helps cut down having alerts vibrate your Note 5 and your watch at the same time.

**5.** Tap to choose whether you want to keep your watch synchronized with your Note 5 over Wi-Fi, via your Google Cloud account. Having this feature turned on allows your watch to stay in-sync even when it is not connected to your Note 5 via Bluetooth.

**6.** Tap to manage the Together feature. The Together feature works with special Together watch faces and allows you to choose a friend to keep in-sync with and share sketches, photos, stickers, and fitness information.

**7.** Features that are used by app developers to debug and troubleshoot their apps. You will not need to use these debugging features.

**8.** Tap the name of your watch to see watch-specific settings.

| | |
|---|---|
| ← Settings | |
| Device settings | |
| Gear Live<br>Connected | 8 |
| General | |
| Calendar settings | 2 |
| Block app notifications<br>Block watch notifications from specific apps | 3 |
| Mute phone alerts & calls<br>Mute calls and notifications on this phone while<br>it's connected to your watch | 4 |
| Cloud sync<br>Sync data between your phone and your watch over Wi-Fi. | 5 |
| Together<br>Manage who your connected watch face is paired to | 6 |
| Debugging over Bluetooth | |
| Device to Debug<br>Gear Live 10C9 | 7 |
| Debugging over Bluetooth | |

9. Tap to disconnect your Note 5 from your watch. Tap again to reconnect.

10. Move the switch to the On position to set your watch to keep a low-resolution monochrome version of the screen on at all times, even when it goes to sleep.

11. Move the switch to the On position to set your watch to wake up when it detects you tilting your wrist.

12. Move the switch to the On position to allow a preview of an alert to be displayed on the bottom of the watch screen. If you move the switch to the Off position, there will be no alert previews; however, you can still swipe up to view alerts.

13. Tap to manage the voice actions for your watch.

14. Tap to see how your watch's battery is performing and how much power each app is taking. Using this screen can help you identify apps that are draining the battery.

15. Tap to see your watch's memory usage, and how much memory each app is using.

16. Tap to resynchronize apps between your Note and your watch. You don't normally need to do this, but if you suspect that an app you recently installed on your Note 5 has not installed a mini-app on your watch, you can tap here.

17. Tap to return to the previous screen.

# Watch Battery Usage

Viewing your watch's battery performance can help to determine how much longer your watch will last on its current charge based on current usage. You can also see which apps and watch faces are using the most battery time. Watch faces with a lot of animation can use a lot of battery charge. If you see a watch face or watch app that is using a lot of battery charge, you may choose to uninstall the app or stop using the watch face to help your watch last longer on a single charge.

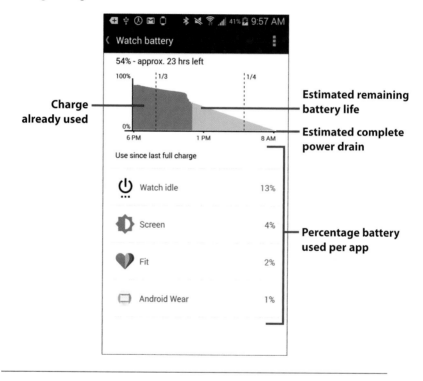

# Watch Memory Usage

Viewing your watch's battery memory usage can help you see if your watch is running out of space, and if it is, which apps and watch faces are using the most memory.

# Install Apps on the Android Wear Watch

Some apps installed on your Note 5 automatically install a watch app on your watch that helps you interact with the app from your watch. There are also dedicated watch apps that you can install from the Google Play Store.

1. In the Android Wear app, tap More next to Essential Watch Apps.

2. Swipe up to see all of the categories of watch apps. The categories are Watch Faces, New Year, Tools, Social, Productivity, Communication, Health & Fitness, Entertainment, Travel & Local, and Games.

3. Tap More to see more apps in a specific category.

4. Tap an app you want to download. Some apps cost money. This example uses Reversi for Wear.

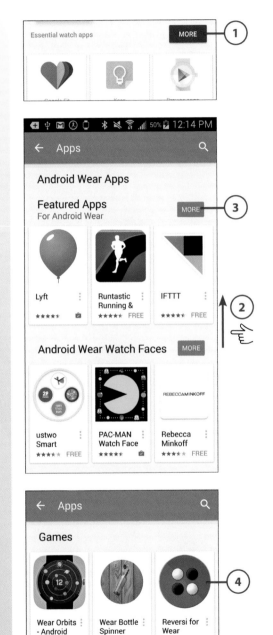

5. Tap Install.

6. Tap Accept to accept any device or information permission the app needs to run. In this example, the app does not need any permissions.

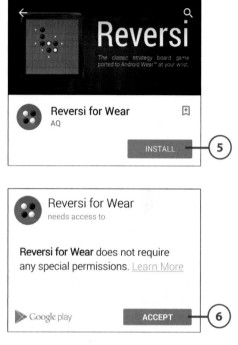

# Using Your Android Wear Watch

Now that we have covered how to set up your watch via the Android Wear app, and you've installed some watch faces and apps, let's take a look at using the watch itself.

## Watch Features

Your Android Wear watch actually runs on the Android operating system. As of the writing of this book, the version of Android running on Android Wear watches is Android 5.1.1 (Lollipop). Your watch either has a round or square face, includes an accelerometer to detect movement, a capacitive touchscreen so you can perform gestures such as tapping and swiping, and a microphone to listen for voice commands. Your watch probably also has a sensor to monitor your heart rate and a pedometer to measure your activity. Your watch relies on your Note 5 for the majority of its functions, including voice commands, so you must always have your Note 5 close by to use your watch. Although most Android Wear watches include a physical button, some do not.

## Navigate Your Watch

Your watch responds to taps and swipes that allow you to navigate the interface, run apps, and see and respond to onscreen information.

1. While your watch is not being used, the screen becomes low resolution, monochrome, and dimmed to save energy.

2. Lift your arm to view your watch, and the screen turns to full color.

3. Swipe notifications up to read them, and in some cases take actions on them. If you have more than one notification, swipe up repeatedly to read all of them.

4. Tap the preview of the notification to show more of it, and scroll down to read all of it.

5. Swipe the notification to the left to see any actions that you can take on the notification. This includes an option to block the app so that you don't see notifications from it again.

6. Swipe the notification to the right to dismiss it. To dismiss most apps while using them on your watch, swipe to the right.

**7.** After you dismiss a notification, if you decide that you didn't want to, you can quickly swipe up from the bottom of the screen to see a dismiss timer. Tap the timer to undo the dismiss before it runs out.

**8.** Swipe down from the top of the screen to see options and settings.

**9.** Tap to toggle through the Notification options. You can choose to be notified on your watch for all notifications, Priority notifications only, or none.

**10.** Swipe left to see more options.

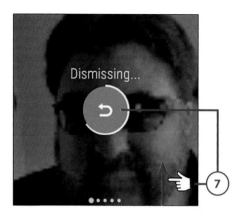

**11.** Tap to put your watch in Theater mode. When in Theater mode, the screen remains blank, you receive no notifications, and the action of lifting your arm to look at your watch is deactivated. Press the watch button to exit Theater mode.

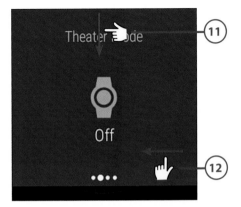

## Alternative Method of Activating Theater Mode

If you double-press your watch's button, you set it to Theater mode. Pressing the button again makes the watch exit Theater mode.

**12.** Swipe left to see more options.

**13.** Tap to set your watch to Brightness boost for five seconds. Brightness boost sets the screen brightness to the maximum for five seconds to help with bright sunlight or other situations where it is difficult to see the watch screen.

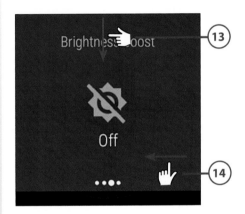

## Alternative Method of Activating Brightness Boost

If you triple-press your watch's button, Brightness Boost is engaged for five seconds.

**14.** Swipe left to see more options.

**15.** Tap to change your watch's settings. See the next section for a description of all settings.

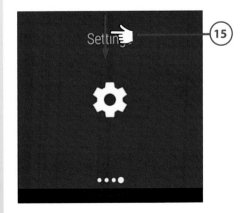

## Adjust Your Watch's Settings

Use this section to adjust your watch's settings. To enter your watch's settings, you can either swipe down from the top of the screen and swipe left until you see the Settings icon, or tap your watch screen and scroll down to Settings.

1. Tap to manually adjust the brightness of your watch's screen.

2. Tap to change your watch face.

3. Tap to change the size of the font used on your watch.

4. Swipe up for more settings.

5. Tap to manage what Wi-Fi network your wach conencts to. Your watch automatically connects to the same Wi-Fi network that your Note 5 is conencted to, but you can switch Wi-Fi networks.

6. Tap to pair your watch with Bluetooth devices such as Bluetooth speakers.

7. Tap to toggle Always-on Screen on or off. When this is off, your watch screen no longer switches to the low-resolution mode when it goes to sleep; instead, it turns off completely.

8. Swipe up for more settings.

9. Tap to turn Wrist Gestures on or off.

10. Tap to toggle Airplane mode on or off. When in Airplane mode, your watch is not able to communicate using Bluetooth to your Note 5.

11. Tap to mange whether you want to enable large fonts or the magnification gesture on your watch.

12. Swipe up for more settings.

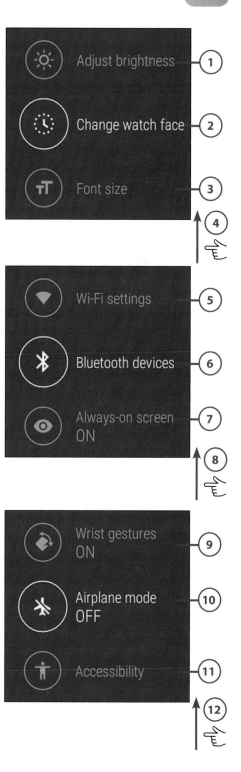

13. Tap to choose whether you want your watch to automatically lock itself when you take it off your wrist. If this is the first time you are enabling this feature, you are asked to draw an unlock pattern. You need to use this pattern to unlock your watch when you put it back on your wrist.

14. Tap to reset your watch. This puts the watch back to the way it came out of the box, and all your saved information will be lost.

15. Tap to restart your watch. All your information remains untouched; your watch just restarts.

16. Swipe up for more settings.

17. Tap to power off your watch.

18. Tap to see information about your watch, as well as whether there is an update for it.

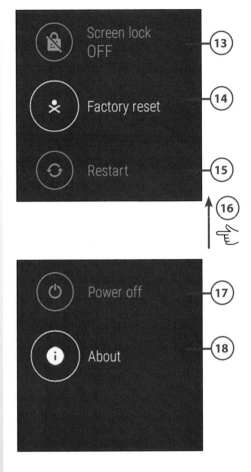

## Use Your Watch and Run Watch Apps

Your watch was designed to be used with your voice. However, you can also manually select functions and apps by tapping and swiping on the screen.

1. Wake up your watch by lifting your arm. Alternatively, you can tap your watch's screen to wake it up.

2. After your watch wakes up and the screen turns to full color, say "OK Google." Alternatively, you can tap the watch screen.

3. Your watch is now listening for a command. Say a command to perform an action or start an app. Use the next section to learn how to use each command and launch watch apps.

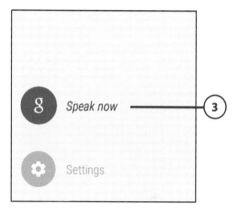

# Use Watch Functions and Watch Apps

Your watch is designed for voice commands. However, if you don't speak, your watch stops listening and allows you to select functions and run apps using the touchscreen. It's your choice how you want to perform the following functions—either by speaking or by touching.

1. Say "Settings," or tap to see the Settings screen.

2. Say "Start *app name*" to start an app. For example, say "Start Reversi" to start the Reversi app installed earlier in this chapter. Alternatively, you can tap the app icon to start it. Remember that with watch apps like Reversi you must say "Start." You can also start watch apps by saying "Run" (for example, "Run Reversi").

3. Say "Start Stopwatch," or tap to start the Stopwatch watch app.

4. Say "Take a note," or tap and speak the text of the note, to take a note. For example, you can say "Take a note to drink more water" and a new note is created with the text "Drink more water." If you have previously installed an app that handles notes, the note is saved to that app. Otherwise, your note is emailed to your Gmail account.

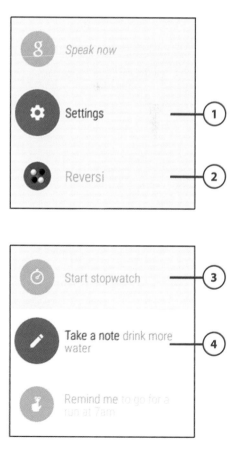

5. Say "Remind me," or tap and speak the reminder to add. For example, you can say "Remind me to go for a run at 7 a.m." and a new reminder is created labeled "Go for a run" set for 7:00 a.m. the next day. You can also set recurring reminders. For example, you can say "Remind me to make coffee at 8 a.m. every weekday."

6. Say "Start a run," or tap to launch the app you installed to handle your runs. Start running and use the watch app you installed to monitor your run.

7. Say "Show me my steps," or tap to show how many steps you have walked. Your watch uses its built-in pedometer to keep track of your steps.

8. Say "Show me my heart rate," or tap to activate your watch's heart rate monitor. Follow the instructions to allow your watch to take your heart rate.

9. Say "Send text," or tap and speak the name of the recipient and the text message to send a text message to someone. For example, you can say "Send a text to Jim, see you later" and a new text message is created to Jim with the text "See you later." If the contact has more than one phone number, you need to say the phone number to use, for example "Send a text to Jim mobile."

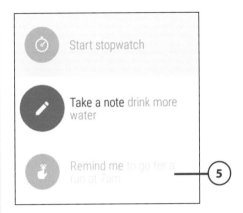

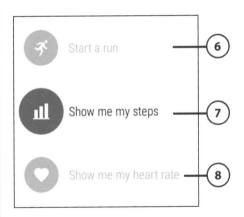

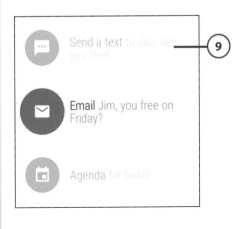

## Contact Recognition

You must enable contact recognition for the Send a Text and Send an Email functions to work. To do this, on your Note 5, tap Settings, Accounts, Google, Accounts & Privacy, and check the box next to Contact Recognition.

**10.** Say "Email," or tap and speak the name of the recipient and message. For example, you can say "Email Jim, you free on Friday?" and a new email will be created to Jim with the body of the message set to "You free on Friday?" If you have more than one person with the same name, and you are not specific, you are prompted to say the person's full name. If the person has more than one email address, you are prompted to say the one to use (for example, Home or Work).

**11.** Say "Agenda" or tap to see your agenda for today.

**12.** Say "Navigate," or tap and speak the desired destination to start turn-by-turn directions to your desired destination. You can say things like "to a pizza place nearby" or "home" or "work," or you can speak an address. Turn-by-turn directions start on your Note 5, with a mini version of them being displayed on your watch.

**13.** Say "Set a timer," or tap and speak the time the timer must use. For example, you can say "Set a timer for 45 minutes." The timer starts on your watch.

**14.** Say "Start stopwatch," or tap to start the stopwatch app on your watch.

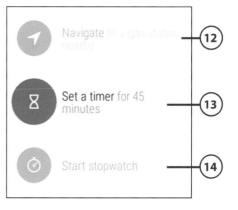

**15.** Say "Set an alarm," or tap and speak when the alarm must be set for. For example, you can say "Set an alarm for 6 this evening." The alarm will be created. Before the alarm is finished being created, you can tap Edit to edit the alarm and even make it recurring by selecting certain days of the week when it must trigger.

**16.** Say "Show alarms," or tap to show the alarms that have been set on your watch. You can edit or remove individual alarms by using the touch screen.

**17.** Say "Call a car," or tap to launch the car pickup service you installed on your Note 5 that supports Android Wear, such as Lyft.

**18.** Say "Play music," or tap to start playing an "I'm feeling lucky" mix on your Note 5. You can also say "Play Depeche Mode" to start playing all songs by Depeche Mode on your Note 5. See the "Play Music from Your Watch" sidebar at the end of this chapter for more information.

**19.** Say "Settings," or tap to see your watch's settings.

**20.** Say "Start," or tap and say the name of a watch app you have installed. For example, if you installed an app called Eat24, you would say "Start Eat 24."

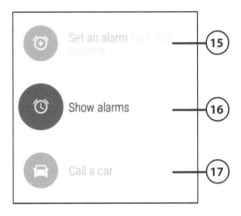

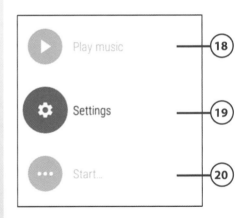

## Reply to an Email Using Your Voice

When you receive a new email notification on your watch, you can reply to the email using your voice. To do this, swipe up the email notification. Swipe the notification to the left twice and tap Reply. Speak your reply. When you stop speaking, your watch sends the reply using the message you dictated.

**Tap to reply.**

Reply

**Speak your reply.**

Reply

Reply
I'm replying to the
email using my voice

# >>>Go Further
## MORE ABOUT NOTIFICATIONS

If there are more than one notifications from an app (this is common for email notifications), you see a plus (+) symbol and a number indicating how many more notifications there are from this app. Tap the number, and all the notifications are shown. Tap the one you want to interact with.

Digg
This Week's Best
Videos: A Ruthless
Dart-Throwing Man,
North Carolina's

+3 more ——— **Tap to see all notifications from the app.**

Some notifications you see come from apps that do not provide any way to interact with them. Your only choice is to have your watch tell your Note 5 to open the corresponding app. You can then continue interacting with the app on your Note 5. To do this, swipe the notification to the left and tap Open on Phone.

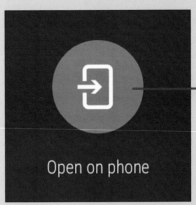

Tap to open the corresponding app on your Note 5.

## >>>Go Further
## PLAY MUSIC FROM YOUR WATCH

It's easy to command your watch to play music that is stored on your Note 5; however, you can also store music on your watch. To do this, open the Google Play Music app, open Settings, and check the box next to Download to Android Wear to download a copy of any music that you choose to your Android Wear watch. To switch to playing music from your Note 5 to your watch, after you say "OK Google, Play music," tap the blue X and tap Android Wear. This then allows you to play only music that is stored on your watch. To hear the music, you need to have a Bluetooth speaker paired with your watch. To switch back to playing music on your Note 5, say "OK Google, Play music," tap the blue X, and tap Phone.

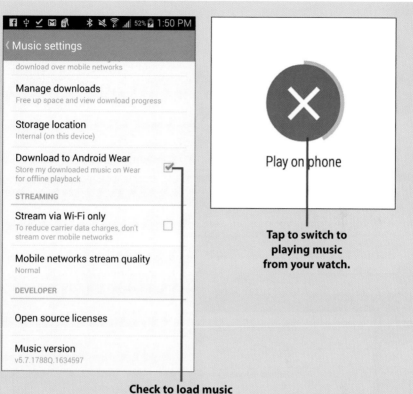

**Check to load music
to your watch.**

**Tap to switch to
playing music
from your watch.**

When you choose to play music from your watch, swipe up and down to scroll through the albums. When you find an album you want to play, swipe left to choose to shuffle the songs on the album. Swipe left again to see the songs on the album. Scroll through the songs and tap one to start playing it. If you try to play music from your phone before you have paired a Bluetooth device capable of receiving the audio, you are prompted to complete the pairing process.

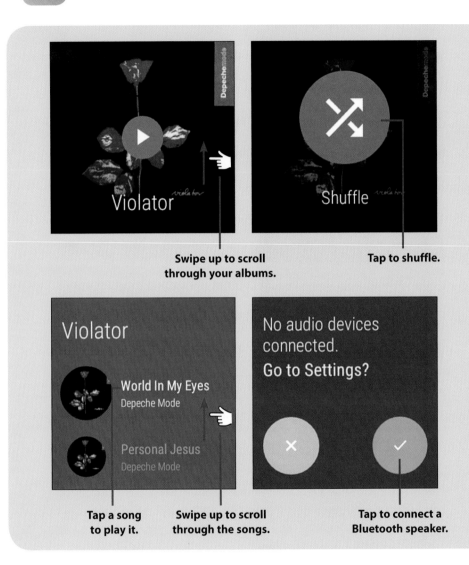

Swipe up to scroll
through your albums.

Tap to shuffle.

Tap a song
to play it.

Swipe up to scroll
through the songs.

Tap to connect a
Bluetooth speaker.

## >>>*Go Further*

## THE TOGETHER FEATURE

Android Wear watches support a feature called Together. Together uses special watch faces to allow you to share sketches, photos, emojis, stickers, and your fitness information with someone else. This could be your spouse, partner, family member, or just a close friend.

To start, you need to pair with someone. You do this from the Android Wear app on your Note 5. Under Watch Faces, tap Together. Tap Pair with a Friend, and choose the method you'd like use to invite them to pair with you.

After your friend accepts your Together invite, his picture appears on your Together watch face. Tap the picture to send your activity, draw a quick sketch, or send emojis, stickers, or photos.

See your battery usage trends.

Learn which features have used the most power.

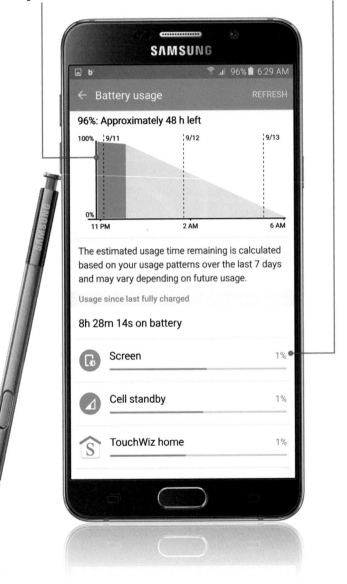

**SAMSUNG**

96% 6:29 AM

← Battery usage                    REFRESH

96%: Approximately 48 h left

100%    9/11           9/12              9/13

0%
11 PM            2 AM              6 AM

The estimated usage time remaining is calculated based on your usage patterns over the last 7 days and may vary depending on future usage.

Usage since last fully charged

8h 28m 14s on battery

Screen                              1%

Cell standby                        1%

TouchWiz home                       1%

In this chapter, you discover how to maintain your Galaxy Note 5 and solve problems. Topics include the following:

→ Updating Android
→ Optimizing battery life
→ Identifying battery-hungry apps
→ Caring for your Galaxy Note 5

# Maintaining Your Galaxy Note 5 and Solving Problems

Every so often, Google releases new versions of Android that include bug fixes and new features. In this chapter, you find out how to upgrade your Galaxy Note 5 to a new version of Android and how to tackle common problem-solving issues and general maintenance of your Galaxy Note 5.

## Updating Android

New releases of Android are always exciting because they add new features, fix bugs, and tweak the user interface. Here is how to update your Galaxy Note 5.

## Updating Information

Updates to Android are not on a set schedule. The update messages appear as you turn on your Galaxy Note 5, and they remain in the Notification bar until you install the update. If you tap Install Later, your Note 5 reminds you at short intervals—30 minutes, 1 hour, or 3 hours—that there's an update. When to install the update is up to you. You might prefer to wait to see whether each new update contains any bugs that need to be worked out rather than applying each update immediately.

1. Pull down the Notification bar to open the Notification shade.

2. Tap Software Update. The Software Update screen appears, showing the details of the update the Galaxy Note 5 has downloaded.

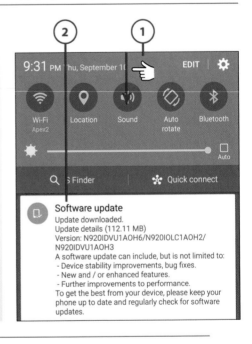

## Manually Checking for Updates

If you think there should be an update for your Galaxy Note 5 but have not yet received the onscreen notification, you can check manually by tapping Settings, About Device, and Software Update. On the Software Update screen, tap Update Now to check for an update.

**Tap Update now to check manually for an update.**

3.  Tap Install.

4.  Tap OK in the next Software Update dialog, which tells you that the device will be rebooted. Your Galaxy Note 5 restarts, installs the update, and then displays the Lock screen.

5.  Unlock the Galaxy Note 5 as usual (not shown). For example, swipe the screen and then type your passcode. A Software Update dialog opens, confirming that the device has been updated successfully.

6.  Tap OK to close the screen. You can then resume using your Galaxy Note 5 normally.

---

Software update

**The update has been downloaded. To install it, tap INSTALL.**

☐ Scheduled software updates

**Update details**

Size: 112.11 MB
Version: N920IDVU1AOH6/N920IOLC1AOH2/
N920IDVU1AOH3
A software update can include, but is not limited to:
- Device stability improvements, bug fixes.
- New and / or enhanced features.
- Further improvements to performance.
To get the best from your device, please keep your phone up to date and regularly check for software updates.
remaining updates: 0

**Notice**

During installation, you cannot use your device at all, even for emergency calls. Icons on the Home screen and device settings may revert to default and may need to be reconfigured after installation. After installation, your data will be preserved but if you stop the installation incorrectly by removing the battery, your device may not work normally. To avoid unexpected data loss, we recommend that you back up important data before installation.

INSTALL

**You can check this box to set a schedule for updates.**    ③

---

**Software update**

Your device will now restart and install updates.

OK

④

## Arranging Scheduled Software Updates

For simplicity, you can set your Galaxy Note 5 to install software updates on a schedule. To do so, check the Scheduled Software Updates box on the Software Update screen.

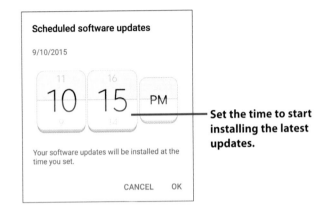

Set the time to start installing the latest updates.

On the Scheduled Software Updates screen, use the dials to set the time you want your Galaxy Note 5 to start installing the latest updates. You then tap the OK button, and your Galaxy Note 5 will run the updates at the time you specified. If there are multiple updates, the Galaxy Note 5 downloads and installs them in sequence, so it might take some time to finish the updates.

## Download Software Updates via Wi-Fi Whenever Possible

Unless you have an unlimited data plan, it's wise to download software updates via Wi-Fi rather than the cellular network. Not only can the update files be large enough to deplete your data plan, but downloading the files via cellular tends to use up more of your precious battery power than downloading via Wi-Fi.

# Optimizing the Battery

Your Galaxy Note 5 contains a lithium-ion battery that provides good battery life as long as you take care of it. You can change the way you use your Galaxy Note 5 to prolong the battery life so that the battery lasts long enough for you to use the phone all day.

## It's Not All Good

**You Can't Change the Battery on the Galaxy Note 5**

Previous Galaxy Note models had a removable back that enabled you to change the battery in seconds, so you could carry around an extra battery or two and switch batteries when running low on power.

The Galaxy Note 5 has a fixed back, so you cannot open the device without surgery. Replacing the battery on the Galaxy Note 5 is a job for a trained technician armed with good tools.

## Take Care of the Battery

There are specific steps you follow to take care of the battery in your Galaxy Note 5 and make it last longer.

Follow these steps to care for your Galaxy Note 5's battery:

1. Try to avoid discharging the battery completely. Fully discharging the battery too frequently harms the battery. Instead, try to keep it at least partially charged at all times (except as described in the next step).

2. To avoid a false battery-level indication on your Galaxy Note 5, let the battery fully discharge about every 30 charges. Lithium-ion batteries do not have "memory" like older battery technologies, but fully discharging the battery once in a while helps keep the battery meter working correctly.

3. Avoid letting your Galaxy Note 5 get overheated because this can damage the battery and make it lose charge quickly. Do not leave your Galaxy Note 5 in a hot car or out in the sun anywhere, including on the beach.

4. Consider having multiple chargers. For example, you could have one at home, one at work, and one in your car. This enables you to always keep your phone charged.

# Monitor Battery Use

Android enables you to see exactly
what apps and system processes are
using the battery on your Galaxy
Note 5. Armed with this information,
you can alter your usage patterns to
extend the Galaxy Note 5's run time
on the battery.

1. On the Apps screen, tap Settings.

2. In the System section, tap Battery
   to display the Battery screen.

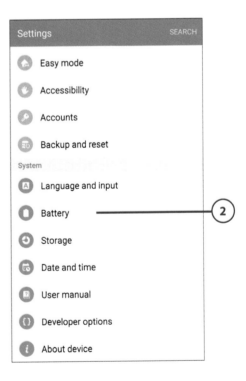

3. Look at the Estimated Usage Time Remaining readout to see approximately how much usage time is left.

4. Look at the Power Saving Mode readout to see how much time you might get by switching on Power Saving mode, which you can do by tapping this button. The next section, "Configure and Use Power Saving Mode," explains Power Saving mode.

5. Look at the Ultra Power Saving Mode readout to see how much time you might get by switching on Ultra Power Saving mode, which you can do by tapping this button. The section "Use Ultra Power Saving Mode," later in this chapter, explains Ultra Power Saving mode.

6. Enable or disable the power readout on the status bar by setting the Show Power on Status Bar switch to On or Off.

7. Tap Battery Usage to display the Battery Usage screen.

8. Look at the usage diagram to see how the battery use has varied during the period monitored.

9. Tap Refresh to update the display with the latest information.

10. Look at the Usage Since Last Fully Charged readout to see how long the Galaxy Note 5 has been running since the battery was last fully charged.

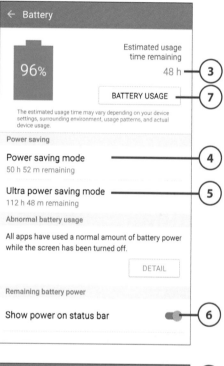

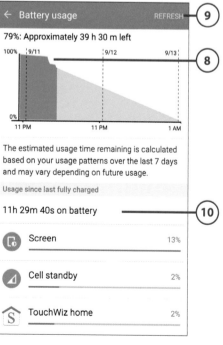

11. Look at the list of features and apps to see which of them have used the most power. The list is sorted by power consumption, so the greediest features and apps appear at the top. Usually, you will need to scroll down to see other features and apps.

12. Tap a feature or an app to see more details about it. For example, tap Screen to display the Use Details screen, which shows the percentage of power the screen has used, the length of time it has been on, and suggestions for adjusting the power usage.

13. Tap the arrow button or the Back button to go back to the Battery Usage screen.

14. Tap the arrow button or the Back button to go back to the Battery screen.

## How Can Seeing Battery Drain Help?

If you look at the way your battery has been draining, you can see when the battery was draining the fastest, and you should be able to remember what apps you were using at that time or what you were doing on your Galaxy Note 5. Based on that, you can change your usage habits—for example, you can plan to charge your Galaxy Note 5 after a session of phone calls. You can uninstall any apps that appear to be power hogs, or you can simply avoid using them when running on the battery.

If you need to extend battery runtime, make sure you turn down the brightness of the screen. You don't have to make the screen unusably dim—even turning down the brightness part of the way can make a huge difference to battery life.

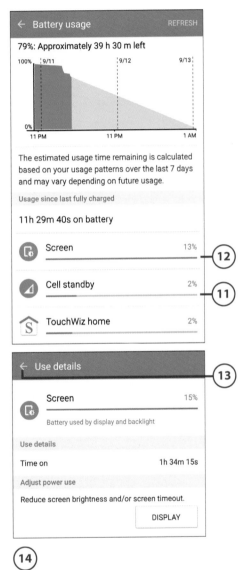

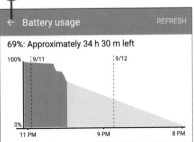

# Configure and Use Power Saving Mode

Your Galaxy Note 5 includes a feature called Power Saving mode that enables you to reduce the amount of power the Note 5 consumes. You can enable Power Saving mode in the Settings app. After enabling Power Saving mode, you can choose whether to start saving power immediately or when the battery level goes down to a certain percentage.

## How Does Power Saving Mode Save Power?

Power Saving mode saves power in four main ways. First, it limits the maximum performance of the processor. Second, it reduces the brightness of the screen and the rate at which the screen refreshes. Third, it disables the light for the soft keys (the Recents button and the Back button) below the screen and disables vibration feedback (such as when you type). Fourth and last, it turns off the screen more quickly after the Galaxy Note 5 receives notifications when you're not otherwise using the device.

For times when the battery is dangerously low, the Galaxy Note 5 also includes a feature called Ultra Power Saving mode that reduces power usage to a minimum by changing the Home screen to grayscale and limiting the number of apps you can use. See the section "Use Ultra Power Saving Mode," later in this chapter, for coverage of this feature.

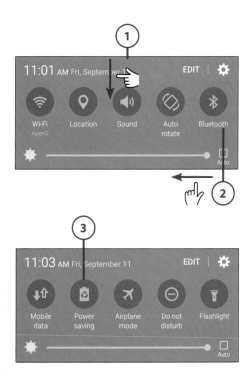

1. Pull down from the top of the screen to open the Notification shade.

2. Scroll the Quick Buttons bar left.

3. Tap and hold Power Saving until the Power Saving Mode screen appears.

4. Set the Power Saving Mode switch to On.

5. Tap Start Power Saving to display the Start Power Saving screen.

6. Tap immediately if you want to start using Power Saving mode immediately. Otherwise, tap the button for the level at which you want to start using Power Saving mode, such as At 50% Battery Power or At 20% Battery Power. When you make your choice, the Power Saving Mode screen appears again.

← Power saving mode

On

**Start power saving**
At 50% battery power

Save battery power by limiting the maximum CPU performance, reducing screen brightness and frame rate, turning off the touch key light, turning off Vibration feedback, and reducing the time before the screen is turned off when notifications are received.

**5** **6** **4**

← Start power saving

○ Immediately

○ At 5% battery power

○ At 15% battery power

○ At 20% battery power

◉ At 50% battery power

## Turning Power Saving Mode On and Off Quickly

When you need to squeeze the most run time out of your Galaxy Note 5's battery, you'll probably want to turn Power Saving mode on and off at a moment's notice. To do so, pull down from the top of the screen to display the Notification shade, scroll the Quick Buttons bar left to display the second set of buttons, and then tap the Power Saving button.

**Tap the Power Saving button to turn Power Saving Mode on or off.**

# Use Ultra Power Saving Mode

Using the regular Power Saving mode can net you much more run time on the battery, but when you're in serious danger of running out of power, you can switch to Ultra Power Saving mode. Ultra Power Saving mode changes the screen to grayscale, restricts you to essential apps, turns off Wi-Fi and Bluetooth, and allows cellular data only when the screen is on. So it's really no fun at all. It's more of a get-you-home measure (or a get-you-to-a-power-source measure)—the Galaxy Note 5's equivalent of a spare tire.

Follow these steps to turn on Ultra Power Saving mode:

1. On the Apps screen, tap Settings.

2. In the System section, tap Battery to display the Battery screen.

3. Tap Ultra Power Saving Mode to display the Ultra Power Saving Mode screen.

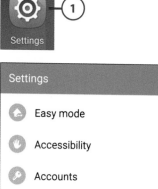

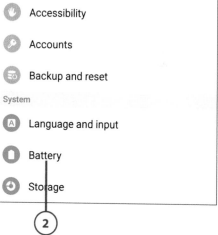

4. Set the Ultra Power Saving Mode switch to On. The Ultra Power Saving Mode Home screen appears.

## Accepting the Terms and Conditions for Ultra Power Saving Mode

The first time you turn on Ultra Power Saving mode, your Galaxy Note 5 displays a Terms and Conditions screen emphasizing that the run time that Ultra Power Saving Mode displays may not be strictly accurate because it depends on your device's network configuration, what you're doing with the device, and a handful of other variables, including the operating temperature (yes, really). You must check the box agreeing to the terms and conditions and then tap the Agree button before you can start using Ultra Power Saving mode.

5. Look at the Battery Percentage readout and the Estimated Max. Standby Time readout to see how long Ultra Power Saving mode might give you.

## Bare-Bones Home Screen

At first, the Home screen displays the icons for only three apps: Phone, Messages, and Internet. You can customize the apps (see the next section) on the Home screen by adding other apps from the meager selection that Ultra Power Saving mode offers; after that, you can remove any apps you've added, but you cannot change the three default apps.

## Customize the Home Screen in Ultra Power Saving Mode

1. Tap one of the Add (+) buttons to display the Add Application screen. Tap the button for the position in which you want to add the app.

2. Tap the app you want to add. The app appears on the Home screen. You can then repeat the steps to add other apps, up to the maximum of six.

3. To remove one of the apps you've added, tap the More button. The menu opens.

4. Tap Remove. The Home screen opens for customization.

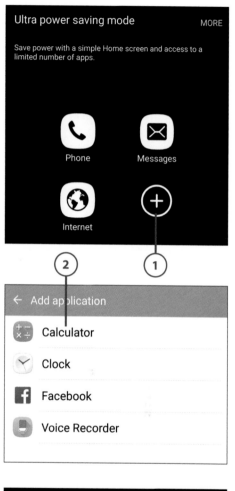

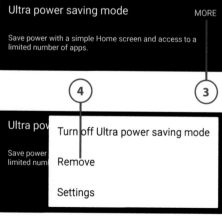

5. Tap Delete (–) for the app you want to remove.

6. Tap OK to stop customizing the Home screen.

## Choosing Settings in Ultra Power Saving Mode

Ultra Power Saving mode enables you to configure a limited range of settings. To do so, tap the More button on the Home screen and tap Settings to display the Settings screen. You can then tap the appropriate button—Wi-Fi, Bluetooth, Airplane Mode, Mobile Networks, Location, Sound, or Brightness—and configure settings as usual.

**Ultra power saving mode**

Tap the Delete button to remove the item from the Home screen.

 Phone

 Messages

 Internet

 Calculator

 Voice Recorder

 Facebook

OK

⑥ ⑤

## Turn Off Ultra Power Saving Mode

1. Tap the More button on the Home screen in Ultra Power Saving Mode.

2. Tap Turn Off Ultra Power Saving Mode. The Galaxy Note 5 turns off Ultra Power Saving Mode, and the normal, colorful Home screen appears once more.

**Ultra power saving mode**    MORE

Save power with a simple Home screen and access to a limited number of apps.

② ①

Ultra po...

Save power
limited num...

Turn off Ultra power saving mode

Remove

Settings

# Manage Apps and Memory

Your Galaxy Note 5 can run many apps at the same time. With Android, you don't normally close apps between uses or after using them; instead, you leave them running in the background, which enables you to switch quickly to a running app when you need to use it again. However, when you want to close apps, you can easily close either individual apps or all the apps you're running.

The Galaxy Note 5 provides two tools for managing apps and memory:

- **Recent Apps list**—You can close one or more apps quickly from the Recent Apps list when you no longer want those apps open.

- **Application Manager**—If you suspect that an app is slowing down your Galaxy Note 5, you can open Application Manager and display the Running screen. From here, you can display the Active App screen for the app and force the app to close.

## Close One or More Apps from the Recent Apps List

The quick way to close one or more apps is by using the Recent Apps list. Follow these steps:

1. From whichever screen you're currently on, tap the Recents button to display the Recent Apps screen.

2. Swipe each app you want to close off the list to the left or right.

3. If you want to close all open apps, tap Close All.

# Force an App or a Service to Close

If closing apps from the Recent Apps screen doesn't solve the problems your Galaxy Note 5 is exhibiting, you might need to force an app or a service to close. This is an action you should take only to resolve problems, not as a regular move.

To force an app or service to close, follow these steps:

1. On the Apps screen, tap Settings to open the Settings app.

2. In the Device section, tap Applications to display the Applications screen.

3. Tap Application Manager to display the Application Manager screen.

4. Swipe left one or more times as needed to display the Running tab. This tab lists the apps that are currently running.

5. Look at the graph to see how much memory is being used by running apps and cached processes, and how much is free.

6. Tap an app to display the Active App screen, which contains more information about the app.

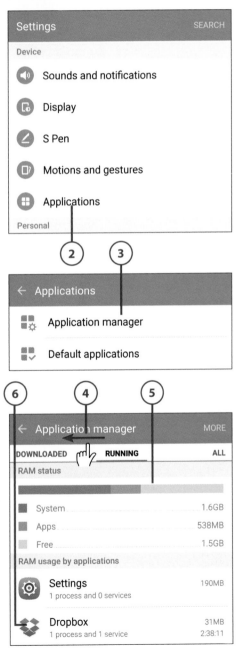

7. Look at the Processes readout to see the processes that this app is using.

8. Tap Report to report an app to Google. You might want to do this if it is misbehaving, using up too many resources, or you suspect it of stealing data. Some apps disable the Report button to prevent reporting.

9. Tap Stop if you believe the app is misbehaving.

## When Should You Manually Stop a Service or an App?

After you have been using your Galaxy Note 5 for a while, you'll become familiar with how long it takes to do certain tasks, such as typing, navigating menus, and so on. If you notice your phone becoming slow or not behaving the way you think it should, the culprit could be a new app you recently installed or a system service that has encountered a problem. Because Android doesn't normally quit an app or a service, the app or service continues running in the background, which might cause your Galaxy Note 5 to slow down. When this happens, it is useful to manually stop the app or service. If stopping one or more apps or services doesn't help, try restarting your Galaxy Note 5.

**Stop system service?**

If you stop this service, some features of your device may stop working correctly until you power it off and then on again.

CANCEL       OK

**Tap OK to confirm you want to stop a system service.**

# Reining in Your Data Usage

If you are worried that you might exceed your data plan in a month, you can set a usage limit on your Galaxy Note 5. You can even prevent apps from using data while they are running in the background rather than in the foreground.

**1.** On the Apps screen, tap Settings to open the Settings app.

2. In either the Quick Settings section or the Connections section, tap Data Usage to display the Data Usage screen.

3. Make sure the Mobile Data switch is set to On to enable data transfer over your Galaxy Note 5's cellular connection.

4. Tap the Set Mobile Data Limit switch to On to enable or disable mobile data limits. When the mobile data limit is enabled, your Galaxy Note 5 automatically cuts off all mobile data usage when the limit you set in step 7 is reached.

5. Tap the Cycle pop-up menu to set the monthly billing cycle your cellular carrier uses for your Galaxy Note 5's account.

6. Tap the red handle and drag the red line up or down to select the mobile data limit you want to impose. This might or might not match your cellular data plan limit.

7. Tap the black handle and drag the black line up and down to set a data usage warning threshold. When you reach or pass this threshold, you see a warning in the Notification bar.

8. Tap Background Data to display the Background Data screen.

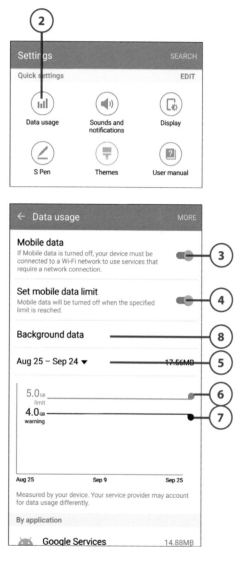

9. Set the switch for each app to On if you want the app to be able to transfer data across the cellular connection when it is in the background or to Off if you want to prevent the app from transferring data in the background.

10. Tap the arrow button or the Back button to return to the Data Usage screen.

11. In the By Application list, tap an app whose data usage you want to examine. The Application Data Usage screen for the app appears.

12. Look at the Data Usage chart to see the data usage for this app specifically.

13. Look at the Foreground readout and Background readout to see the breakdown of data usage in the foreground and background.

14. Tap the arrow button or the Back button to return to the Data Usage screen.

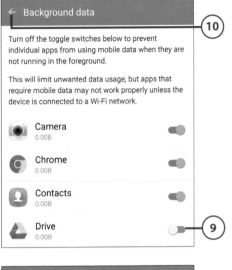

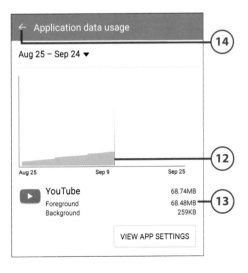

# Caring for the Galaxy Note 5's Exterior

Because you need to touch your Galaxy Note 5's screen to use it, it picks up oils and other residue from your hands. You also might get dirt on other parts of the phone. Here is how to clean your Galaxy Note 5 and how to avoid damaging its multipurpose jack:

- Wipe the screen with a microfiber cloth. You can purchase these in most electronic stores, or you can use the one that came with your sunglasses.

- To clean dirt off other parts of your phone, wipe it with a damp cloth. Soap and chemical cleaners can damage your Galaxy Note 5, so never use them.

- When inserting the connector on the USB cable, try not to force it in the wrong way. If you damage the pins inside your Galaxy Note 5, you will need to use a wireless charger.

## Protecting Your Galaxy Note 5's Exterior

Another way to care for your Galaxy Note 5's exterior is to protect it with a case. Many different types of cases are available from both brick-and-mortar stores and online stores. To protect the screen, you can apply a screen protector. When choosing a screen protector, make sure it is thin enough for the S Pen to work effectively.

# Getting Help with Your Galaxy Note 5

There are many resources on the Internet where you can get help with your Galaxy Note 5 and Android. Here are five sites to explore:

1. Visit Samsung's official Galaxy Note 5 site at www.samsung.com/global/galaxy/galaxy-note5/.

2. Visit Google's official Android website at www.android.com.

3. Check out Android blogs such as these:

- Android Central at www.androidcentral.com/

- Android Guys at www.androidguys.com/

- Androinica at http://androinica.com/

Measure your stress level using the sensor built in to the Galaxy Note 5.

In this chapter, you discover how to use the powerful S Health app that comes with your Galaxy Note 5. Topics include the following:

→ Performing initial setup
→ Configuring S Health to suit your needs
→ Tracking your activities, diet, and vital signs

# Using S Health

Your Galaxy Note 5 includes Samsung's S Health app for tracking health and activity information. S Health offers three overarching fitness goals, a wide range of built-in trackers that you can use to track everything from your heart rate to your caffeine intake, and several training programs focused on running. S Health can also interoperate with third-party apps that are designed to analyze health and activity information and to derive reports or recommendations from them.

## What Is S Health For?

Samsung's terms and conditions make it clear that S Health is "intended for fitness and wellness purposes only" and not for diagnosing, mitigating, treating, curing, or preventing disease or conditions.

Similarly, please be clear that this book does not offer health or diet advice, and that even if you manage to construe any of its contents as such, you should not follow it without seeking professional medical advice.

# Performing Initial Setup

Before you can start using S Health, you must agree to its terms, conditions, and disclaimers. If you want to store your data online, you must also sign in to your Samsung account and connect S Health to the account; so if you don't yet have a Samsung account, you must create one.

1. On the Apps screen, tap S Health. The introductory screen appears.

2. Check the upper I Agree check box.

3. Tap the lower I Agree check box.

4. Tap the Next button. The Welcome screen appears, running through a sequence of healthful activities accompanied by supposedly suitable colors.

**Tap Terms and Conditions to read S Health's many terms and conditions.**

S Health is for fitness and wellness, not medical purposes.

Terms and conditions

☑ I agree

To provide aspects of its functionality, S Health may collect data on the following:

👣 Profile
☐ Sensors and usage
○ Location

Privacy Policy

☑ I agree

NEXT →

**Tap Privacy Policy to read the Privacy Policy – S Health Supplement.**

5. Tap the Sign In button if you want to sign in to your Samsung account. Signing in enables you to store your health data online and access it from other devices. See the nearby sidebar titled "Is It Safe to Store My Health Data Online with Samsung?" for advice about whether to store your data online.

6. Tap the Enter ID field and type the ID for your Samsung account—for example, the email address you used to set up the account.

7. Tap the Enter Password field and type your password. You can check the Show Password check box if you need to verify you've typed the password correctly.

8. Tap the Sign In button. The S Health dashboard screen appears, displaying a Welcome to S Health! banner and items you can add to the dashboard.

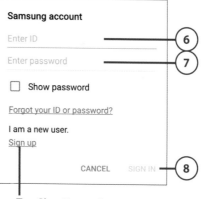

**Welcome!**

S Health is an app that can help you manage your health and exercise better.

With a Samsung account, you can back up and restore your health data easily.

SKIP                    SIGN IN → ⑤

**Tap Skip to store your S Health data only on your Galaxy Note 5.**

Samsung account

Enter ID ——— ⑥

Enter password ——— ⑦

☐ Show password

Forgot your ID or password?

I am a new user.
Sign up

              CANCEL    SIGN IN — ⑧

**Tap Sign Up to sign up for a Samsung account.**

## It's Not All Good

### Is It Safe to Store My Health Data Online with Samsung?

The S Health app encourages you to store your health data online on Samsung's S Health server—but should you do so? Storing your data online has clear advantages, such as being able to access your data from any device or restore your data if you change your phone. But it also raises concerns about your privacy that you should think about first.

There are three main concerns here. The first concern is that you are giving Samsung your information and allowing Samsung to manipulate it in any way specified by the terms and conditions to which you agree. As with any site or service, the terms and conditions might change, and any change may or may not be in your favor. So you might want to revisit the Terms and Conditions page periodically to verify exactly what you're permitting. (After setup, you can view the Terms and Conditions by tapping More, tapping Settings, tapping About S Health, and then tapping Terms and Conditions on the About S Health screen. This screen also has a link to the S Health Supplement to Samsung's Privacy Policy.)

The second concern is that someone might hack Samsung's servers and get access to your information. Recent history has shown that very few companies and organizations can secure their networks effectively against determined hackers, so it's worth taking this threat seriously.

The third concern is simply the amount of data you are giving Samsung (and any potential hacker). The S Health Supplement to Samsung's Privacy Policy makes clear that S Health collects data including your name, date of birth, height, photo, location, stress level, body temperature, blood glucose level…, and on and on. There's nothing sinister in this—collecting sensitive health data is much of the point of the app. But however noble and benevolent the app's aims, the net result is that Samsung ends up with a huge amount of data about you, some of which is definitely sensitive and some of which is potentially sensitive.

So you must decide whether the benefits to storing your health data online with Samsung outweigh the real and potential drawbacks. There's no single answer that's right for everyone.

# Customizing the S Health Dashboard

Now that you've finished initial setup, the S Health Dashboard appears. The Dashboard combines readouts showing your activities and progress with quick access to all your items.

Before you start using S Health, you should set up the Dashboard with the goals, trackers, and programs you want to use.

## What Are Goals, Trackers, and Programs?

S Health uses three types of components for tracking and logging your activities: goals, trackers, and programs.

A goal has daily targets and long-term aims. There are three goals, which you can enable or disable as needed. The first goal is the Be More Active goal, which has a target number of active minutes in a day. The second goal is the Eat Healthier goal, which has a target number of calories for you to consume, and also tracks the nutritional content of what you eat. The third goal is the Feel More Rested goal, which logs your sleep hours.

S Health includes a wide range of trackers, including Steps, Walking, Running, Cycling, Sports, Food, Water, Caffeine, Sleep, Heart Rate, and Stress. Some trackers use the sensors built into your Galaxy Note 5, but others require you either to use a third-party device that can communicate with S Health or to log data manually. For example, you can use a sleep monitor to log your sleep hours automatically, or you can enter them in the Sleep tracker automatically. For other trackers, such as Food and Caffeine, you must enter your consumption manually, because—fortunately—no automated monitor is available.

You can also add third-party trackers to S Health to enable yourself to track other fitness or health metrics.

A program is a training program designed to get you to perform a specific race. As of this writing, S Health has four programs: Baby Steps to 5K, Run 5K, First Attempt at 10K, and Run 10K. (K stands for kilometers.)

## Add Goals to the Dashboard

Begin your customization of the S Health Dashboard by choosing which of the three goals to add to it. Each goal appears in a temporary box at first, enabling you easily to either add the goal or remove it.

# Add or Remove the Be More Active Goal

1. Tap the Let's Go button if you want to view tips on how to get started with S Health.

2. Tap the × button to close the Welcome to S Health banner.

3. Tap the Add button on the Be More Active box to display the Be More Active screen.

4. Drag the Active Minutes per Day slider until your target number of active minutes appears in the box.

5. Tap the Start button. The Be More Active widget appears on the Dashboard, showing your progress toward the Be More Active goal.

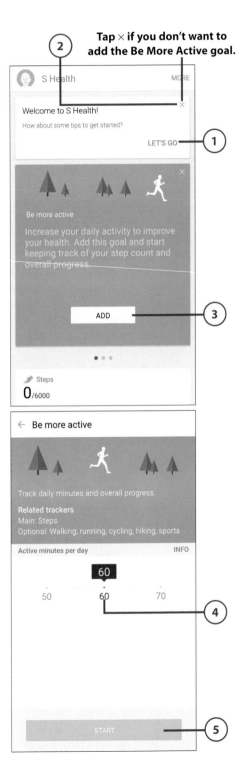

Tap × if you don't want to add the Be More Active goal.

6. Swipe left on the Be More Active widget to display the Eat Healthier box. You can then set up the Eat Healthier goal as explained in the next section—if you want to do so.

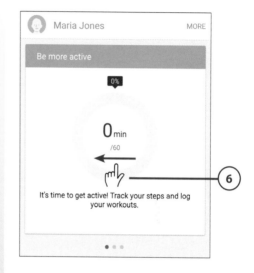

## What Does the Active Minutes per Day Setting Count?

The Active Minutes per Day setting in S Health counts light, moderate, and vigorous activity. An example of light activity is walking, and S Health uses the Steps tracker as the main related tracker for the Be More Active goal. Moderate activity includes things like cycling or swimming, both at a medium pace rather than a lung-busting sprint. Vigorous activity includes running, cage-fighting, and other pursuits that exhaust you in short order.

Fitness and medical authorities argue endlessly about how much activity and exercise people need, but many agree that a minimum of 30 minutes of moderate-intensity activity per day is a good target.

## Add or Remove the Eat Healthier Goal

1. Tap the Add button on the Eat Healthier box to display the Eat Healthier screen.

**Tap × if you don't want to add the Eat Healthier goal.**

2. Drag the Daily Calories (Cal) slider until your target intake appears in the box.

3. Tap the Start button. The Eat Healthier widget appears on the Dashboard, showing your progress toward your calorie target.

4. Swipe left on the Eat Healthier widget to display the Feel More Rested box. You can then set up the Feel More Rested goal as explained in the next section.

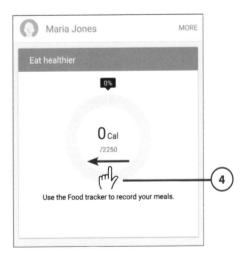

# Add or Remove the Feel More Rested Goal

**Tap ✕ if you don't want to add the Feel More Rested goal.**

S Health's third goal is the Feel More Rested goal. This goal requires you to either log your sleep hours manually or wear a device that can record your sleep data and sync it with S Health.

1. Tap the Add button on the Feel More Rested box to display the Feel More Rested screen.

2. Drag the Bedtime slider until your target bedtime appears in the box.

3. Drag the Wake-Up Time slider until your target wake-up time appears in the box.

4. Tap the Start button. The Feel More Rested widget appears on the Dashboard, showing a rating dial for your sleep.

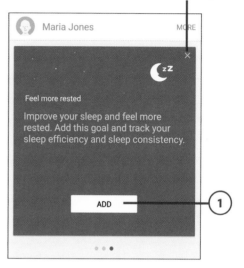

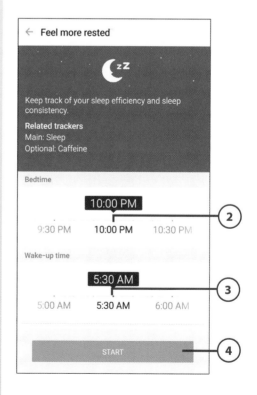

## Navigating Among Goals

Now that you have added your goals to the Dashboard, you can swipe left or right to navigate from one goal to another. The goals wrap around, so you can swipe left from the last goal to display the first goal or swipe right from the first goal to display the last goal.

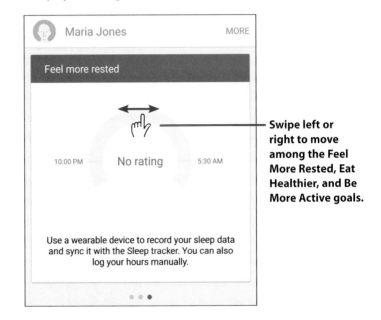

Swipe left or right to move among the Feel More Rested, Eat Healthier, and Be More Active goals.

You find out more about how to add data to the Eat Healthier goal in the section "Record Your Food Intake," later in this chapter. See how to add sleep data in the section "Record Your Sleep Hours," even later in this chapter.

# Set Up the Dashboard with the Trackers and Programs You Need

After choosing which—if any—of the three goals to use on your Dashboard, you can set up the trackers you want to use. The Dashboard comes with several trackers preconfigured and suggests other trackers you might want to add, but you can remove any tracker or suggested tracker and use only those you actually want.

While adding trackers, you might also want to add one of the training programs that S Health includes, such as the Run 5K program. Programs appear at the top of the Dashboard in the Goals area, so you swipe left or right to move among your programs and your goals.

1. From the Goals section at the top of the Dashboard, swipe up to scroll down until you see the Trackers section.

2. You can tap the Measure button on a tracker that uses the Galaxy Note 5's measurement devices. Such trackers include Heart Rate, $SpO_2$, and Stress.

3. You can tap the Start button on a tracker that measures your activity. Such trackers include Running.

4. You can tap × to remove a suggested tracker from the Dashboard.

5. Tap the Add button on a tracker such as the Food tracker to add data to the tracker. For example, for the Food tracker, you can add a meal or a snack.

6. At the bottom of the Dashboard, tap the Manage Items button to display the Manage Items screen. This screen has three tabs: the Trackers tab, the Goals tab, and the Programs tab.

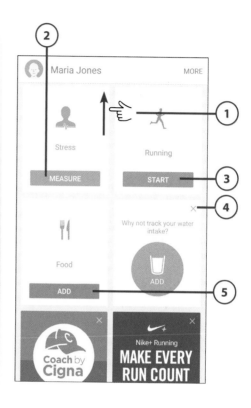

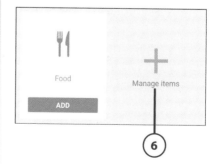

7. Set a switch to Off to remove that tracker from the Dashboard.

8. Set a switch to On to add that tracker to the Dashboard.

9. Tap Programs to display the Programs screen, which you use for adding specific training programs to S Health.

10. Tap the program you want to add. This example uses Run 5K.

Tap Goals to display the Goals screen and change your goals.

Notes indicate which trackers are tied to your goals.

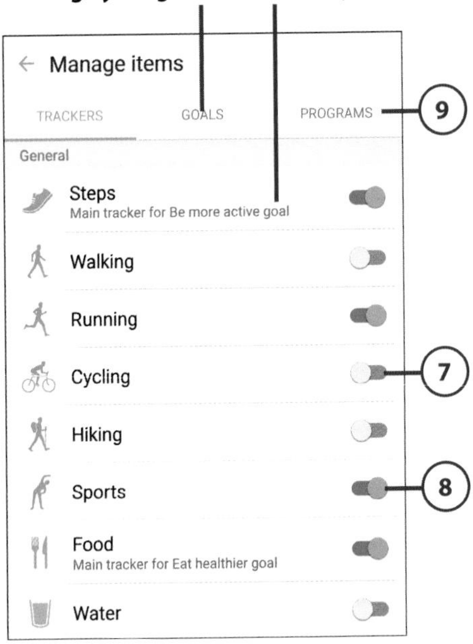

**Manage items**

TRACKERS     GOALS     PROGRAMS — 9

General

Steps
Main tracker for Be more active goal

Walking

Running

Cycling — 7

Hiking

Sports — 8

Food
Main tracker for Eat healthier goal

Water

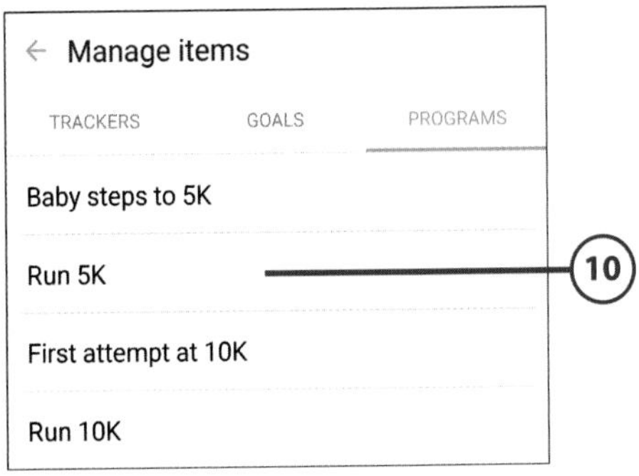

**Manage items**

TRACKERS     GOALS     PROGRAMS

Baby steps to 5K

Run 5K — 10

First attempt at 10K

Run 10K

11. Tap the Start button and choose your start date.

12. In the Workout Days bar, tap the buttons to select the days you want to work out. (Note: If you don't conform to the specified number of days for the workout, S Health will chide you.)

13. Tap the Add Program button. S Health adds the program and then displays the Dashboard again.

## Drag Your Dashboard Items into Order

Apart from the goals and programs at the top of the Dashboard, you can drag any of the other items into your preferred order. To move an item, tap and hold it until it becomes mobile, and then drag it to where you want it. Drop the item on another item to make the two items switch places.

← Run 5K

This program will help beginning runners improve their stamina. After 10 weeks, you should be able to run either 5 km (3.1 mi) at a time or for 30 minutes without stopping. Are you ready?

**Related trackers**
Running

Program overview

Total workouts   Number of weeks
30               10

Start        –    Wed, Oct 14, 2015    ⑪

End               Sun, Dec 20, 2015

Workout days ————⑫
3 workouts per week

S  M  T  W  T  F  S

Choose your workout days.

ADD PROGRAM ————⑬

# Configuring S Health to Suit Your Needs

S Health has a ton of configuration options, and it's a good idea to set them to suit your needs before you spend a lot of time using the app.

First, you might want to set your profile so that S Health knows basic information such as your gender, height, and weight.

# Set Your Profile

1. Tap your photo or the placeholder icon to display the My Page screen. Until you enter your details, this displays default profile information for a male born the first day in 1980.

2. Tap the Edit button to display the screen for editing the profile.

3. Tap the Name field and type your name the way you prefer it to appear.

4. Tap the Photo icon if you want to add a photo to the profile. You can either take a photo with the camera or use a photo that's already on your Galaxy Note 5.

5. On the Gender line, tap the Male option button or the Female option button, as appropriate.

6. On the Birthday line, tap the date button, and then use the controls to pick your official birthday.

7. On the Height line, enter your height. You can tap the pop-up arrow button to switch between centimeters and feet-and-inch measurements.

8. On the Weight line, enter your weight. (Be honest.) You can tap the pop-up arrow button to switch between kilograms and pounds.

9. On the Activity Level line, tap the button that corresponds to your activity level, from 1 (Little to No Activity) to 5 (Very Heavy Activity).

10. Tap the Save button to save the changes you've made. The My Page screen appears again, now showing the information you entered.

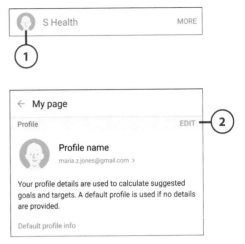

11. Tap the arrow button or the Back button below the screen. The Home screen appears again.

# Choose Settings for S Health

To choose settings for S Health, you first open the S Health Settings screen, which you can reach from the Home screen in the S Health app. From the S Health Settings screen, you can configure account settings, unit settings, notifications settings, and data permissions settings. You can also erase all of your S Health data if necessary.

## Display the S Health Settings Screen

1. In S Health, tap the More button to open the menu.

2. Tap Settings to display the S Health Settings screen.

## Choose Account Settings for S Health

1. On the S Health Settings screen, tap Account. The Account screen appears, showing controls for configuring how to sync your account.

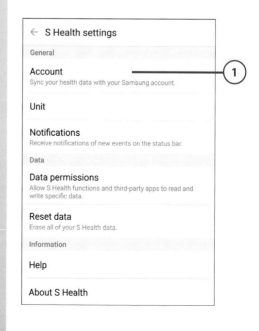

2. Tap your account to display the Samsung account screen. From here, you can tap Profile to display your account information profile, or tap Terms and Conditions if you want to revisit the terms and conditions.

3. Tap Sync Now to sync your account data to the S Health server. The Syncing readout appears under your account name as S Health syncs the data. Then the Last Synced readout appears, showing the date and time of the last sync.

4. Set the Auto Sync switch to On if you want S Health to sync your data automatically. This is normally a good idea if you want to store your S Health data online.

5. Set the Sync via Wi-Fi Only switch to On if you want to prevent S Health from syncing via cellular connections. This is a good idea if you have a limited data plan.

6. Tap the arrow button or the Back button below the screen to return to the S Health Settings screen.

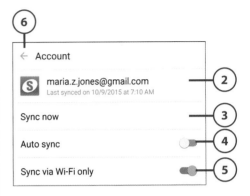

← Account

S maria.z.jones@gmail.com
Last synced on 10/9/2015 at 7:10 AM — **2**

Sync now — **3**

Auto sync — **4**

Sync via Wi-Fi only — **5**

## Choose Unit Settings for S Health

1. On the S Health Settings screen, tap Unit. The Unit screen appears, showing controls for choosing the measurement units to display for height, weight, temperature, distance, and blood-glucose levels.

← S Health settings

General

Account
Sync your health data with your Samsung account.

Unit

**2.** Tap Height and then tap "cm" or "ft, in" on the pop-up menu.

**3.** Tap Weight and then tap "kg" or "lb" on the pop-up menu.

**4.** Tap Temperature and then tap °C or °F on the pop-up menu.

**5.** Tap Distance and then tap "km" or "mi" on the pop-up menu.

**6.** Tap Blood Glucose and then tap "mg/dL" or "mmol/L" on the pop-up menu.

**7.** Tap the arrow button or the Back button below the screen to return to the S Health Settings screen.

(7)

← Unit

Height — (2)
ft, in

Weight — (3)
lb

Temperature — (4)
°C

Distance — (5)
mi

Blood glucose — (6)
mmol/L

## What Are the Blood Glucose Measurement Units?

S Health gives you a choice of two measurement units for blood-glucose levels: mg/dL and mmol/L. Normally, you would choose whichever measurement unit your monitoring device or healthcare professional uses.

Milligrams per deciliter (mg/dL) is the standard for measurement used in the U.S. and in much of Europe. A normal fasting blood-glucose measurement for a person without diabetes is in the range 70 mg/dL to 99 mg/dL. A fasting measurement is taken after eight hours with no food.

Millimoles per liter (mmol/L) is the standard for measurement used in the UK. A normal fasting blood-glucose measurement for a person without diabetes is in the range 4 mmol/L to 6 mmol/L.

# Choose Notifications Settings for S Health

1. On the S Health Settings screen, tap Notifications to display the Notifications screen.

2. Set the Notifications switch to On if you want to receive notifications from S Health.

3. Set the Inactive Time Alerts switch to On if you want the Steps Tracker feature to alert you when you have been inactive for a specific length of time during the time period you specify.

4. If you set the Inactive Time Alerts switch to On, tap the Set Inactive Time Alerts button to display the Track Inactive Time screen. If you set this switch to Off, skip to step 8.

5. Tap Time of Day to display the Time of Day screen. Here, you can set the Always switch to On if you want S Health to give you inactive time notifications all the time. Usually, you'd want to set the Always switch to Off and use the From button and To button to specify the hours during which you want to receive inactive time notifications. Tap the arrow button or the Back button below the screen to return to the Track Inactive Time screen.

6. Tap Notification Interval and then tap the interval on the pop-up menu to specify how frequently S Health should notify you about being inactive. Your choices are 30 Min, 1 Hr, 1 Hr 30 Min, and 2 Hr.

7. Tap the arrow button or the Back button below the screen to return to the Notifications screen.

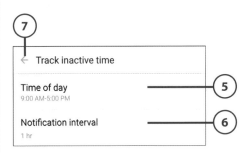

8. Set the Food Logging Reminders switch to On if you want S Health to raise notifications reminding you of the Eat Healthier goal.

9. Set the Sleep Logging Reminders switch to On if you want S Health to raise notifications reminding you of the Feel More Rested goal.

10. Set the Program Reminders switch to On if you want to receive notifications from apps reminding you of your goals.

11. Set the Earned Reward Alerts switch to On if you want to receive notifications from goals and trackers telling you about the rewards you have earned.

12. Tap the arrow button or the Back button below the screen to return to the S Health Settings screen.

## Choose Data Permissions Settings for S Health

If you have added third-party fitness and health apps to your Galaxy Note 5, you can use the Data Permissions screen in S Health settings to control which data each app can access.

1. On the S Health Settings screen, tap Data Permissions to display the Data Permissions screen. This screen contains an entry for each third-party app for which you can set data permissions.

### Which Apps Work with S Health?

You can find a list of apps that work with S Health by going to http://shealth. samsung.com, navigating to the Expand It heading, and clicking the Learn More link.

---

**(12)**

← Notifications

On ⬤

**Inactive time alerts** ⬤
Receive alerts from the Steps tracker during a set time period.

**Set Inactive time alerts**
9:00 AM-5:00 PM / 1 hr

**Food logging reminders** ⬤—**(8)**
Receive reminders for the Eat healthier goal.

**Sleep logging reminders** ⬤—**(9)**
Receive reminders for the Feel more rested goal.

**Program reminders** ⬤—**(10)**
Receive reminders from each program.

**Earned reward alerts** ⬤—**(11)**
Receive notifications of earned rewards from goals and trackers.

---

Data

**Data permissions** ————**(1)**
Allow S Health functions and third-party apps to read and write specific data.

**Reset data**
Erase all of your S Health data.

Information

**Help**

**About S Health**

2. Tap the app for which you want to set data permissions.

3. Set the app's master switch to On to enable the other controls.

4. In the Allowed to Write area, set any switch to On if you want the app to be able to write this type of data to S Health's database.

5. In the Allowed to Read area, set any switch to On if you want the app to be able to read this type of data from S Health's database.

6. Tap the arrow button or the Back button below the screen to return to the Data Permissions screen.

7. Tap the arrow button or the Back button below the screen to return to the S Health Settings screen.

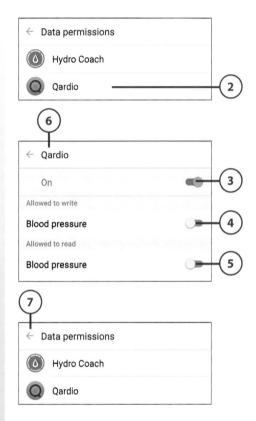

## Erase Your S Health Data

If you decide to stop using S Health, you can erase your S Health data from both your Galaxy Note 5 and from the S Health server. As you would likely expect, deleting the data gets rid of it permanently, so you cannot recover it afterward.

1. On the S Health Settings screen, tap Reset Data to display the Reset Data screen.

2. Read the warning.

3. Tap the Reset button. S Health displays a warning dialog.

4. Tap the Reset button. The Samsung Account screen appears.

5. Tap Confirm Password and type your password.

6. Tap the Confirm button. S Health deletes your data. The app then closes, and the Home screen appears.

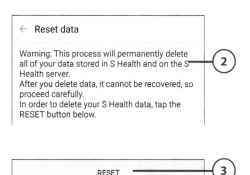

← Reset data

Warning: This process will permanently delete all of your data stored in S Health and on the S Health server.
After you delete data, it cannot be recovered, so proceed carefully.
In order to delete your S Health data, tap the RESET button below.

RESET

All of your S Health data stored on the device, as well as in S Health and on the S Health server, will be permanently deleted. The deletion process may take some time. You will not be able to sign into your account until all of the data is completely deleted.

CANCEL    RESET

← Samsung account

maria.z.jones@gmail.com

Confirm password

☐ Show password

Forgot your ID or password?

CANCEL    CONFIRM

## What Happens If I Delete the S Health App?

You can delete the S Health app from your Galaxy Note 5 in the same way you can delete most other apps, but be warned that deleting S Health does not delete your data from the S Health server. The data stays on the S Health server so you can resume using S Health on another device or after restoring it on your Galaxy Note 5 (if you have deleted the app to resolve configuration or performance issues).

# >>>Go Further
## CONNECT ACCESSORIES TO S HEALTH

Running on your Galaxy Note 5, S Health includes powerful features of its own, but you can extend its capabilities further by connecting accessories. As of this writing, your options include Samsung Gear smartwatches, heart-rate monitors from various manufacturers, step trackers, bike speed and cadence sensors, body-composition monitors, blood-glucose monitors, and other items.

To see the list of accessories your version of S Health supports, tap More to display the menu, and then tap Accessories to display the Accessories screen. You can then tap the accessory you want to learn more about or you want to connect to S Health.

| ← Accessories | SORT BY | |
|---|---|---|
| **Steps** | | |
| Samsung Activity Tracker EI-AN900A | | |
| Samsung | | |
| Samsung Gear | | |
| Samsung | | |
| Samsung Gear 2 | | |
| Samsung | | |
| Samsung Gear 2 Neo | | |
| Samsung | | |
| Samsung Gear Fit | | |
| Samsung | | |
| View more | ⌄ | |
| **Sports** | | |
| Samsung Activity Tracker EI-AN900A | | |
| Samsung | | |

**Tap Sort By to switch the sorting between Manufacturer Name and Trackers.**

**Tap an item to display more information about it.**

**Tap View More to view more items in a category.**

If you have an accessory that's supposed to be compatible with S Health, but that accessory doesn't appear in the list, make sure that S Health is updated to the latest version. See Chapter 11, "Working with Android Apps," for instructions on updating apps.

# Tracking Your Activities

Once you have gotten S Health set up with the goals, trackers, and programs you need, you will find tracking your activities largely straightforward. This section shows you quick examples of working with goals, trackers, and programs.

## Work Toward Your Goals

S Health puts your goals and programs at the top of the Dashboard so that you can reach them instantly.

## Measure Progress Toward the Be More Active Goal

The Be More Active goal appears prominently at the top of the Dashboard, so you can quickly see your progress toward your daily activity goal.

1. View the readouts in the Be More Active box to see a summary of your progress.

2. Tap the Be More Active box to display the Be More Active screen.

3. You can tap the Trends tab button to display the Trends tab, which shows your activity trends. You can view the data by days, by weeks, or by months.

4. You can tap the Rewards tab to see any rewards you have earned. Rewards are digital badges that commemorate your activity accomplishments, not thick slices of triple-frosted chocolate cake.

5. View the Calories Burned timeline to see the different amounts of calories you burned at different hours of the day.

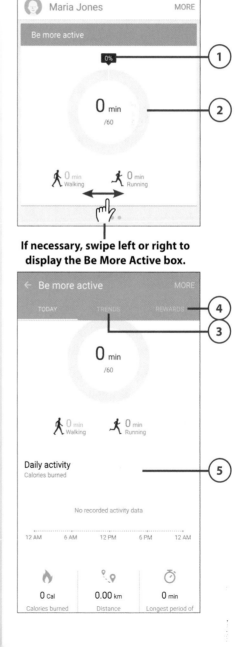

**If necessary, swipe left or right to display the Be More Active box.**

6. View the Calories Burned read-out, the Distance readout, and the Longest Period of Active Min readout to see the details of your activity.

7. Tap the arrow button or the Back button below the screen to return to the Dashboard.

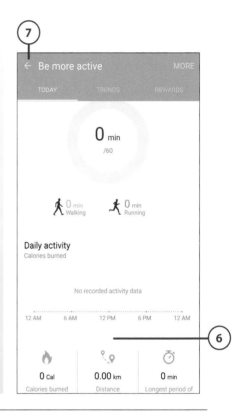

## View Your Step Count and Calories Burned

To view the number of steps you've taken today and learn how many calories you've burned, tap the Steps tracker on the Dashboard.

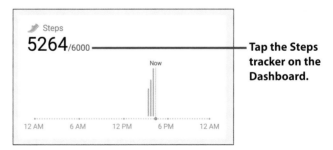

Tap the Steps tracker on the Dashboard.

The Steps screen appears, showing your progress towards the day's step count of 6000 steps, the distance you have covered, the number of calories you have burned, and the number of steps you have taken at a healthy pace. S Health displays the Healthy Pace icon after you maintain a pace of 100 steps a minute or faster for 10 minutes.

You can see how much you walked at which hours.

You can see how far you've walked.

You can see how many calories you've burned by walking.

You can see how many steps you've taken at a brisk pace.

## Record Your Food Intake

If you have enabled the Eat Healthier goal, you need to enter your consumption into S Health.

1. Tap the Eat Healthier box on the Dashboard to display the Eat Healthier screen.

See your current progress toward your calorie goal.

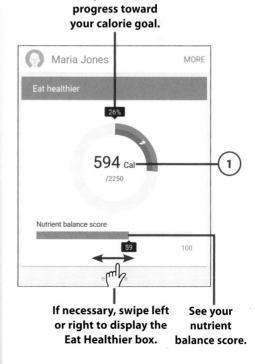

If necessary, swipe left or right to display the Eat Healthier box.

See your nutrient balance score.

2. Tap the meal or snack you want to add; this example uses lunch. The Morning Snack icon appears below the Breakfast icon; the Afternoon Snack icon appears below the Lunch icon; and—as you might guess—the Evening Snack icon appears below the Dinner icon. You are not required to eat all of these.

3. On the Search tab of the screen for the meal, such as the Lunch screen, tap the Search for Food or Restaurant box.

4. Type as much of the word is need-ed to produce suitable matches in the pop-up menu.

5. Tap the best match to display a list of options for that food item.

**Tap Frequent to see food items you've frequently entered.** **Tap Favorites to display food items you've added to your favorites.**

**S Health suggests your recent foods, in case leftovers are on the menu.**

6. Tap the appropriate match on the list to display serving-size options and nutritional details about this food item.

7. Tap the star icon if you want to add this food item to your favorites.

8. Drag the slider to adjust the amount of the food item you have ingested.

9. If necessary, tap the pop-up menu to switch between weight and calories for the serving.

10. Look at the nutritional composition of the food item.

11. Look at the details of the food item. You need to scroll down to see the full list of horrors.

12. Tap the Done button to finish adding this food item to your meal or snack. The meal or snack screen then appears again, showing a green circle with a check mark to the right of the item.

13. Repeat steps 3 through 12 to add the remaining items you consumed for the meal or snack. (I'm sure you can guess what I'm adding next—that's right, fries.)

14. Tap the Next button when you finish adding food items. The screen for the meal or snack appears.

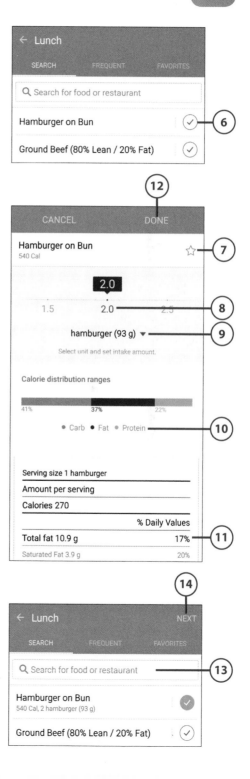

15. If necessary, tap the Time button and specify when the meal took place. S Health won't let you set times in the future.

16. Tap the Done button to finish entering your meal. The Eat Healthier screen appears, now showing the meal or snack you added.

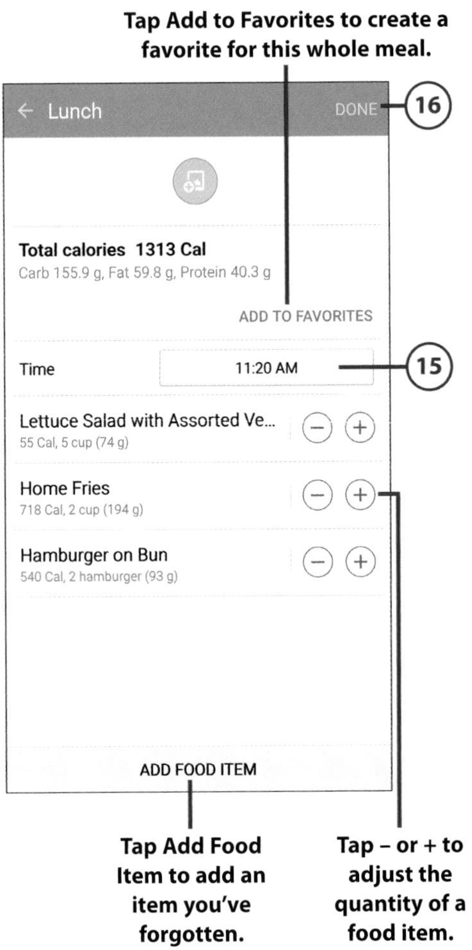

**Tap Add to Favorites to create a favorite for this whole meal.**

← Lunch                    DONE —(16)

Total calories **1313 Cal**
Carb 155.9 g, Fat 59.8 g, Protein 40.3 g

ADD TO FAVORITES

Time                    11:20 AM —(15)

Lettuce Salad with Assorted Ve...      ⊖ ⊕
55 Cal, 5 cup (74 g)

Home Fries                             ⊖ ⊕
718 Cal, 2 cup (194 g)

Hamburger on Bun                       ⊖ ⊕
540 Cal, 2 hamburger (93 g)

ADD FOOD ITEM

**Tap Add Food Item to add an item you've forgotten.**

**Tap – or + to adjust the quantity of a food item.**

## Take the "Perfectly Balanced Meal" Message with a Pinch of Salt

When you enter a meal, S Health evaluates it against certain nutritional criteria and assigns it a score out of 100. If the score is high enough, S Health might display the Perfectly Balanced Meal message.

**Tap OK and entertain healthy skepticism.**

If you get this message, take it with a pinch of (virtual) salt. The example meal that produced this message—two hamburgers, a double order of fries, and five cups of salad—is not one that most dieticians would recommend.

**17.** Tap the arrow button or the Back button below the screen to return to the Dashboard.

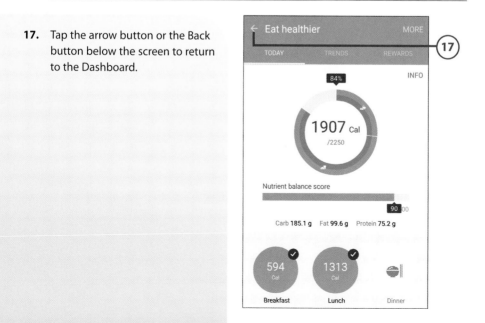

# Record Your Sleep Hours

If you have enabled the Feel More Rested goal, you must either wear a sleep-tracking device that can communicate your sleep hours to S Health automatically or you must log those hours manually. This sections covers logging the hours manually.

1. In S Health, tap the Feel More Rested box to display the Feel More Rested screen.

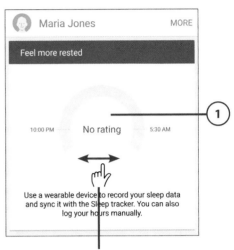

**If necessary, swipe left or right to display the Feel More Rested box.**

## Start Recording Sleep Hours from a Notification or the Sleep Tracker

S Health might display a notification prompting you to record your sleep hours. If so, tap the notification in the Notifications panel to display the screen for logging your sleep hours.

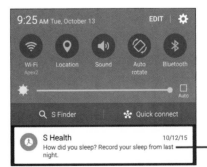

**Tap the "How did you sleep?" prompt to log your sleep hours.**

You can also start recording your sleep hours by tapping the Sleep tracker on the Dashboard. By doing so, you can avoid the steps of visiting the Feel More Rested screen and returning from it.

2. In the Sleep Details area, tap the Tap Here to Record Sleep Manually prompt.

3. Tap the Bedtime button and use the resulting controls to specify the time you went to bed.

4. Tap the Wake-Up Time button and use the resulting controls to specify the time you awoke.

5. Tap the Save button. The Feel More Rested screen appears again, now showing your sleep performance.

**You can tap Trends to view your sleep trends.**

**You can tap Rewards to see any rewards you've earned in your sleep.**

← Feel more rested     MORE

TODAY     TRENDS     REWARDS

10:00 PM    No rating    5:30 AM

Use a wearable device to record your sleep data and sync it with the Sleep tracker. You can also log your hours manually.

Sleep consistency

10:00 PM

5:30 AM

T   F   S   S   M   T   W

Sleep details

Tap here to record sleep manually — (2)

CANCEL     SAVE — (5)

Enter the time you went to sleep.

Bedtime

WED, OCT 14, 2015, 11:00 PM — (3)

Enter the time you woke up.

Wake-up time

THU, OCT 15, 2015, 5:30 AM — (4)

6. Tap the arrow button or the Back button below the screen to return to the Dashboard.

## Monitor Your Vital Signs

The S Health trackers that use the monitoring devices built into the Galaxy Note 5 enable you to monitor vital signs such as your heart rate, your oxygen saturation, and your stress. This example shows you how to measure your heart rate, but you use the SpO₂ tracker and the Stress tracker in the same way.

1. On the Dashboard, tap the Measure button on the Heart Rate tracker. The Heart Rate screen for measuring appears, prompting you to place your finger on the sensor.

2. Place the pad of your finger on the sensor. You need to cover the entire sensor, but you don't need to press hard.

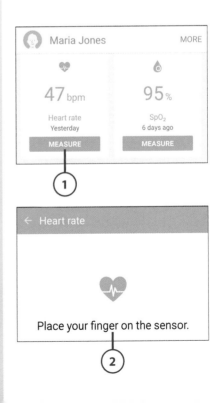

**3.** A progress indicator appears while the tracker measures your heart rate. A screen showing your heart rate then appears.

**4.** Tap the Notes field and type any notes needed.

**5.** In the Select Current Status area, tap the icon that corresponds to your current condition: General, Resting, After Exercise, Before Exercise, Excited, Tired, In Love, Surprised, Sad, Angry, Fearful, or Unwell.

**6.** Tap the Save button to save the data. The Heart Rate screen appears, showing your data.

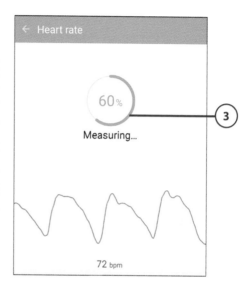

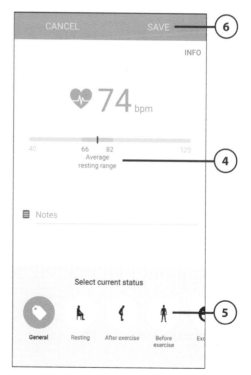

7. Tap the arrow button or the Back button below the screen to return to the Dashboard.

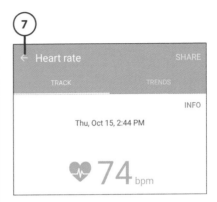

# Track a Workout

S Health enables you to track your workouts for analysis or posterity. This section shows an example of a walking workout.

1. On the Dashboard, tap the Start button for the appropriate tracker. This example uses the Walking tracker.

2. On the Track screen for the tracker, tap the pop-up menu to choose a target. For example, for walking, you can choose among Distance Target, Duration Target, Burned Calorie Target, and Basic Workout. This example uses Distance Target.

3. Tap the + button and – button to set the target, such as the distance.

4. Tap the Start button to start the workout. S Health displays details of your progress and encourages you with announcements.

5. When you finish the workout, tap Stop. S Health displays the Results screen, which shows statistics and achievements.

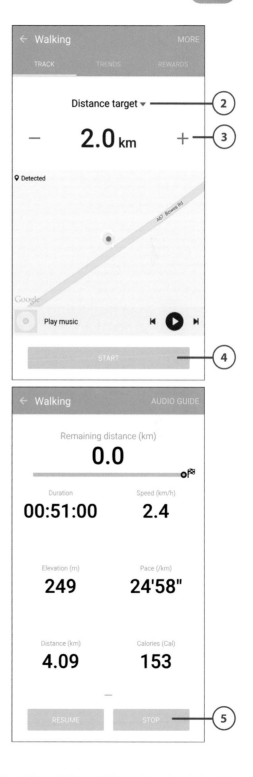

# Index

## J-K

## L

# N

## U

# X-Z